湖北文理学院特色教材基金资助出版

湖北文理学院校级重点教研项目《地方本科院校英语专业教学资源建设与优化研究》阶段性成果

翻译工作坊教程（英汉互译）

Translation Workshop Tutorials

◉主 编 卢 颖

南京大学出版社

图书在版编目(CIP)数据

翻译工作坊教程：英汉互译 / 卢颖主编. — 南京：
南京大学出版社，2016.8(2021.2 重印)
ISBN 978-7-305-17294-6

Ⅰ. ①翻… Ⅱ. ①卢… Ⅲ. ①英语－翻译－教材
Ⅳ. ①H315.9

中国版本图书馆 CIP 数据核字(2016)第 171215 号

出版发行　南京大学出版社
社　　址　南京市汉口路 22 号　　　　邮　编　210093
出 版 人　金鑫荣

书　　名　**翻译工作坊教程(英汉互译)**
主　　编　卢　颖
责任编辑　张淑文　　　　　　编辑热线　025-83596997

照　　排　南京南琳图文制作有限公司
印　　刷　南京人文印务有限公司
开　　本　787×1092 1/16　印张 10.75　字数 262 千
版　　次　2016 年 8 月第 1 版　2021 年 2 月第 4 次印刷
ISBN 978-7-305-17294-6
定　　价　32.00 元

网址：http://www.njupco.com
官方微博：http://weibo.com/njupco
官方微信号：njupress
销售咨询热线：(025) 83594756

前　言

翻译工作坊(Translation Workshop)是"类似于商业性的翻译中心,由两个或两个以上的译者集中在一起进行翻译活动"。在翻译时,译者可以合作交流,共同翻译并解决实际过程中的问题。翻译工作坊的运行模式可以应用于翻译教学中,以加强学生对翻译理论的运用,提高翻译技能及效率,培养学生职业翻译能力素养。"翻译工作坊"作为一种教学方式,是近几年翻译教学和翻译研究发展到新的阶段的产物。目前,它已成为高等学校翻译专业硕士(MTI)和翻译学硕士研究生(MA)的必修课程之一。部分本科院校的翻译专业也开设了该课程。该课程通过"在操练中学习翻译""在合作中学习翻译""在讨论中学习翻译"的方式,不断提高学生的翻译能力。但是,目前国内与"翻译工作坊"课程配套的教材较少。《英汉翻译理论与实践》方面的教材琳琅满目,虽然可以用来当做"翻译工作坊"课程的教材,但是多数英汉互译的教材所涉及的译例都偏重文学性和理论性,不适合用作"翻译工作坊"课程的配套教材,该课程需要有适合课程本身性质的配套教材,要求实践性强,译例文体范围广(旅游文化翻译、碑记文字翻译、商务合同翻译、公告标识语翻译、公司简介翻译、时事要政翻译、教育文献翻译、会议翻译、讲话稿翻译、企事业单位理念翻译、报纸杂志翻译等),难度适合学生翻译,配有两种以上参考译文,译例典型,适合小组合作并讨论完成等。在这样的背景下,本教材应运而生。教材的编写以实现翻译工作坊环境下交互式翻译教学模式为总体建设目标,目的在于革新英语专业的翻译教学,强调以学生为中心、以实践为根基,以计算机辅助翻译为技术导向,通过学生间的协作交流,培养学生的团队合作精神,为地方经济培养应用型专业翻译人才。

教材的编写遵循以下三个原则:

1. 案例或练习的选择具有普遍性、实用性;

第一,普遍性。案例的选择具有一定的普遍性,使教材的推广不受区域的限制。第二,实用性。本教材分为14章,除了第1章对翻译工作坊基本理论的介绍外,其它13章均为实践翻译案例。每章节按照主题或文体的不同配有案例,内容主要涉及旅游、文化、法律、标识语、公司简介、外贸洽谈、报纸杂志、时事要政、学校简介、学术论文、公文、广告、会议发言辞、公司简介。这些领域都是与就业市场关系密切的专业，了解这些领域的翻译对学生未来的就业及职业翻译能力的培养有积极作用。

2. 教材的难度和体例适合本科阶段使用，适合翻译专业或翻译方向培养应用型翻译人才。教材以案例教学法和任务驱动教学法为基础，体例为：相关翻译理论和翻译技巧介绍—案例—翻译前的准备—任务—练习—参考答案。教材配有丰富的练习及答案，案例和练习每篇在 1000 字左右，方便学生课下进行大量的翻译实践。本教材练习题答案放在南京大学出版社网站(www. njupco. com)的高校教材中心的课件下载中，供读者下载参考。

(1) 相关翻译理论和翻译技巧介绍是对每章涉及的翻译文本的文体、翻译理论和背景知识的介绍；练习是帮助学生复习每章节知识的辅助习题；

(2) 案例部分是结合每章具体的教学目标选取的具有典型意义的案例，使学生可以理论结合实际，了解翻译工作坊的实施环节，熟悉翻译特定文体文本时的应对方案，在教师的指导下学生进行协作翻译。通过教师的引导和协调，教师和学生一起分析案例以培养学生独立评析不同译文的能力；

(3) 任务驱动部分指每章节在案例后附有学生自主完成的任务。此部分是根据英语专业本科生的英汉语言的实际水平设定的具体翻译任务。翻译任务主要结合每章的翻译教学目标，给出不同文体的文本，要求学生 3—5 人一组完成翻译、讨论、协作、定稿的各个环节。

3. 教材自身体现了教学的实现路径，符合教学实践的推进。自编教材以实现翻译工作坊环境下交互式翻译教学模式为总体建设目标，根据授课方式设计了小组进行翻译案例练习前需要的准备工作，如：分组、该案例的文化、社会或历史背景、课前小组需讨论的问题、翻译中会遇到的难点、每章节术语的解释及翻译、翻译评析的要点等。这有利于教师安排教学计划，有利于授课过程中师生互动，有利于学生养成良好的翻译习惯。

教材的编写注重理论性和实践性相结合的原则，适合翻译专业本科生、翻译自学者及广大英语翻译爱好者使用。但由于时间仓促、水平有限，不足之处在所难免，敬请国内外专家学者及广大读者批评指正。

编　者

Contents 目录

第十一章　学校及下属学院简介翻译

第十二章　时事政要翻译

第十三章　学术论文翻译

第十四章　广告翻译

参考文献

第一章

翻译工作坊及翻译工作坊环境下的翻译教学

社会的不断进步与国际交流的日益频繁扩大了国际市场对复合型翻译人才的需求。国内众多高校都开设了英语专业,部分高校甚至在本科阶段已经开设翻译专业,虽每年都有成千上万的毕业生涌入市场,但仍无法满足社会对翻译人才的需求,导致这一现象的主要原因是学生的翻译实践能力未能满足翻译市场的要求。学校教师的翻译教学模式直接影响学生翻译实践能力。传统的"教师为中心,文本为基础"的翻译教学模式极大程度上限制了学生翻译应用能力的培养。计算机信息技术的不断更新推动了翻译方式和翻译工具的革新。计算机辅助翻译(CAT)已经成为各翻译机构及公司必要的应用技术。在教学中模拟翻译工作坊(translation workshop)的运作机制进行交互式教学,可培养学生协作翻译能力,提高翻译效率,增强学生职业翻译素养,增加学生在翻译市场的适应力。

第一节 翻译工作坊

译者,顾名思义即翻译的人,历来都被理解为单数形式。一部作品、一篇说明书、一份合同的翻译,传统意义上人们都理解为由一位译者完成。大部分文学作品的译著基本上都是由一位译者独立完成的。因为无论就文本解读、译者风格、术语的一致还是翻译思想而言,一位译者相对于多位译者作品更具连贯性和完整性。但是无论中国还是西方,大规模的翻译总是涉及多位译者的参与,如中国的佛经翻译和西方的圣经翻译,均涉及几十人甚至几百人。多人完成翻译任务较一人完成翻译任务,具有速度上的优势,符合现代经济快节奏的发展需求,多人合作翻译也逐渐形成一种翻译模式,存在于社会翻译实践中——翻译工作坊。

"翻译工作坊"是一群从事翻译活动的人聚集在一起,就某项具体翻译任务进行见仁见智的广泛而热烈的讨论,并通过不断协商,最终议定出该群体所有成员均接受或认同的译文的一种活动。"翻译工作坊"类似于商业性的翻译中心,由两个或两个以上的译者集中在一起进行翻译活动。在翻译时,译者可以合作交流,共同翻译并解决实际过程中的问题。翻译工作坊的运行模式和程序可以应用于翻译教学,作为翻译教学的实践环节,通过实践学习,以加强学生对翻译理论的运用,提高翻译技能及效率,培养学生职业翻译能力素养。翻译工作坊模式下的翻译教学,强调以学生为中心,以实践为根基,以计算机辅助翻译(CAT)为技术导向,通过学生间的协作交流,培养学生的团队合作精神,从而为社会培养职业化的翻译人才。

第二节　翻译工作坊环境下的翻译教学

1. 传统翻译教学

　　翻译教学一直被认为是传授自下而上的语言技能。传统的翻译教学模式主要是以教师为中心,教师"手把手"传授翻译技巧,这种模式会导致一些弊端。第一,忽视了学生主体性的发挥,无法激发学生的创造性。在这种模式下,教师是课堂的主体,教师讲解时间过长,内容抽象并且过程单调,学生在真实语言环境下进行翻译实践的机会较少,从而导致学生缺乏双语对比、文体修辞和语篇翻译的相关实践知识。这种教学模式忽视了学生主体性的发挥,虽然教学程序按部就班,精细严密,但是学生处于被动接受的静坐地位,因而丧失了主观能动性,缺乏翻译的应变性和创造性,容易减弱学生的翻译热情,影响翻译教学效果。第二,翻译知识"填鸭式"教学导致学生获得的翻译知识缺乏全面性。教师一般按部就班地讲解某一翻译理论或翻译技巧,学生亦步亦趋地模仿运用,通过不断重复和机械性训练达到"刺激—反应—强化"的效果,其结果是强行灌输的知识导致学生"消化不良",学生获得的知识零碎片面,难以将理论和实践相对应。第三,翻译实践教学过程缺乏"宏观操控",过分强调"微观"翻译技巧的传授,导致学生无法独立运用所学技巧于翻译实践中。传统翻译教学强调翻译中增、减、分、合等微观翻译技巧,机械性地把技巧公式般的传授给学生,导致学生在进行翻译实践时仍不清楚怎样具体运用所学技巧。这种重语言微观现象的转换技巧,轻语言宏观结构把握的教学模式无法培养学生实际翻译能力,不能达到良好的教学效果。因而在传统翻译教学模式下,教师忽视学生实际翻译能力的培养,是"知识传授型"教学的典型体现。不能达到良好的教学效果,更不能有效培养学生的翻译能力,学生在就业市场的竞争力就差。

2. 翻译工作坊教学模式

　　传统翻译教学一直沿袭传授自下而上的语言技能,教学以教师为中心,忽视学生的主体地位,无法有效培养学生的翻译实践能力和创造性。林克难提出翻译教学应从"以教师为中心向学生为中心过渡",以消除传统翻译教学所带来的弊端。在翻译工作坊的模式下,更有利于创造师生互动的学习氛围,通过师生间、学生间的学习交流,可以培养学生自主学习能力,尤其可以消除传统课堂上学生的紧张情绪,进而更好地参与到教师设计的各种教学环节中。在计算机辅助翻译(CAT)的环境下,可以实现课堂模拟职业翻译的过程,与作坊式翻译环境结合,真正构建一个以职业翻译能力培养为目标、以协作能力开发为目的的实践平台。另一方面,教师通过监看翻译过程,可以监控并总结学生翻译过程中的错误,并为教师翻译教学提供广泛的教学资料库,有利于教师设计个性化教案,从而更好地进行翻译教学。

第三节　翻译工作坊课程教学模式

1. 教学目标设计

　　教学目标包括翻译教学所需讲解的理论基础及翻译技巧;课程所要实现的具体目标及阶段性目标。目标系统的设定非常重要,是翻译工作坊教学的基础及关键。

2. 教学方案设定

　　教学方案是翻译工作坊教学模式的核心,教师根据教学目标选择相应的翻译项目,项目的选定要具备专业性强、文体多样化、教学环节实践性强的特点。教学方案的设定要突出体现教师作为指导者、组织者、监管者及中心协调者的作用。

3. 翻译团队组成

　　翻译团队是翻译教学活动的主体,基本由课程参与者组成,可以是翻译课的学生,亦可以是课下自由结合的翻译小组。翻译团队的组成可以是固定的,也可以是自由结合的,通过翻译团队在翻译工作坊环境下进行翻译实践学习,共同解决翻译过程中遇到的问题。

4. 翻译实践场地

　　翻译实践场地是教学进行的前提,必须能够满足翻译工作坊教学的要求。一般包括装有 CAT 软件的电脑、多媒体设备、网络设备以及电子互动平台。提供现代化信息交流手段,满足学生与教师间的小型讨论、过程演示与小型报告的需求。

第四节　翻译工作坊教学特点

　　翻译工作坊教学具有如下特点:

　　1. 翻译工作坊的运行模式和程序应用于翻译教学中,可以加强学生间的合作交流,同时加强学生对翻译理论的运用,提高翻译技能及效率;

　　2. 翻译工作坊教学以培养学生职业翻译能力为目的,大量的翻译实践可以提高翻译速度,增强学生职业化素养,使学生更适应社会对翻译人才的要求;

　　3. 翻译工作坊教学以学生为主体,可以激发学生的学习兴趣,调动其积极性,培养译者间的合作互助,使之参与更多的翻译实践;

　　4. 翻译工作坊教学改善了翻译实践教学的环境,这一革新可提高教学质量,培养学生的职业翻译技能,使学生在就业市场具备独特的专业技能。

第二章

旅游翻译

随着中国经济改革的进一步推进和快速发展,人民收入逐步提高,旅游作为一种绿色产业越来越受到国家和地方政府的青睐。旅游业的迅速发展吸引了国内及国际友人来华观光游览。越来越多的国人也开始走出国门去欣赏异国景观,体验不同民族的文化活动。中国旅游业将面临巨大的挑战。除了旅游设施等方面的筹建和规划,更重要的是如何准确地把我国悠久的文化传播出去。国际旅游的促销传播及文化交流离不开翻译。旅游翻译的复杂性、多样性、文化性及特殊性也要求翻译人员对其进行深入研究,从跨文化传播、接受美学、旅游文本的功能性、交际翻译等多角度分析解读文本,翻译出适合国际旅游市场需求的翻译文本。

第一节　旅游翻译的定义

中国旅游不仅历史久远,也是世界上具有最早文字记载的国家。"旅"和"游"二字在山东昌乐骨刻文中发现,是东夷平民旅游娱乐活动最早的记录,也是中国旅游文化最早的体现。"旅"是旅行,外出,即为了实现某一目的而在空间上从甲地到乙地的行进过程;"游"是外出游览、观光、娱乐,即为达到这些目的所做的旅行。二者合起来即旅游。旅行偏重于行,而旅游不但有"行",且有观光、娱乐含义。

从翻译的范围来看,旅游翻译包括一切与旅游相关的文本翻译及口译。旅游翻译的范畴涉及旅游广告翻译、旅游宣传卡翻译、旅游公关文本翻译、旅游网站翻译、景点牌示解说翻译、导游图翻译、景区公示语翻译,等等。这些范畴涉及广告翻译、公示语翻译及历史、文化、文学等领域的翻译。因而旅游翻译是多元素集合下的文本和口头翻译的交际活动。

从翻译的本质来看,陈刚教授在其专著《旅游翻译与涉外导游》一书中给出以下定义:

旅游翻译应是为旅游活动、旅游专业和行业进行的翻译(实践),属于专业翻译。概括地说,旅游翻译是一种跨语言、跨社会、跨时空、跨文化、跨心理的交际活动。

本书讨论的是文本翻译相关的原则和方法,因而对旅游文本的概念和内涵要有清楚的认识。旅游文本是指"涉及旅游(接待)一线人员(尤其是导游翻译或涉外导游)在工作中经常碰到的、约定俗成的那些应用型文本,包括旅游指南、旅游行程、旅游委托书、旅游意向书、旅游合同、旅游广告、旅游表格、导游解说词、景点介绍、参观点介绍、博物馆解说词、旅游推销手册、旅游宣传册、旅游地图、旅游宣传标语、文艺演出节目单、餐厅菜单、宾馆指示牌/标志、公园指示牌、参观点标语、各类通知、路标、地名、各种(旅游)会展/文本、各种(旅游)会议文本等"。翻译信息的复杂化和多样化、目的语读者的国际化要求旅游文本翻译具有较高的准确性和较广泛的跨文化传播功能。

第二节　旅游翻译的原则和标准

旅游文本翻译属于应用翻译学中的专业类翻译。近 15 年来,旅游翻译的研究主要集中在以下十大研究视角:跨文化交际理论、文本类型理论、翻译目的论/功能翻译理论、语用学理论(语用失误、语用等效、关联论、语境理论、合作原则)、美学/接受美学理论、平行文本比较/篇章对比/语料库、译者主体性理论、生态翻译理论、信息理论、变译理论。具体的旅游文本翻译技巧体现为:增补、删减、直译、释义/解释、音译加注、改写/译、音译、意译、类比/借用、转译、直译加注、重组、变译、归化、直译加音译、交际翻译法、语义翻译法、异化、意译加注释、意译加音译、概述、替换。研究者从不同研究视角探讨旅游文本的翻译方法,从各个方面关注旅游翻译的方法和技巧,但如果不综合系统地研究,很可能导致翻译的片面性和主观性。任何一个旅游文本都不能简单地被归属哪一种翻译类别或使用哪一种翻译技巧或方法。旅游翻译的原则和标准决定着译者对翻译策略的选择,因而确定明确的翻译标准和原则是首要和必需的。

一、旅游翻译的标准

第一,动态性。

旅游文本涉及文学、历史、政治、科技、地理、文化等各个领域,旅游翻译具有多样性、综合性、实践性强等特征。翻译的标准不是静态的,是与翻译文本的特点和属性相适应的。文本特征和受众的接受度是调节其平衡的两个重要因素。

第二,多元互补

翻译标准多元化并不是翻译标准无限化(无数个标准),也不是翻译标准虚无化,而是追求无限中的有限性。鉴于上述旅游文本文体特征的多样性,翻译时仅持有一种翻译标准是无法达到翻译目的的。思维方法上的单向性会使译者缺乏翻译视野的全面性,翻译标准的多元化可以使译者在无限标准中缩小范围,根据语篇分析的结果确定有限标准的体系,进而产出更好的翻译作品。

二、旅游翻译的原则

第一,内涵方面保证文化传播、信息传播的客观性及准确性;
第二,文本形式上达到源语形式特征的保留与目的语读者接受度的契合。

第三节 案例及习题

一、英译汉：英国国家博物馆有关中国整体形象的牌示解说

1. 英文原文

China

The Chinese have created the single most extensive and enduring civilization in the world. The language, spoken and written in the same forms over nearly four thousand years, binds their vast country together and links the present with the past, expressing a unified culture unmatched elsewhere.

In contrast, the land of China is one of great geographical diversity. Bordered by mountains, steppes and deserts, the immense central plains are watered by great rivers, supporting a dense population, a large part of which has always been tied to the land, but which has also proved itself extraordinarily skilled in the production of material goods of a high standard.

In spite of the vast size of the country, and the periodic eruptions of social unrest within or invasion from outside, China's rulers have always sought a single, strong, and unified state administered by and educated elite. The bonds of society have been held in place by language, codes of law, custom and ceremony, as well as by the wide distribution of the products of the arts and manufacturing.

注：英国国家博物馆是世界上历史最悠久、规模最宏伟的综合性博物馆，位于英国伦敦。它收藏了世界各地的许多文物和图书珍品，藏品之丰富、种类之繁多为全世界博物馆所罕见。18世纪至19世纪中叶，英帝国向世界扩张，对各国进行文化掠夺，大量珍贵文物运抵伦敦，数量极多，英国国家博物馆盛不下，只得分藏于各个博物馆。埃及文物馆是其中最大的陈列馆，有7万多件古埃及各种文物，代表着古埃及的高度文明。希腊和罗马文物馆、东方文物馆的大量文物反映了古希腊罗马、古代中国的灿烂文化。本段文字就选自大英博物馆有关中国整体形象的牌示解说。该解说上还配有中国地图。

2. 翻译工作坊课程规划

第一，文本解读。

（1）大英博物馆的背景了解；

（2）英语牌示解说词的文体特征；

（3）牌示解说词的文体功能；

（4）目的语读者的需求指向；

(5) 根据所学翻译理论,提出相应的翻译策略,并讨论如何将其应用到译文中。

第二,分组翻译(六人一组)。具体要求如下:

(1) 六人组下分为三组(1/2/3 每小组两人),原文三段 A/B/C,1 组翻译段落 A,2 组翻译段落 B,3 组翻译段落 C,每组中的两人独立进行翻译。

(2) 1、2、3 组分别在组内对各自的译稿进行修改,拟初稿;

(3) 将初稿合并,六人进行小组讨论,统一术语,纠查错误,拟定稿;

(4) 各组提交定稿。

第三,翻译教学讨论。

(1) 以上各组分别由代表进行报告演示,结合所学翻译理论对相关术语及翻译技巧进行解释;

(2) 小型讨论,评议并找出译文中的错译及误译,并剖析原因;

(3) 教师给出参考译文,结合学生译文进行评析,讲解相关翻译技巧。

3. 参考译文

中 国

中国创造了世界上独具特色、博大精深、隽永灿烂的文化。统一的语言文字历经四千多年传承提炼,不仅将幅员辽阔的国家紧密地连接在一起,而且将独特的文化传统薪火相传,展现给世界一个统一的、无与伦比的民族文化。

与统一的文化相反的是中国的广阔地域和不同的地理环境。中国的边境线多与高山、平原和沙漠接壤,而其中部平原河流纵横,人口稠密。在中部平原,很多人以土地为生,但他们凭着精湛的手艺制造了许多精工制品。

尽管地域广阔,国内时有动乱,并经常受到外族的侵略,中国的君主帝王们仍一直努力创建一个由知识精英治理的集权、统一、强大的国家。独特的语言、法律、习俗和礼仪,以及大量的手工艺品像条条纽带把这个古老的民族紧密地联接在一起。

4. 英译汉翻译练习

(1) 美国自由女神的铭文题词

The New Colossus

By Emma Lazarus

Not like the brazen giant of Greek fame,

With conquering limbs astride from land to land;

Here at our sea-washed, sunset gates shall stand

A mighty woman with a torch, whose flame

Is the imprisoned lightning, and her name

Mother of Exiles. From her beacon-hand

Glows world-wide welcome; her mild eyes command

The air-bridged harbor that twin cities frame.

"Keep ancient lands, your storied pomp!" cries she

With silent lips. "Give me your tired, your poor,
Your huddled masses yearning to breathe free,
The wretched refuse of your teeming shore.
Send these, the homeless, tempest-tost to me,
I lift my lamp beside the golden door!"

注："The New Colossus" is a sonnet by Emma Lazarus(1849—1887)，written in 1883 and, in 1903，engraved on a bronze plaque and mounted inside the Statue of Liberty. 从 1945 年，刻有这首诗歌的铜板从《自由女神像》的内部被移到雕像的主要入口处。

（2）　　　　　**Thirlmere—Home of great water**

Welcome to Thirlmere, home of great water. Thirlmere is not a natural lake but a reservoir which contains about 11 per cent of the North West's water supply—about one glass of water in every nine comes from here. Thirlmere's fascinating history and staggering beauty have earned critics and admirers throughout its life. There's lots to see whether you like local history, native wildlife, fantastic feats of engineering or just somewhere nice to take the kids. We also have two of the finest rock climbing crags in the Lake District-Raven Crag, near the dam, and Castle Rock, at Legburthwaite, which are granted free access for ever.

Take a look around and enjoy yourself. There are information panels in every car park to guide you and give you an insight into the life and times of Thirlmere. All we ask is that you take care while you're here. Hundreds of thousands of people will enjoy a drop of Thirlmere today. It's your water. Help us keep it clean by not leaving litter or lighting fires.

Download our free visitor leaflet at uniteduitities. com/thirlmereservoir

注：瑟米尔水库位于英国坎布里亚郡的阿勒代尔自治市，属于英国的湖区。它由南到北，北端修有大坝，东临 A591 大道，西侧修有一条小路。瑟米尔水库建于 19 世纪，由曼彻斯特公司承建，负责为新兴工业城市——曼彻斯特提供水源。瑟米尔水库长 96 英里，目前仍为曼彻斯特地区供水。

二、汉译英：襄阳南漳水镜庄风景区牌示解说

1. 汉语原文

白马洞、水镜祠

白马洞镶嵌在玉溪山峭壁之中，冬暖夏凉，气候宜人，可容千人。司马徽先生隐居时，曾在这里读书、弹琴、会友。清乾隆七年（1742 年），南漳知县徐彦在白马洞口依山势而建水镜祠。1936 年，县参议夏云清重新修缮门楼，并亲自撰写"彝水环绕，明镜高悬"的石联。上联

和下联的第二个字,巧妙地运用了"水、镜"二字,把水镜先生的雅号包含其中。1954 年、1981 年南漳县人民政府拨专款再次重修。现"水镜祠"匾额为原中国书协主席沈鹏先生所题。

相传白马洞通四川,深不可测。很久以前,洞内有匹白马,昼伏夜出,损坏庄稼,百姓聚众捕捉,众人缚住白马后,到襄阳马市出售,遇四川一马商,称此马是他在四川峨眉山丢失,应予以归还。于是双方争论不休。有一长者从中调停,让两人以据定夺。马商一声嗯哨,马即近前亲昵,不断自明,白马归原主。于是有了白马洞通四川的神秘传说。现洞内塑有司马徽与好友庞德公当年对弈及其学生诸葛亮、庞统、徐庶的塑像。

注:此段源自三国著名水镜先生司马徽的故居"水镜庄风景区"牌示解说词。司马徽,字德操,河南颍川人,东汉末年,北方战乱,他寓居襄阳即现在的南漳县水镜庄。因庞统"先生数典如流水,心清似明镜,真乃水镜先生矣"得水镜先生之称,水镜庄也因司马徽居住而取得其名。

2. 翻译工作坊课程规划

第一,文本解读。

(1) 汉语牌示解说词的语言特征;

(2) 目的语读者的审美接受对翻译结果的影响;

(3) 根据所学翻译理论,提出相应的翻译策略,并讨论如何将其应用到译文中。

第二,分组翻译(六人一组)。具体要求如下:

(1) 六人组下分为两组(1/2 每小组三人),原文三段 A/B,1 组翻译段落 A,2 组翻译段落 B,每组中的两人独立进行翻译;

(2) 1、2 组分别在组内进行对各自任务的译稿及修改,拟初稿;

(3) 将初稿合并,六人进行小组讨论,统一术语,纠查错误,拟定稿。

(4) 各组提交定稿。

第三,翻译教学讨论。

(1) 以上各组分别由代表进行报告演示,结合案例说明英汉牌示解说词语言特征的异同;

(2) 所有同学对各组所提出的翻译策略进行讨论;

(3) 教师给出参考译文,结合学生译文进行评析,讲解相关翻译技巧。

3. 参考译文

Baima Cave and Shuijing Temple

Embedded in the cliff of Yuxishan Mountain, Baima Cave, which can hold 1,000 people, has a pleasant environment, warm in winter and cool in summer. When Sima Hui was living in seclusion, he was ever reading books, playing the Guqin and meeting friends here. In the 7th year of Qianlong Period in Qing Dynasty (1742), Xu Yan, magistrate of Nanzhang County, established Shuijing Temple in the mouth of Baima Cave according to the mountain shape. In 1936, Xia Yunqing, senator of Nanzhang County, renovated the gate tower and wrote a poetic couplet on stone "Yi water surrounding, bright mirror hung". The second characters in the first line and second line of the couplet are respectively "Water", namely "Shui" in Chinese and "Mirror", namely "Jing" in Chinese, the combination of which is exactly the art name of Mr. Shuijing. In 1954 and 1981, People's Government of Nanzhang County appropriated special funds to make renovations. The current horizontal inscribed board of "Shuijing Temple" was written by Mr. Shen Peng, former chairman of China Calligraphers Association.

A story goes that Baima Cave connects to Sichuan province and is unfathomable. Long time ago, a white horse in the cave hided by day and came out by night for food, so a curious man gathered a crowd to catch the horse and sell it in horse market of Xiangyang city, while a horsecouper came to say that the horse was his and lost in Emei Mountain, Sichuan province, and asked for return. Thus, a lengthy argument was incurred. Then, an elder acted as mediator and made a final decision depending on evidence. After the horsecouper had whistled, the horse approached hime intimately. It is self-evident that the horse belonged to the horsecouper and it was returned to him finally. Thus, the mysterious legend that Baima Cave connects to Sichuan province turns up. In the cave, there are statues of Sima Hui and his friend Pang Degong, who are playing the game of Go, and his disciples, such as, Zhuge Liang, Pang Tong, and Xu Shu.

4. 汉译英翻译练习

（1）　　　　　　　　　　　**草庐**

草庐，是司马徽先生生活起居，待客交友，开堂讲学之地。约建于公元 206 年，1998 年复修。当年水镜先生为避战乱在此隐居。先生身居草庐，生活简朴，过着农桑生活，但仍心系天下大事，开堂讲学，教书育人，著有《司马诫子书》等。先生常和襄阳名士庞德公，黄承彦等来往密切，有诸葛亮，徐庶等十多名优秀弟子。汉昭烈帝刘备访水镜庄，先生荐贤为贤，使之得到"伏龙"（诸葛亮），"凤雏"（庞统）辅佐，终书"三分天下"史篇。

（2）　　　　　　　　　　　**荐贤堂**

荐贤堂，是水镜先生举荐"伏龙"（诸葛亮）、"凤雏（庞统）"的旧址。此堂始建于清乾隆七年，后毁于战乱，1987 年复修。公元 206 年，寄居新野的刘备投奔襄阳刘表，遭刘表内弟蔡瑁与夫人所妒。公元 207 年某一春日，蔡瑁在襄阳设下"鸿门宴"，企图谋杀刘备，刘备察觉后从西门逃走，马跃檀溪，来到南漳，访问水镜先生，请先生辅佐。

先生辞曰："儒生俗仕，不识时务，识时务者在乎俊杰"。此间自有"伏龙"、"凤雏"二人得一人可安天下。今堂内塑有刘备、司马徽、书童塑像一组，再现当年荐贤情景。

第三章

地方文化翻译

第一节　地方文化及其翻译

给"文化"下定义非常困难,各个领域的众多学者都尝试给其一个严格精确的定义,但迄今仍未有公认的定义。文化可以是社会学、历史学、人类学的研究范畴,也同时可涉及地理、风俗、文学、艺术、意识形态、思维方式等等。

广义文化指人类在社会历史发展过程中所创造的物质财富和精神财富的总和。它包括物质文化、制度文化和心理文化三个方面。广义的文化,着眼于人类与一般动物、人类社会与自然界的本质区别,着眼于人类卓立于自然的独特的生存方式,其涵盖面非常广泛,所以又被称为大文化。随着人类科学技术的发展,人类认识世界的方法和观点也在发生着根本改变。对文化的界定也越来越趋于开放性和合理性。

对文化的不同定义无不体现出广义的文化是综合多种社会现象的复杂整体。不同角度对文化的阐释折射出文化概念的动态性。人类在不断地认识和改造自然,人类创造的物质文化和精神文化也是在不断更新完善的。从地域的角度划分,文化可分为地方文化和主流文化。而地方文化又与特定区域紧密联系。所谓地方文化,从广义上说,是某一地区在其社会历史发展过程中所形成的物质和精神成果的总和。因此地方文化是指地方特色文化,具有明显地方特征、独特艺术风格,能够反映当地人民群众生产斗争、生活方式、风俗习惯,并已形成相当大的影响和优势,具有一定审美价值的、为群众喜闻乐见的文化项目。

可见,地方文化与地方的历史、民风、生活方式、风俗、地理特征、文学艺术等方面息息相关。地方文化的翻译也会涉及以上各方面的领域,因而地方文化的翻译不仅要对英汉双语掌握娴熟,还要对各地的历史、风俗、地理等特征有所了解。文本的解读也要从不同角度进行,翻译时尤其注意不同文体的不同语言特征,把握特定文体的英汉语言差异,以适合各自文体特征的翻译理论为基础,采取相应的翻译策略,翻译的结果既忠实原文,又要照顾目的语读者的各种需求。

11

第二节　地方文化的翻译原则

　　文化翻译是一项艰难的任务。之所以说它艰难,不仅仅因为文化所包含的领域广泛,还因为文化翻译直接影响到文化信息是否能准确的传播出去。文化和翻译是相互影响的,译者的翻译观和对文化的理解度直接影响了文化的传播,异国文化的特质性又极大影响了译者的翻译操作。对文化的翻译研究,可以分为三个层次:宏观层面的社会操控;中观层面的语言形式;微观层面的文化语句。社会操纵体现在社会文化大环境对翻译实践的影响。社会文化大环境包括社会组织形式、社会意识形态及风俗习惯等等。这些社会因素制约或影响着译者的翻译视野和翻译思想,对翻译实践有着直接或间接的影响。

　　语言和思维是密切相关的。不同的语言形式和结构可以反映语言使用者的思维方式。特定民族语言使用者的文化心理特征和思维模式都可以从其语言的句法、词法层面中体现出来。翻译真正要解决的就是将语言形式对理解及翻译的影响抹除,将其内涵准确的传递出去。

　　文化语句是那些比较凝练的体现在语言中的文化因素的词或句。如果说语言形式体现文化的形式是隐含的,那么文化语句则是直接体现的,是显性的。对于这类词句的翻译如果有对等语就用对等语翻译,没有对等语的词位空缺,则要解释性地翻译给读者。

　　综上所述,处理文化信息的时候要关注社会、语言形式和文化语句三个层面,涉及地方文化的翻译也同时要从这三个层面出发,从地方社会意识形态、地方语言形式及地方特色文化语句三个角度考虑翻译策略的选择,从而进行有效、高质量的翻译。

第三节　案例及习题

一、英译汉

1. 英语原文

Broad Street

　　In the 13th century Broad Street was used for horse trading, but the advent of many handsome buildings has since given it a distinguish air. These include ① Balliol College, founded in the 1260s by John De Balliol as a penance for insulting the Bishop of Durham, ② 16th century Trinity College, built on the site of an earlier college which educated the monks of Durham and, ③ Exeter College, founded in 1314 by the Bishop of Exeter, a prominent courtier subsequently murdered by enemies of the King. At the eastern end of the street is The Clarendon Building ④, the 18th century University Printing House (now part of the Bodleian Library) and The Sheldonian Theatre ⑤, the University's ceremonial hall designed in 1663 by Sir Christopher Wren when he was professor of Astronomy here. Beside it is the 17th century building occupied by The Museum of the History of Science ⑥ which formerly housed the Ashmolean Museum and the first chemical laboratory in England. 50 Broad Street ⑦ is the original Blackwell's Bookshop opened in 1879 by Benjamin Blackwell, founder of the world-famous family business which now has seven bookshops in the central Oxford alone.

Behind the modest façade of The Oxford Story ⑧, Europe's longest dark ride traces the history of the University and introduces famous faces and events from 800 years of town and marks the spot where Protestant Bishops Latimer, Ridley and Cranmer were burned at the stake in 1555 and 1556 for rejecting the doctrine of the Catholic Church. The Martyrs' Memorial in St. Gile was erected to their memory in 1841—3.

2. 翻译工作坊课程规划

第一,文本解读。

(1) 牛津大学城市和大学合二为一的背景;

(2) 目的语读者的需求、归纳语言特点并分析地方文化语句如街道名、主教名的翻译策略;

(3) 根据所学地方文化翻译原则,提出相应的翻译策略。

第二,分组翻译(六人一组)。具体要求如下:

(1) 各组首先对相似语言结构及文化词找出,提出一致的翻译;

(2) 组内进行翻译并修改,拟初稿;

(3) 将初稿合并,六人进行小组讨论,统一术语,纠查错误,拟定稿。

(4) 各组提交定稿。

第三,翻译教学讨论。

(1) 由代表进行报告演示,重点指出译文如果在社会意识形态、语言形式和文化语句三方面解读文本并翻译的;

(2) 所有同学对各组所提出的翻译策略进行讨论;

(3) 教师给出参考译文,结合学生译文进行评析,讲解相关翻译技巧。

3. 参考译文

宽　街

在 13 世纪,宽街主要用于马匹交易,但之后在这条大街上修建的许多著名建筑使这条大街举世闻名。这包括① Balliol 学院,Balliol 学院由 John De Balliol 在 13 世纪 60 年代建造。这座学院是 John De Balliol 用来向 Durham 的主教谢罪的,因为他侮辱了主教大人。② 三一学院。三一学院是 16 世纪在 Durham 神学院的基址上建筑起来的。③ 是由 Exeter 主教在 1314 年建造的 Exeter 学院。作为朝廷重臣,Exeter 主教后来被国王的敌手杀害。宽街的东端是 Clarendon 楼④。18 世纪时这里是牛津大学的印刷厂(现在它的一部分是 Bodleian 图书馆)和 Sheldonia 剧院⑤。Sheldonia 剧院是牛津大学举行典礼仪式的地方,

1663 年由 Christopher Wren 勋爵设计建造。当时 Christopher Wren 勋爵是牛津大学的天文学教授。剧院的旁边是一座 17 世纪的建筑⑥，该建筑最初是 Ashmolean 博物馆和英国最早的化学实验室所在地，现在该建筑是科学历史博物馆。宽街 50 号⑦是 Blackwell's 书店的原址。Blackwell's 书店是世界著名的家族企业，在牛津市中心就有 7 家书店。Blackwell's 书店创建于 1879 年，其创始人是 Benjamin Blackwell 先生。

在庄重无华的"牛津故事"⑧的后面是欧洲最长的甬道。在此可以寻踪牛津大学的历史以及牛津城 800 年中的重要人物和历史事件。在宽街 Balliol 学院外的十字架就记录了新教主教 Latimer、Ridley 和 Cranmer 因为拒绝接受天主教教义而被钉在十字架上火焚的惨剧。1841—1843 年人们为了缅怀他们，在 St. Gile 建立了英烈纪念堂。（程尽能，吕和发 2008:312）

4. 翻译练习

(1)   **Fish and Chips**

The dish became popular in wider circles in London and South East England in the middle of the 19th century. (Charles Dickens mentions a "fried fish warehouse" in *Oliver Twist*, first published in 1838), while in the north of England a trade in deep-fried chipped potatoes developed. The first chip shop stood on the present site of Oldham's Tommyfield Market. It remains unclear exactly when and where these two trades combined to become the fish-and-chip shop industry we know. A Jewish immigrant, Joseph Malin opened the first recorded combined fish-and-chip shop in London in 1860 or in 1865; a Mr. Lees pioneered the concept in the North of England, in Mossley, in 1863.

The concept of a fish restaurant, as opposed to take-away, was introduced by Samuel Isaacs (born 1856 in Whitechapel, London; died 1939 in Brighton, Sussex) who ran a thriving wholesale and retail fish business throughout London and the South of England in the latter part of the 19th century. Isaacs' first restaurant opened in London in 1896 serving fish and chips, bread and butter, and tea for nine pence and its popularity ensured a rapid expansion of the chain.

(2)   **Deer Gate Mountain**

The particular Hsiang-yang locale with which Meng Hao-jan has been most notably associated is Deer Gate Mountain (Lu-men Shan) which stood distant from the city a full ten miles southeast, overlooking to its west the Han River. Meng's biographies in the official histories note that he lived at Lu-men in seclusion. His association with the mountain is expressed best in the following poem, and "old-style verse (ku-t's shih)" written in the heptasyllabic meter.

A Song on Returning at Night to Deer Gate

A sounding bell from a mountain temple—day now is darkling;

At the head of Fish-weir Crossing—a clamor of quarrelsome crossers.

The others follow the sandy shore toward the river village,

I for my part board a skiff, going home to Deer Gate.

As the splendor of Deer Gate's moon discloses misty trees,
Suddenly I arrive at Lord P'ang's place of hidden retreat.
Cliffside door and pinetree path, for long still and silent—
Here there is only an obscure one who comes and goes on his own.

二、汉译英:"三国文化"讲座^①

1. 原文

各位老师、各位同学:

下午好!

很荣幸今天有这样一个机会给大家做讲座。希望通过这个讲座大家能记住三个词:襄阳、隆中、湖北文理学院。

襄阳位于湖北省西北部,拥有 2800 多年的建成史。长江最大的支流汉江穿城而过,把襄阳分为襄阳和樊城,江北为樊城,江南为襄阳。(图片汉江、码头)我们现在所在的位置就是襄阳。可能很多外国朋友都听说过襄阳。历史上的襄阳就是我们现在襄阳的中心城区。人们经常赞叹古襄阳"固如金汤",易守难攻。这是因为襄阳城东、西、南均有高大的城墙,城墙外还有全国最宽的护城河,城北是汉江。(图片:古城墙、古城墙夜景、护城河)襄阳城坚固的防御体系,使得襄阳城自古都是兵家必争之地。

襄阳既是群雄逐鹿的古战场,也是历史文人骚客荟萃之地,孕育了楚国诗人宋玉、战国时期政治家伍子胥,唐代诗人杜审言、孟浩然、张吉、皮日休和宋代书画家米芾等文人名士,留下了诗仙李白、诗圣杜甫等贤达雅士的足迹和传颂千古的诗章。

说起襄阳,不得不提到一个人,那就是被誉为"中华民族智慧的化身"的诸葛亮。位于襄城城西的隆中山环境清幽、古木参天。诸葛亮 17 岁至 27 岁在此隐居躬耕,饱读诗书。刘备"三顾茅庐"和"隆中对"的千古佳话就发生在这里。闻名中外的《三国演义》120 回中,有 31 回和襄阳有关。

图片 1:牌坊。位于隆中山口,正中雕刻着"古隆中"三个大字。

图片 2:牌坊。背面写着"三代下一人",意思是说诸葛亮是夏、商、周以后的近千年来唯一的人物。

图片 3:诸葛蜡像

图片 4:武侯祠。是后人为纪念诸葛亮而修建的祠宇,依山而建,雄伟壮观。

图片 5:草庐。

草庐是诸葛亮日常会见宾朋的地方,三顾茅庐的故事就发生在这里。刘备是汉景帝子中山靖王的后代,到他这一代,家庭已经衰败。作为皇室一脉的刘备,虽然有建功立业的雄心和气质,但是缺乏出谋划策、运筹帷幄的谋士。在司马徽的推荐下,刘备决定到隆中拜访

---

① 该讲座是湖北文理学院文学院刘群教授给该校国际交流生进行的一次当地文化讲座。

诸葛亮。三顾茅庐的故事在史书上没有详细的记载，但《三国演义》却把这些情节描绘得具体生动。第一次，刘备来到隆中山打听诸葛先生，谁知诸葛亮踪迹不定，不知到何处去了。第二次来隆中，正值严寒隆冬、瑞雪霏霏，谁知诸葛亮又不在家，外出闲游去了。诸葛亮两次不见刘备，并不是故意抬高身价，而是他选择明主的慎重和考验刘备是否有求才建业的决心。通过两次考验，诸葛亮决定出山辅助刘备。公元207年冬天，刘备第三次上隆中山，诸葛亮在自己简陋的茅屋里热情接待了他，并畅谈了自己统一天下的谋略。此后，诸葛亮便离开了隐居十年的隆中山，跟随刘备到新野，走上了风云变幻的历史舞台，辅佐刘备建立三分天下的蜀汉政权。

图片6：三顾茅庐

图片7：六角井。草庐宅院内的生活用井，这是草庐故址所在的实物佐证。

图片8：躬耕田。

诸葛亮在隆中过着自食其力的生活。他盖起了草庐，用老龙洞的泉水灌溉田地，亲自耕种。人们知道古时种庄稼总是"望天收"，可是在隆中冲却两样了，不论天旱、地涝，躬耕田里的庄稼总是长得很茂盛，年年是好收成。周围的庄稼人都感到很惊奇：一个白面书生，竟种出了一片好庄稼！更奇怪的是，他的农活安排与周围老乡不一样。庄户人是按常规年复一年地种麦子、稻子、苞谷。他却有时种稻子，有时种苞谷。凡是诸葛亮种稻子这年，就风调雨顺；凡是诸葛亮种高粱、苞谷或其他杂粮时，这年天气就反常。这样年复一年的过去，躬耕田就成了周围庄稼人的样板田了。诸葛亮种苞谷时，老百姓就不种稻子，诸葛亮种水稻时，就意味着风调雨顺，大家也都种稻子。诸葛亮根据气候规律而掌握的一套种植技术，逐渐被隆中周围的庄稼人学到手。如今，隆中一带仍旧是襄阳区的主要产粮区，并且种出的粮食和外地不一样，传说这都是诸葛亮当年留下来的良种。如果你到隆中尝一尝当地产的大米饭，真是又甜又香。

其实，三国故事的真正源头并不在隆中，而是在水镜庄。水镜庄位于南漳县城南。西汉末年名士司马徽在此隐居，因司马徽又称水镜先生，山庄因此又叫水镜庄。相传刘备在襄阳遇险，马跃滩溪一路逃到南漳，在水镜庄于司马徽相遇。司马徽举荐诸葛亮于刘备，这才产生了后来的"三顾茅庐"的故事。所以说，三国文化的真正源头是水镜庄。三国鼎立，更使水镜先生明昭千古。

图片1：三国源。

图片2：司马徽像。

图片3：司马徽和刘备。

大家能不能用汉语说出我们学校的名称？凡是来过隆中的人，都会记住湖北文理学院。湖北文理学院是一所本科院校，有19个院系，本科专业33个，一万多名学生在此苦读勤学。讲座结束后，大家还要参观校园，我相信：大家亲眼看到的校园肯定比图片上的更漂亮。让我用两句话总结今天的讲座：访三国故里，到诸葛亮读书的地方学汉语。

2. 翻译工作坊课程规划

第一，文本解读。

（1）分析上文的语言特征；

（2）留学生对译文的心理期待；

（3）结合社会因素、语言结构和文化语句三个方面提出相应的翻译策略。

第二，分组翻译(六人一组)。具体要求如下：

（1）把全文所有的文化词、地名选出来，进行术语统一翻译；

（2）组内进行翻译、修改，拟初稿；

（3）将初稿合并，六人进行小组讨论，统一术语，纠查错误，拟定稿。

（4）各组提交定稿。

第三，翻译教学讨论。

（1）以上各组分别由代表进行报告演示，说明影响文化翻译的三个方面如何指导本组翻译策略的选择的；

（2）所有同学对各组所提出的翻译策略进行讨论；

（3）教师给出参考译文，结合学生译文进行评析，讲解相关翻译技巧。

3. 参考译文

Ladies and gentlemen,

Good afternoon!

It's my great honor to have the opportunity to give the lecture on the culture of Three Kingdoms, a special historical period in the Chinese history. And I hope "Xiangyang" "Longzhong" and "Hubei University of Science and Arts" will give you a deep impression.

Xiangyang city is Located in the northwestern Hubei province and enjoys a history of over 2800 years with a splendid culture. Hanjiang River, the major tributary of Yangtze River, divides the city into two districts: Fancheng district in the north of the Hanjiang River and Xiangcheng district in the south. Now we are in Xiangyang that maybe some foreign friends have heard about (Picture: Hanjiang River and wharf). Now, the center area of Xiangyang city is the site of ancient Xiangyang. In the history, Xiangyang city is invulnerable because of the solid city wall and the city moat which is the widest in China. (Picture: ancient Xiangyang wall, the night view of the ancient Xiangyang wall, the city moat.). Just because of the strongly fortified defense system, Xiangyang city has been a strategic point.

Xiangyang not only was a crucial spot to arms, but also attracted the attention of the famous scholars and the men of letters, such as Song Yu(宋玉), a poet of ancient Chu kingdom, Wu zixu(伍子胥), a statesman of the period of Warring States, Du Shenyan(杜审言), Meng Haoran(孟浩然), Zhang Ji(张吉) and Pi Rixiu(皮日休), who were the brilliant poets of Tang dynasty, Mi Fu（米芾）, a calligrapher and an artist of Song Dynasty. And the great poets Li Bai and Du Fu had been traveled here and wrote the great poems.

When people talk about Xiangyang, one figure has to be mentioned—"Zhuge Liang" who has been praised as the "embodiment and the symbol of the Chinese wisdom". At the age of 17—27, Zhuge Liang lived at ancient Longzhong Mountain in seclusion, which is covered with pine and cypress trees and embellished with tranquil environment. For ten years, he led a simple peasant life—farming by day and studying by night. The story of "*Three Visits to the Thatched Cottage*" and the "*Longzhong Plan*" originated from there. In the well-known literary work—*the Romance of the Three Kingdoms*, Xiangyang has been mentioned in 31 chapters of 120 chapters.

Pictures：

1. The Memorial Arch in Longzhong Mountain passes with three Chinese characters in the middle "Gu Long Zhong" (ancient Longzhong)

2. At the back of the Memorial Arch, there are five Chinese characters "San Dai Xia Yi Ren", which means Zhuge Liang is the only important figure since the Xia Dynasty, Shang Dynasty and Zhou Dynasty during the nearly one thousand years.

3. The wax statue of Zhuge Liang.

4. Temple of "Wuhou" or "Temple of Marquis Wu", built by the later generations in memory of Zhuge Liang who was granted the honored title of Marquis Wu after his death.

5. The thatched cottage, where Zhuge Liang met his guests and friends. The story of "*Three Visits to the Thatched Cottage*" happened there, which goes that：Liu Bei, one of the offspring of the King of Zhongshan of Han Dynasty, decided to restore Han Dynasty. But he felt it would be impossible without the help of a smart adviser. By the recommendation of Sima Hui, Liu Bei was determined to visit Zhuge Liang. Although the story has no detailed historical record, it was depicted vividly in *The Romance of the Three Kingdoms*. When Liu Bei for the first time went to Wolonggang in Longzhong Mountain, hoping to invite Zhuge Liang to be the military adviser, Zhuge Liang, however, was not there; then in a cold snowy winter day, Liu Bei visited Zhuge Liang for the second time, but still he was not at home. The reason why Zhuge Liang refused to see Liu Bei is that he needed a second thought on choosing a wise and ambitious master to serve. At last, Liu Bei paid the third visit to the thatched cottage without complaint and finally succeeded in hiring Zhuge Liang to be his military adviser. It was in his thatched cottage that Zhuge Liang come up with *The Plan to Unify China*, and decided to be out of seclusion. Afterwards, Zhuge Liang assisted Liu Bei to get the "tripartite balance" and with his help, Shu Kingdom was finally established in Chinese history.

6. Three visits to the thatched cottage.

7. Hexangular well, a domestic well that Zhuge Liang used when he lived in Longzhong Mountain, and it is the proof of Zhuge Liang's living there.

8. Farmland. The thatched cottage Zhuge Liang lived in was built by himself. He not only farmed by himself, but also irrigated the field with the water from the "Old Dragon Cave". Zhuge Liang was such an excellent farmer that he could get the good harvest from year to year no matter it was dry or water logging. The ploughmen around the mountain wondered how could an inexperienced scholar get good harvest every year! But the facts told them Zhuge Liang actually knew the weather very well and could get the law of the weather changes, therefore, when Zhuge Liang planted corn, they did the same, when he

planted the paddy, they followed. Today, Longzhong area has been a major grain-producing area, where the grains are different from those from other area. People believe that it is Zhuge Liang who improved the seeds that can grow up to the better grains. If you travel here, don't forget to taste the boiled rice esp. locally produced, and you will find it is very delicious.

The story of *Three Kingdoms* actually originates from Village of Shuijing, located in the south of the Nanzhang county. The name of Shuijing Village is from Sima Hui, a personage of West Han Dynasty, who secluded there and was called Mr. Shuijing. It is said that when Liu Bei fled to Nanzhang from Xianyang, he met Sima Hui who recommended Zhuge Liang, to help him restore Han Dynasty. Then comes the story of *Three Visits to the Thatched Cottage*.

Pictures：

1. Source of the story of *Three Kingdoms*

2. The Image of Sima Hui

3. Sima Hui and Liu Bei

Ladies and Gentlemen, could you tell the name of Hubei University of Science and Arts in Chinese? No one will forget Hubei University of Science and Arts if he goes to Longzhong. Hubei University of Science and Arts is an interdisciplinary university which has 19 departments and colleges and provides 33 bachelor programs. Now there are more than ten thousand students studying hard here. After the lecture, you can have tour of the campus and I believe that it will be more beautiful than the picture. Finally, let me conclude this lecture into：traveling the hometown of Zhuge Liang and studying Chinese at the place where Zhuge Liang studied.

4. 翻译练习

(1)　　　　　　　　　　清明上河园

清明上河园是中国著名八朝古都开封的一座大型历史文化主题公园,占地600余亩,坐落在开封城风光秀丽的龙亭湖西岸。它是依照北宋著名画家张择端的传世之作《清明上河图》为蓝本建造的,于1998年10月28日正式对外开放。《清明上河图》是中国古代一幅弥足珍贵的社会民俗生活长卷,画中反映了开封作为中国北宋时期都城的社会生活、市井风情和城建格局。虽然它所反映的只是开封的一部分,但管中窥豹,可见一斑,由此也不难推想其他街市的大略形貌。有趣的是,千年前,张择端把它从现实搬到了画卷,千年后,开封人又把它从画卷搬到了现实。徜徉其中,常令人有"一朝步入画卷,一日梦回千年"的时光倒流之感。

清明上河园的南苑展现了北宋时期的市井百态和民俗风情,在这里您可以了解民间工艺的传奇魅力,体验市井百态的多姿多彩,感知民俗文化的深厚内涵。北苑集中体现了北宋时期的皇家院林及宫廷娱乐,在这里您可以感受皇宫城内的神圣巍峨,领略皇家院里的美轮美奂,感叹北宋皇城的瑰玮壮丽。

（2）

束河古镇

束河古镇位于丽江古城 4 公里处,是纳西先民在丽江坝子中最早的聚居地之一,是茶马古道上保存完好的重要集镇,古道、泉水、人家,是束河的传统风貌。茶马文化、纳西文化、农耕文化、生态文化,是束河的特色景观。束河古镇是纳西族从农耕文明向工商文明过渡的活标本,是对外开放和马帮活动形成的集镇建筑典范,1997 年被联合国教科文组织列为世界文化遗产丽江古城的重要组成部分。

第四章

法律英语翻译

第一节　法律英语

　　法律语言作为一种应用型语言在国际舞台发挥着重要的作用。随着中国国际地位的不断提高，法律方面的英汉-汉英翻译需求大量增加。作为一种应用性、交际性较强的文体，法律语言具有权威性、严肃性和强制性的特点，在翻译时，要尽量保留法律文本原有的特征，在忠实原文的同时，注意把握法律文本的功能性及交际性原则。

　　为了更准确、忠实地翻译法律文本，有必要对法律英语的语言特点进行分析研究。具体来讲，法律英语具有正式、专业和简洁三个主要的语言特点。

1. 正式性

　　法律文书属于书面语言，因而法律英语使用的法律词汇均属于正式的法律术语，句法也采用正式、客观的语法形式进行表达，体现法律文本正式的一面。

　　（1）使用正式的法律用词，以显示合同的正规、庄严、准确、规范以及威严的语言特点。

　　例：It hereby covenants that the Consignee guarantees the payment of all bills and accounts for goods.

　　　　兹订立契约，代销人保证付清货物的一切票据及账款。

　　其中 covenant 一词是法律用词，表示签订法律约束力的正式合约，同时体现了该句的正式性和威严性。

　　例：If any of the terms and conditions of this Agreement is substantially breached by either Party, the other Party shall have the right to terminate this Agreement.

　　　　如果当事人任何一方实质性破坏了本协议中所签订的条款或条件，那么另一方有权终止该协议。

　　Terminate 意思为"终止"，在法律文书中代替 stop，体现严肃、正式的文体特征。

　　（2）使用某些特定的语态、句式等。

　　例：All the payments shall be made in the U. S. Currency by the Buyer to the Seller by telegraphic transfer to the Seller's designated account with the Bank of China, Beijing,

China.

买方应该以美元支付卖方货款，并以电汇的方式汇至卖方指定的在中国银行北京分行的账户。

被动语态的使用体现了正式、客观的文体特征。

例： In Witness Whereof, the Parties hereto have caused this Agreement to be executed on the day and year first before written in accordance with their respective laws.

本协议于上面所签订的日期，由双方根据各自的法律签订，开始执行，特立此据。

In Witness Whereof 即"特此立据，一次立证"，"in accordance with"较"according to"更正式。这些特殊短语的使用使该句具有正式、严肃的特点。

2. 专业性

（1）法律术语

很多法律文本使用了大量的法律术语，需要译者具备较强的专业性。例如"合同的转让"用 assignment of contract 而不是用普通词 transfer，"约定违约金"用 penalty，"中止合同"用 suspension of contract，"不可抗力"用 Force Majeure，"stipulaiton"表示规定、条款，原告 plaintiff，被告 defendant 等。译者在翻译时，遇到不了解的专业术语要通过查阅专业书籍或者上网考证，做到真正理解原文的意思再进行翻译。

（2）拉丁语的使用

现代法律文书中仍在使用一些拉丁语。中世纪拉丁语随着古罗马帝国的扩张在欧洲各国成为欧洲统一语言。罗马帝国覆灭后，拉丁语仍被使用于教会语言，英语受到拉丁语的深刻影响，法律文法中的继承关系采用了一些拉丁语，具有权威、严肃和正式的风格，这些拉丁文往往给读者一种庄严甚至神圣的感觉。例：alibi（不在犯罪现场），a fortiori（更加，更不必说），ad litem（专为某一诉讼目的），agent ad litem（诉讼代理人），ab initio（自始），void ab initio（自始无效），viz（即），ex delicto（由于侵权，源自侵权）等等。

（3）特殊结构：同义词连用

一些法律文件出现了两个或三个同义词连用来表达同一意思的结构。这是由于有的词有多个意思，为确保所用词语不被曲解，将两个或三个同义词并用，来保证内容准确严谨的特点。

例： Any such consent shall not relieve the Contractor from any liability and obligation under this Contract.

任何此类同意均不应该解除合同规定的承包人的责任和义务。

Liability 和 obligation 在句中是同义词。其他如 null and void（无效），terms and conditions（条款），acknowledge and agree（确认并同意），authorize and grant（授权与授予）等。

（4）某些特定用法的短语

法律文本要求较高的正式度，有些短语在法律文本中经常使用。如 whereas（鉴于），now therefore（特此，因此），in compliance with（已从，按照），in question（该，这），in favor of（以……为受益人），the above-mentioned，aforesaid（上述的），provided that（但是，但规定），be entitled to（有权，有资格）等。

3. 简洁

有些法律文本中使用了一些古体词语，如 hereto，thereafter，whereby，hereby，herein，hereinbefore，therefrom，whereby 等，这些特殊副词的使用是为了避免重复，使行文显得正式、准确、简洁。

例： The minimum royalty herein specified shall be paid by ZZZ to AAA.

于此规定的最低使用费（租费）应由乙方付给甲方。

又如"should＋主语＋动词结构"。此结构属于省略 if 的非真实条件句。在法律英语尤其在合同英语中使用这种条件句表明发生条件句中所述情况的可能性很小，如果该条件句所述情况发生了，那么主句所设的事宜必须完成。

例： Should any of the stipulations to the Contract be altered, amended, supplemented or deleted, the same shall be negotiated between and agreed upon by both parties and written documents shall be signed by the representatives of both parties.

本合同条款的任何变更、修改或增删，须经双方协商同意，并由双方代表签署书面文件为有效。

第二节　法律英语的翻译标准及原则

由于法律英语具有正式、专业及简洁的语言特点，在翻译实践中译者对翻译策略的选择也需更加慎重。法律文本的翻译不仅要体现法律文体的特点，还要保持法律的权威性、强制性和严肃性。因而需确定一定的翻译标准并结合翻译目的、文本功能和译者主体性三个方面来确定翻译的策略。

一、翻译标准

1. 准确严谨

对于法律名词、术语和用语以及文本内容，要求译者做到准确、严谨、无漏洞。译文要忠实再现原文含义，不能有丝毫马虎。

2. 规范通顺

根据原文的内涵意义，用规范通顺的译语表达出来。

3. 文体对应

根据原语的语言特点，译语也同样需做到正式、专业及简洁。

二、翻译策略的选择

1. 语用原则

法律翻译的目的是"做出能够通过保证一致的解释和适用而保留单一法律唯一性的文本"。从语用学的角度出发，法律翻译应遵循四条语用原则：（1）原语文本功能决定法律翻译的策略；（2）法律翻译是法律机制中的交际行为；（3）译文应传达原文的法律意图；（4）译者在法律翻译交际活动中扮演着积极参与的角色。因而，译者灵活采用直译或意译的方法来进行翻译。

2. 静态对等

香港理工大学的李克兴博士提出在翻译法律文本的时候，要尽量实现"静态动态"。与奈达所提出的动态对等（即在词汇、句法、语篇、文体四个方面动态对等）不同的是，"真正的静态对等的译本要求深层意思、表层意思、语言结构、风格、格式与原文的这些方面完全对等，还要求译文最大程度地再现原文作者的写作意图。"静态对等要求译文与原文严格对等，不可以灵活处理，如 to kill two birds with one stone 译为"一石二鸟"为静态对等，而译为"一箭双雕"则为动态对等。用静态对等策略翻译的译文可经得住回译的考验，更加保证了译文的准确性。

3. 损失补偿

由于法律文本的翻译对译文质量要求极高，对准确性的把握尤其重要。中英法律文本在语言、文化、结构等方面都会有所不同，因而译者可以采用补偿策略以弥补不对等的现象。归化和异化、重复、删减等翻译方法可以酌情运用到翻译实践过程中，译者最终的目的是实现原文在法律文化、意义、风格方面的对等，将翻译的损失降到可以接受的范围，即不影响交际的目的，最大程度上实现忠实原文、静态对等。

第三节　案例及习题

一、英译汉

1. 原文

Mediation

Mediation is defined as a private, voluntary negotiation process using a trained neutral third party to facilitate a final, contractual binding settlement between parties involved in a dispute. Unlike litigation and arbitration, which consist of a formal evidentiary hearing, mediation is a semiformal negotiation between the parties without the use of evidence or witnesses. While litigation and arbitration are presided over by a judge who renders a decision in the case, mediation is facilitated by a specially trained neutral advisor who is not empowered to decide the case, only to assist the parties in negotiating effectively. Mediation is also unlike litigation in that it is non-adversarial. Indeed, the most effective mediators build a process in which parties understand their role as active participants and collaborate to resolve the dispute. Unlike a trial or arbitration, mediation often results in a mutually agreeable outcome.

Mediation, now readily available throughout the United States, has several advantages over traditional adversarial forms of dispute resolution. First, it is less costly than evidentiary processes. Mediation is normally completed in a matter of hours through a series of one to three conferences. It may occur much earlier and with much less preparation in a dispute than in a trial or arbitration. Furthermore, mediation is not a formal evidentiary process requiring extensive use of expert witnesses or demonstrative proof. Indeed, the process is most effectively accomplished without introduction of evidence or witnesses, relying instead on the parties to negotiate in good faith. As a result, the costs associated with the use of expert witnesses, trial counsel, and case preparation are substantially reduced or even eliminated. Costs are further controlled because parties traditionally share the comparatively minimal fees of hiring a mediator.

Second, the process is more efficient than most evidentiary processes. One of the principal attractions of mediation is the speed with which parties can resolve their disputes. Because mediators are present to manage negotiation, not to represent a party or render a legal decision, they need not prepare extensively to conduct the conference. As a result, one can be mediator on relatively short notice. In addition, mediation requires less preparation by the parties than formal processes, so they are able to participate sooner. Finally, overcrowded court dockets throughout the United States often delay trials for years. Private mediation can be accomplished virtually on demand.

2. 翻译工作坊课程规划

第一,文本解读。
(1) 从词汇、句法两方面分析法律英语的语言特征在上文中的体现;
(2) 了解美国关于"调解"的过程和法律背景,指出与中国现状的区别;
(3) 考虑汉语读者对该段内容的理解力,结合法律英语、法律汉语的特征提出相应的翻译策略。
第二,分组翻译(六人一组)。具体要求如下:
(1) 找出法律专业术语,进行术语翻译的统一;
(2) 组内进行翻译、修改,拟初稿;
(3) 将初稿合并,六人进行小组讨论,统一术语,纠查错误,拟定稿。
(4) 各组提交定稿。
第三,翻译教学讨论。

（1）由代表进行报告演示，结合法律英语的语言特征、翻译标准和中美关于"调解"方面的异同说明本组所用翻译策略的原因；

（2）所有同学对各组所提出的翻译策略进行讨论；

（3）教师给出参考译文，结合学生译文进行评析，讲解相关翻译技巧。

3. 参考译文

调 解

调解是争议双方当事人在受过训练的中立第三人的帮助下，自愿私下协商以最终达成有契约约束力的协议过程。和包括有正式听证程序的诉讼和仲裁不同，调解是当事人之间不使用证据或证人的半正式协商解决争议程序。诉讼和仲裁由法官主持并做出裁决，而调解是在一个受过特殊训练的中立咨询人的协助下进行的，中立者无权断案，仅协助当事人进行有效的协商。调解有别于诉讼的另一方面是其非对抗性。的确，最有效的调解人能够在调解过程中使争议双方建立起主动参与意识并积极合作、解决争议。而和审理或仲裁不同的是，调解往往导致双方都满意的结果。

调解如今在全美国是一种便捷可得的争议解决途径。同传统的对抗性争议解决方式相比，调解有几个优点。首先，它比听证程序省时省力省钱。完成调解通常只是一至三次协商、几个小时的事情，它比审理和仲裁及时得多，也只需少得多的准备。再者，调解不是正式的听证程序，不需要大量的专家证人或物证。的确，这种程序没有引入证据或证人，而是依靠争议双方的真诚协商最为有效地达到其目的。这样，用于专家证人、辩护律师以及案件准备方面的花费大大减少了，甚至全部省掉了。由于争议双方传统上共同分担聘请调解人的相对来说极少的费用，办事成本便得到了进一步的控制。

其次，调解比大多数听证程序更有效率。调解的主要吸引力之一就在于当事人解决争议的快捷性。由于调解人只是主持谈判，既不代理任何当事人，也不作出任何法律裁决，他们不用为协商会做大量的准备。这样，当时人只需提前相对较短的时间聘雇调解人即可。另外，调解不像正式程序那样要求当事人做很多的准备工作，因而当事人能够更早地参与协商。最后，全美国法院积案过多，往往使审判耽搁数年，而私下调解却能做到一经要求便可进行。

4. 翻译练习

（1）   **AGREEMENT**

This Agreement is made between _____ for and on behalf of the Government of the Republic of Singapore (hereinafter referred to as "the Government") of the first part and _____

WHEREAS：

1. The Student has been admitted to the NATIONAL UNIVERSITY OF SINGAPORE (hereinafter referred to as "the Institution") for a course in Bachelor of Science (hereinafter referred to as "the Course") leading to the PASS DEGREE.

2. The Student has applied for a grant (hereinafter referred to as a "tuition grant") to

enable the Student to pay all or part of the fees of the Course or such other course which the Student may be allowed to pursue (in place of the Course) at the Institution.

3. The Student has expressed his/her willingness to accept the tuition grant upon the terms and conditions set out in this Agreement.

4. The Sureties have agreed to be bound by the terms and conditions set out in this Agreement.

NOW IT IS HEREBY AGREED as follows:

1. In consideration of the premises and at the request of the Sureties and in consideration of the Sureties agreeing to pay the Government on demand the amount of damages specified in the schedule hereto in any of the cases set out in Clause 3 hereunder, the Government hereby covenants:

   (a) that it shall grant the Student a subsidy, which shall be disbursed to the Institution directly, and which amount shall be based on the rate applicable to the Course, which rate the Government may vary from time to time. The subsidy rate applicable to the Student's Course for the prevailing academic year shall be posted in The Tuition Grant Scheme section on the official website of the Ministry of Education, Singapore.

   (b) that it shall pay the tuition grant to the Institution in such manner, in such amount and at such times as it thinks fit.

2. (1) In consideration of the premises and with the approval and the consent of the Sureties, the Student hereby covenants:

   (a) that he/she shall enter upon and diligently continue in the Course, during which, he/she shall continue to receive the tuition grant in accordance with Clause 1;

   (b) that he/she shall diligently seek:

      (i) employment in Singapore-based companies immediately upon the completion of the Course;

      (ii) re-employment in Singapore-based companies immediately upon his/her resignation or dismissal from or cessation of his/her employment;

   (c) that he/she shall inform the Government (submitting evidence at the same time of all efforts to seek employment or re-employment) if he/she is unable to obtain employment within three (3) months after completion of the Course or re-employment within three (3) months after his/her resignation or dismissal from or cessation of his/her employment;

   (d) that he/she shall unless unable to obtain any employment within one (1) year after completion of the Course or re-employment (within one (1) year after his/her resignation or dismissal from or cessation of his/her employment) work in Singapore-based companies for a period or periods totaling in the aggregate three (3) years (hereinafter referred to as the "Bonded Period") upon the completion of the Course;

(e) that he/she shall, during the Bonded Period, inform the Government of the particulars of his/her initial employment, change of employment, resignation or dismissal from or cessation of his/her employment as the case may be.

(2) For the purpose of this Clause:

(a) The term "employment" shall include such self-employment as may be approved by the Government.

(b) The expression "completion of the Course" shall include, as the case may be, a completion of any other course or courses of study which the Government allows the Student to pursue whether in place of or in addition to the Course.

3. In consideration of the Government having at the Student's and Sureties' request agreed to give the Student a tuition grant, it is hereby agreed and declared that if the Student:

(a) refuses or in the opinion of the Government willfully renders himself/herself unable to work in accordance with the provisions of clause 2(1) (d) of this Agreement; or

(b) has been convicted by a court of law in any country during the Course or the period before he/she commences serving the bond, of an offence involving dishonesty or moral turpitude, which offence, in the opinion of the Government renders him/her unsuitable for appointment to the Government or any organization; or

(c) is dismissed from the service of, or has his/her service terminated by his/her employer for misconduct, negligence or incompetence in his/her duties before the expiry of the Bonded Period; or

(d) having been conferred citizenship or permanent resident status, subsequently renounces or ceases to be the same, whether before or after the date of this Agreement, and is unable to obtain an employment pass or other pass enabling him/her to work in accordance with the provisions of clause 2(1) (d) of this Agreement or has his/her employment or other pass revoked thereby rendering him/her unable to work in accordance with the provisions of clause 2(1) of this Agreement; or

(e) breaches any of the other covenants of the Agreement; then, and in any such cases the Student and the Sureties shall be jointly and severally liable for themselves and their respective heirs, executors or assigns to pay the Government on demand the amount in damages specified in the Schedule hereto;

PROVIDED that the Government may at its discretion, in such manner as it thinks fit, reduce the amount due under clause 3 (a), (b), (c), (d) and (e) by the same proportion as the number of the completed months worked bears to the Bonded Period.

4. In consideration of the Government having at the Student's and Sureties' request agreed to give the Student a tuition grant, and—the Student having prior to this grant made a declaration that all information stated by him/her in his application for the tuition grant is true and accurate to the best of his/her knowledge, it is hereby further agreed that:

   (a) if any of the information furnished by the Student in his/her application for the tuition grant is in any way false, incorrect or inaccurate; or

   (b) if the Student has willfully suppressed any fact which is in the opinion of the Government material, then the Student and the Sureties shall be jointly and severally liable for themselves and their respective heirs, executors or assigns to pay the Government on demand the amount in damages specified in the Schedule hereto.

5. It is hereby further agreed as follows:

   (a) Notwithstanding anything to the contrary hereinbefore contained, the Government may, at its discretion, at any time suspend the tuition grant or revoke this Agreement, as appropriate, without assigning any reason thereof in the event that the Student is suspended or expelled by the Institution or leaves it or is excluded from the Institution or any part thereof or from any courses or subjects or from any examinations. Any suspension of the tuition grant or a revocation of this Deed shall not render the Government liable for any damages, loss, expenses, claims, demands or cost of any kind whatsoever, and shall be without prejudice to the right of action of the Government in respect of any prior breach by the Student of any of the terms and conditions herein contained.

   (b) The Sureties shall not be discharged or released from their liability hereunder by any arrangement made between the Government and the Student with or without the consent of the Sureties or by any alteration in the obligations undertaken by the Student hereunder or by any forbearance whether as to payment, time or performance or otherwise by either the Government or the Student.

6. The Student with the consent of the Sureties hereby further undertakes:

   (1) to absolve the Government including its servants and agents from all liability to the Student or his/her personal representative in respect of any loss, damage, injury or death however caused or occasioned (whether or not by any act or by any omission or neglect of the Institution or its servant or agents)

which he/she may sustain by reason of or during his/her tenure of the Course or such other course which he/she may be allowed to pursue; and

(2) to indemnify and keep harmless the Government against all proceeding, suits, actions, claims, demands, cost and expenses whatsoever which may be taken or made against the Government or incurred or become payable by the Government in respect of injury (whether fatal or otherwise) to any person or damage or loss to any property occasioned directly or indirectly by any act, omission or other default by the Student while on or otherwise in relation to or arising out of the Course or such other course which he/she may be allowed to pursue.

7. Any forbearance whether passive or express on the part of the Government in enforcing any of its) remedies for any breach by the Student of any one or more of the terms and conditions herein contained or any other act or thing which but for this clause would operate as a release of the Student or the Sureties shall not in any way affect or prejudice the joint and several liability of the Sureties or the continuing liability of the Sureties or either of them or their estates.

8. It is further expressly agreed by and between the Student and the Sureties and the Government that if at any time during the currency of this Agreement either of the Sureties shall die or cease to reside within or remain out of their respective Country of Residency for more than twelve (12) consecutive months or shall become insolvent (the duty of reporting any such events to the Government being hereby placed on the Student) then and in such an event the Student and the remaining Surety or either of them shall substitute a new Surety who is acceptable to the Government and who shall be ready and willing to substitute for and take over the obligations herein contained of the Surety who has died, ceased to reside within or remained out of their respective Country of Residency as aforesaid or has become insolvent.

PROVIDED that in the event that no such substitute Surety can be found, the Government may at its option at any time thereafter terminate this Agreement and the Student shall thereupon cease to have any further claim to any benefits under this Agreement or to any right to damages, expenses, claims, demands or cost of any kind whatsoever without prejudice to his/her obligations under this Agreement.

9. In consideration of the premises, the Student also irrevocably consents to and authorises the disclosure by the relevant Government ministry or statutory board, to the Ministry of Education, of any information whatsoever relating to him/her as is necessary for the purpose of ascertaining whether he/she has complied with all the terms of this Agreement, in particular, whether he/she has complied with clause 2(1) of this Agreement.

10. It is hereby agreed and declared that the Schedule to this Agreement shall be read with and shall form part of this Agreement.

11. The Government having agreed to bear the expense of providing the proper stamp duty in respect of this Agreement, this Agreement is exempted from such duty under Section 35(a) of the Stamp Act (Cap 147).

12. The parties hereto agrees that this Agreement shall be deemed to be made in Singapore and shall be governed by the laws of Singapore and the courts of Singapore shall have jurisdiction to decide all questions arising hereunder.

(2) **BRASS CUP 5.56**

Cu Zn28	Material Specification		Page(s):1	
	Number:**LB31.00015**		Of:1	
Name: **BRASS CUP 5.56**			Chemical Formula:**Cu Zn 10**	
Revision:	a	b	c	d	e	f

The brass cups Cu Zu 10 number LB31.00015 must in accord with the terms as follow:

1. Chemical Composition
   a. Cu:89~91%
   b. Zn:Remainder
   c. Fe:Max. 0.05%
   d. Sn:Max. 0.03%
   e. Al:Max. 0.03%
   f. Ni:Max. 0.20%
   g. As:Max. 0.02%
   h. Pb:Max. 0.05%
   i. Sb:Max. 0.01%
   j. Bi:Max. 0.04%
   k. Other ingredient:Max. 0.01%(DIN 17660/According to DIN 17660)

2. Physical & Mechanical properties
   The surface of cups should be free from: Oil, dirt, holes, splits, cracks, scales, flaws at radius, lamination, corrosion, bulg, dents, irregular edges.
   a. Grain size:0.025 + 0.04 mm
   b. Hardness after annealing and washing (According to DIN 17670)

3. Dimension/tolerances   See drawing

4. Packing
   Inside: Max. 25kg & Silicagel in a plastic and cotton bag.
   Outside: Max. 500kg in a metallic container.
   Max. On the Pallet:2 metallic container of approx. 1,000 kg on the Pallet.
   Making, content such as: Product name, weight in container, lot/batch number, contract number, handling method & symbol.

Berat:1.55 gram.

31

（续表）

Remarks：For bullet jacket of cal. 5.56×45 mm(MU5-TJ & MU4-TJ)			
Synonym：MESSING 90 CUPS		Reference：	
Prepared by	Inspected by	Approved by	
Function	Staff of Sub Eng Dept.	Head of Eng Dept.	Deputy VP. For Ammunition Division	Vice President for Ammunition Division
Name				
Date	April 12 2006	April 12 2006	April 13 2006	April 13 2006
Signature				

01PDB177　　　　　　　　　　　　　　　　LB31.00015-CuZn10-4TJ/5TJ

二、汉译英

1. 原文

聘用合同

澳大利亚堪培拉 AA 大学外语系（聘方）聘请李明教授（受聘方）为中国古典文学教师。双方本着友好合作的精神特签订本合同，其条款如下：

1. 聘期为一年，自 2013 年 9 月 1 日起，至 2014 年 8 月 31 日止。

2. 受聘方的工作任务，经双方协商确定为：

1）担任汉语教师、研究生和进修生的培训工作；

2）担任高年级中国古典文学教师，指导学生开展汉语课外活动；

3）编写汉语教材和补充读物；

4）每周授课 8~10 课时。

3. 受聘方的工作时间每周 5 天，每天 7 小时。受聘方按照中国、澳大利亚两国政府规定的节假日放假，寒假按本校校历规定。

4. 聘方每月支付给受聘方工资 2 000 澳元，并按照澳大利亚政府对在澳工作的外籍教师的规定提供各种福利待遇。

5. 受聘方在入境、离境或过境时，必须遵守澳大利亚政府有关外国人居住、工资福利及旅行等的法律、规章，并遵守聘方的工作制度。

6. 双方均不得无故撤销合同。如果聘方要求中途终止合同，除按上述条款承担工资福利待遇外，须给受聘方增发 3 个月的工资作为补偿金，并于 1 个月内安排受聘方及其家属回国并承担有关费用。

如果受聘方中途提出辞职,聘方自同意之日起即停发工资;受聘方不再享受各项福利待遇;受聘方及其家属回国的一切费用均由本人自理。

7. 本合同自受聘方到校之日起生效,到聘期届满时失效。如一方要求延长聘期,必须在合同期满前一个月书面向对方提出,经双方协商同意后另签延聘合同。

8. 本合同用中英两种文字写成,两种文本具有同等效力。

聘方:　　　　　　　　　受聘方:

签字地:中国广州

签署日期:2013 年 8 月 10 日

2. 翻译工作坊课程规划

第一,文本解读。

(1) 合同汉语的词汇、句法特征。同时需要了解合同英语中的被动语态、shall 的用法、长句的使用。分析英汉合同的语言特征异同;

(2) 了解雇佣合同的相关条款;

(3) 根据合同英语、合同汉语的语言特征提出相应的翻译策略。

第二,分组翻译(六人一组)。具体要求如下:

(1) 找出上述合同中的法律专业术语、合同术语、雇佣关系术语,进行术语翻译的统一;

(2) 组内进行翻译、修改,拟初稿;

(3) 将初稿合并,六人进行小组讨论,统一术语,纠查错误,拟定稿。

(4) 各组提交定稿。

第三,翻译教学讨论。

(1) 由代表进行报告演示,结合英汉合同语言特征异同说明本组所用的翻译策略;

(2) 所有同学对各组所提出的翻译策略进行讨论;

(3) 教师给出参考译文,结合学生译文进行评析,讲解相关翻译技巧。

3. 参考译文

Employment Contract

The foreign Language Department of the AA University, Canberra, Australia (the engaging party) has engaged Professor Li Ming (the engaged party) as a teacher of the Chinese classics. The two parties, in the spirit of friendship and cooperation, hereby sign this Contract subject to the following terms and conditions:

1. The term of service is one year beginning on September 1, 2013 and ending on August 31, 2014.

2. The work of the engaged party is decided through mutual consultation as follows:

1) Training teachers of Chinese, research students and students having advanced studies;

2) Conducting senior Chinese classics classes and advising students on extracurricular

activities of Chinese;

   3) Compiling Chinese textbooks and supplementary teaching material;

   4) Having 8 to 10 teaching periods a week.

   4. The engaging party pays the engaged party a monthly salary of 2,000 Australian dollars and provides him with various benefits as prescribed by Australian Government for foreign teachers working in Australia.

   5. The engaged party shall abide by the laws and regulations of the Australian Government concerning residence, wages and benefits, and travel for foreigners when entering, leaving and passing through the territory of the country, and shall follow the working system of the engaging party.

   6. Neither party shall cancel the Contract without reasonable causes. If the engaging party finds it imperative to terminate the Contract, then, in addition to bearing the above-mentioned wages and benefits, it shall pay the engaged party three months' extra salary as compensation allowance, and arrange at its own cost for him and his family to go back to their country within one month.

   If the engaged party submits his resignation in the course of his service, the engaging party will stop paying him salary from the date when his resignation is approved by the engaging party, and the engaged party will no longer enjoy the benefits. When leaving Australia, the engaged party and his family will have to pay for everything themselves.

   7. This Contract comes into effect on the first day of the engaged party's arrival at AA University and ceases to be effective at its expiration. If either party wishes to renew the Contract, the other party shall be notified in writing one month before it expires. Upon agreement by both parties through consultation, a new contract may be signed between two parties.

   8. This Contract is made in English and Chinese, both versions being equally valid.

The engaging party: _____   The engaged party

Signed at Guangzhou, China on August 10, 2013

4. 翻译练习

（1）   分销协议书

   本分销协议由 PETRA 石油公司（以下简称为公司）和_____（以下简称为分销商）于_____（生效日）共同签署，根据本协议进行销售和分销产品。公司和分销商在本协议统称为当事人。

   鉴于：

   公司的业务范围为生产相关产品。公司有意销售并为该产品开拓市场。分销商有意购买公司产品并进行转售。

   协议双方有意签订分销协议用以管控双方关系的期限。

   故，经双方谨慎思虑，互相认同，双方同意以下条款：

   第一条

术语界定

1. "产品"指的是该协议附表 A 中所列的所有或任何一种产品。在该协议的有效期内，公司可随时根据情况单方面决定取消部分产品。

2. "分销区域"指的是本协议附表 B 中所解释的地理位置。

3. "公司商标"指的是本协议附表 C 中的产权、商标、商标名称以及服务商标。在本协议的有效期内，公司随时根据市场销售情况单方面决定对公司商标进行增加或取消。

第二条

约定

4. 分销权：若分销商对本协议的条款认可，公司授权分销商，分销商接受分销权并作为该产品在分销区域内的非独家分销商。除非本协议中明确提出，否则分销商不得复制或销售该产品，不得授权或分销该产品。

未经公司事先书面同意，分销商不得报盘、销售、授权销售或分销来自其他任何实体而非直接从公司获得的产品。

从协议期的第二年开始，双方对协议第二年和以后数年的销售目标达成一致。销售目标应以历史销售和计划销售为基础，形成书面文件，并作为附表 D 附于本协议之后。

5. 区域外分销：分销商应将相关产品仅销售给分销区域内的客户。未经公司事先书面同意，分销商不得在分销区域外进行市场营销或销售。如果任何分销区域内的客户，在分销区域外也有经营场所，或者任何分销区域内的客户欲将产品再次销售于区域外时，分销商可以销售产品并将产品寄送于客户。

6. 国民账户：为销售产品便利，公司可与客户建立国民账户。包括价格条款在内的此国民账户的协议条款可提供给分销区域内的各个客户。若分销商选择销售产品于该客户，分销商应履行客户与公司所签订的国民账户协议；反之，经销商可选择不销售产品给该客户并退出上述国民账户协议。若分销商选择退出国民账户协议，公司有权将该账户转让给另一经销商。

7. 二级分销商：只在经得公司事先书面同意的情况下，分销商可任命二级分销商代表其进行销售。由任何经销商所引起的一切赔偿，责任仅由分销商承担。与二级分销商所签署的与本产品相关的任何协议应与本协议一致。未经分销商事先书面同意，公司不得参与与任何二级分销商的商业活动。

8. 独立承包地位：由本协议所确立的公司与分销商的关系应为独立承包关系。公司和分销商均不能为某一员工、代理人、合伙人或两者的合资公司或与另一方的合资公司。分销商不能是公司以任何事由为目的的代理人或代表，分销商或任何分销商的经理、部门主管、代理人或员工均不能成为公司的代理人或员工。公司不能是分销商以任何事由为目的的代理人或代表，公司或任何公司的经理、部门主管、代理人或员工均不能成为分销商的代理人或员工。

分销商未被授予并不应承担或创造代表公司或以公司为名的责任或义务的权利。公司未被授予并不应承担或创造代表分销商或以分销商为名的责任或义务的权利。

9. 运营及相关费用：分销商自主管控本协议项下属于分销商的各种费用。分销商应对其所有费用及员工负责。分销商应自费提供执行本协议可能需要的办公场所及设施、雇佣及培训员工。未经公司事先同意，分销商不应产生由公司负责的相关费用。

10. 其他未授予权利:公司未授予分销商任何其他除本协议规定外的权利、职位或利益。除本产品及本产品销售区域外,公司未授予分销商与本产品相关的其他任何权利、职位或利益。

（2）　　　　　　　　　　**房屋租赁合同**

本合同双方当事人

出租方（甲方）:

承租方（乙方）:

根据国家有关法律、法规和本市有关规定,甲、乙双方在平等自愿的基础上,经友好协商一致,就甲方将其合法拥有的房屋出租给乙方使用,乙方承租使用甲方房屋事宜,订立本合同。

一、建物地址

甲方将其所有的位于襄阳市区的房屋及其附属设施在良好状态下出租给乙方使用。

二、房屋面积

出租房屋的登记面积为_____平方米（建筑面积）。

三、租赁期限

租赁期限自____年____月____日起至____年____月____日止,为期年,甲方应于____年____月____日将房屋腾空并交付乙方使用。

四、租金

1. 数额:双方商定租金为每月_____元整（含管理费）。乙方以_____形式支付给甲方.

2. 租金按_____月为壹期支付;第一期租金于_____年_____月_____日以前付清;以后每期租金于每月的_____日以前缴纳,先付后住（若乙方以汇款形式支付租金,则以汇出日为支付日,汇费由汇出方承担）;甲方收到租金后予书面签收。

3. 如乙方逾期支付租金超过七天,则每天以月租金的 0.3‰ 支付滞纳金;如乙方逾期支付租金超过十天,则视为乙方自动退租,构成违约,甲方有权收回房屋,并追究乙方违约责任。

五、押金

1. 为确保房屋及其附属设施之安全与完好,及租赁期内相关费用之如期结算,乙方同意于_____年_____月_____日前支付给甲方押金_____元整,甲方在收到押金后予以书面签收。

2. 除合同另有约定外,甲方应于租赁关系消除且乙方迁空、点清并付清所有应付费用后的当天将押金全额无息退还乙方。

3. 因乙方违反本合同的规定而产生的违约金、损坏赔偿金和其他相关费用,甲方可在押金中抵扣,不足部分乙方必须在接到甲方付款通知后十日内补足。

4. 因甲方原因导致乙方无法在租赁期内正常租用该物业,甲方应立即全额无息退还押金予乙方,且乙方有权追究甲方的违约责任。

六、甲方义务

1. 甲方须按时将房屋及附属设施（详见附件）交付乙方使用。

2. 房屋设施如因质量原因、自然损耗、不可抗力或意外事件而受到损坏,甲方有修缮并承担相关费用的责任。如甲方未在两周内修复该损坏物,以致乙方无法正常使用房屋设施,乙方有权终止该合约,并要求退还押金。

3. 甲方应确保出租的房屋享有出租的权利,如租赁期内该房屋发生所有权全部或部分转移、设定他项物权或其他影响乙方权益的事件,甲方应保证所有权人、他项权利人或其他影响乙方权益的第三者能继续遵守本合同所有条款,反之如乙方权益因此遭受损害,甲方应负赔偿责任。

4. 甲方应为本合同办理登记备案手续,如因未办理相关登记手续致该合同无效或损害乙方租赁权利,应由甲方负责赔偿,且甲方应承担该合同相关的所有税费。

七、乙方义务

1. 乙方应按合同的规定按时支付租金及押金。

2. 乙方经甲方同意,可在房屋内添置设备。租赁期满后,乙方将添置的设备搬走,并保证不影响房屋的完好及正常使用。

3. 未经甲方同意,乙方不得将承租的房屋转租或分租,并爱护使用该房屋。如因乙方过失或过错致使房屋及设施受损,乙方应承担赔偿责任。

4. 乙方应按本合同规定合法使用该房屋,不得擅自改变使用性质。乙方不得在该房屋内存放危险物品。否则,如该房屋及附属设施因此受损,乙方应承担全部责任。

5. 乙方应承担租赁期内的水、电、煤气、电话费、收视费、一切因实际使用而产生的费用,并按单如期缴纳。

八、合同终止及解除的规定

1. 乙方在租赁期满后如需续租,应提前一个月通知甲方,由双方另行协商续租事宜。在同等条件下乙方享有优先续租权。

2. 租赁期满后,乙方应在_____日内将房屋交还甲方;任何滞留物,如未取得甲方谅解,均视为放弃,任凭甲方处置,乙方决无异议。

3. 本合同一经双方签字后立即生效;未经双方同意,不得任意终止,如有未尽事宜,甲、乙双方可另行协商。

九、违约及处理

1. 甲、乙双方任何一方在未征得对方谅解的情况下,不履行本合同规定条款,导致本合同中途终止,则视为该方违约,双方同意违约金为_____元整,若违约金不足弥补无过错方之损失,则违约方还需就不足部分支付赔偿金。

2. 若双方在执行本合同或与本合同有关的事情时发生争议,应首先友好协商;协商不成,可向有管辖权的人民法院提起诉讼。

十、其他

1. 本合同附件是本合同的有效组成部分,与本合同具有同等法律效力。

2. 本合同壹式贰份,甲、乙双方各执一份。

3. 甲、乙双方如有特殊约定,可在本款另行约定。

第五章

公示语翻译

第一节　公示语的语言特征

公示语(public signs)是给公众在公众场合看的语言文字,为人们生活中最常见的实用语言,是一种公开和面对公众的、以达到某种交际目的的特殊文体。公示语几乎随处可见,例如路标、广告牌、商店招牌、公共场所的宣传语、旅游简介等等。随着中国国际化程度的逐步深化,公示语的翻译也越来越受重视。

一、公示语的主要功能

1. 示意功能

示意功能主要表现为一种信息提供服务。示意功能包括指示、提示、限制和强制四个应用示意功能。主要提示读者应该如何做、如何规范行为、有些行为是禁止甚至是强制性的。

2. 语用功能

语用功能包括提供信息、引发兴趣或促进行动、服务社会及警示规范四个语用功能。语用功能更多是服务性的,如提供一些消费及服务信息,通过公益公告服务社会、树立城市形象,规范公众行为举止预防犯罪等。

二、公示语具有的语言特点

1. 简洁

由于公示语具有提示信息的语用价值,因而,一般以最简单的词汇和句式最准确和直接的传达信息。句子一般长度较短,祈使句型经常用于公示语中。例如:"请爱护公共设施"(Please Take Care of Public Properties.);"勿将物品放入扶梯间隙处"(Don't Put Objects in the Escalator Gap.);"下车时请注意安全"(Watch Your Step While Getting Off)等。

2. 大量使用名词、动词、动名词、短语和缩略语

服务、指示、说明性质的公示语大量使用名词。例如:"入境检查"是"Passport Control"、"安全检查"是"Security Check"、"候机楼"是"Terminal Building"等。而限制性、强制性的公示语大量使用动词或动名词。如"禁止靠近"是"Keep Clear"、"请节约用水"是"Please Conserve Water"、"请勿挤靠"是"Keep off the Door"、"禁止随地吐痰"是"No Spitting"等。各种短语也大量应用于公示语。如"售完"是"Sold Out"、"入住登记"是"Check In"等。一些旅游和公共设施经常用到缩略词,如"P"表示"停车场"、"VIP"表示"贵宾"等。

3. 互文性

法国后结构主义文艺批评家朱莉娅·克丽斯蒂娃(Julia Kristeva)认为:"每一个文本都是由对其他文本的援引而构成的镶嵌图案,每一个文本都是对其他文本的吸收和转换"。也就是说,文本和文本间有着极大的关联性,反映在文化、历史、语言等各个层面,这种关联就是互文性。公示语不仅仅是信息的传递和行为的约束,公示语的语言中还包含了一个国家的历史、文化及其他各个方面的综合信息,它不仅与创造者的创作意图有关,还与创造者的文化历史背景有着深厚的联系。如"售票处""挂号处"等处所,我国使用"处"而不用"办公室"来表达。一些涉及历史文化的公示语更具有互文性,如"草庐"(Thatched cottage),"荐贤堂"(Talents-recommending Hall)等。

第二节 公示语的翻译原则

公示语具有示意和语用功能,使用起来简洁直接,具有互文性,名词、动词、短语等使用频繁。根据这些特征,本着"信、达、雅"的翻译标准,公示语的翻译要遵循以下五个原则:

一、简洁易懂

公示语一般使用简单直接的语言表达,翻译的时候也要注意文体上的对应,不使用生僻词,尽量做到简单短小,直接易懂。如"谢绝小费"直接译为"No Tipping",名词短语结构简单,不会产生歧义。"市内公交汽车专用"译为"City Buses Only"三个名词就直接简单的表明了意义。

二、语气和谐,信息度与原文切合

公示语传达一定的信息,服务于公众。翻译时,当信息传达的度超过或不及会导致语气与原文不切合。如火车站的售票处如果译为"Ticket",信息度就较弱,译为"Ticket Booking"就可以适度的表达原文的信息量。"顾客止步"如译为"Guest no further"语气过为生硬,译为"Staff Only"比较委婉,语气较为和谐。

三、准确体现语用价值

公示语有一定的语用价值，翻译时要特别注意公示语的交际功能。如"小心滑倒"本是一种关心提醒，当译为"Don't Fall Down"就成为一种命令，损坏了原文的交际目的。译为"Watch Your Step"或"Slippery"就更为恰当些。

四、术语匹配

公示语中可能会涉及一些比较专业的领域。翻译专业的词汇时要特别注意使用行内术语。如"眼科医院"不能译为"Eye Hospital"而应使用术语"Ophthalmology Hospital".

五、文化兼容

翻译是一种跨文化交际行为，在翻译公示语时，要重视其中包含的文化内涵。如"夫妻肺片"不能直译为人的肺片，而应该了解中国该道菜的食材和做法后译为"Sliced beef and ox tongue in chili sauce".

第三节　案例及习题

一、英译汉

1. 案例

金融公示语

(1) Chinese Depository Receipt（CDR）

(2) Stakeholder

(3) Variable Interest Entity（VIE）

(4) Open outcry

(5) Price-to-book ratio

(6) Delivery

(7) Turnover rate

(8) Global depositary receipt（GDR）

(9) Strike price

(10) Interest-rate swap

(11) Bear position

(12) Designated securities

(13) Derivatives

(14) Limit order

(15) Book runner

(16) Underlying securities

(17) Debt-to-equity ratio

(18) Loan to deposit ratio＝outstanding loans÷balance of deposits. It is calculated according to relevant provisions of PBOC. Of which, the balance of deposits include due to customers and due to financial institutions such as financial holding companies and insurance companies(Annual Report of BOC：2012).

(19) The financial statements of BEA China, which comprise the balance sheet as at 31st December, 2010 as well as the income statement and cash flow statement for the year 2010, are prepared in accordance with the requirements of the Accounting Standards for Business Enterprises （2006） promulgated by the Ministry of Finance of the People's Republic of China and have been audited by the Shanghai Branch of KPMG Huazhen Certified Public Accountants (Annual Report of BEA：2010).

(20) The instruments used to manage interest rate risk include interest rate swaps and other derivatives. (BEA 2009：210).

(21) The bank successfully managed the electronic system for the transactions of the RMB interest rate derivative products, improved market-making capability and transacted RMB interest rate swap of RMB 33. 3 billions. (BOC Share A 2008：58).

2. 翻译工作坊课程规划

第一,文本解读。
(1) 分析上述公示语的语言特征；
(2) 目的语读者的范围；
(3) 结合社会因素、中英公共设施的不同、目的语公示语语言特征三个方面提出相应的翻译策略。

第二,分组翻译(六人一组)。具体要求如下：
(1) 按照所提出的翻译策略,各组成员分别进行翻译；
(2) 组内进行翻译、修改,拟初稿；
(3) 将初稿合并,六人进行小组讨论,统一术语,纠查错误,拟定稿。
(4) 各组提交定稿。

第三,翻译教学讨论。
(1) 以上各组分别由代表进行报告演示,说明本组翻译策略选择的依据；
(2) 所有同学对各组所提出的翻译策略进行讨论；
(3) 教师给出参考译文,结合学生译文进行评析,讲解相关翻译技巧。

3. 参考译文

(1) 中国存托凭证
(2) 权益人
(3) 可变利益实体
(4) 口头唱价

（5）市净率

（6）交付/收割

（7）换手率

（8）全球存托凭证

（9）行权价格/行使价

（10）利率调期/利率掉期

（11）空头/空仓

（12）标的证券/指定证券

（13）衍生品/衍生工具

（14）限价委托

（15）配售经办人/簿记管理人

（16）基础证券/指定证券

（17）股本金比率/债务

（18）货存比＝贷款余额÷存款余额，货存比按照中国人民银行的规定计算。其中，存款余额包括客户存款以及保险公司和金融控股公司等同业存款（中国银行年度报告：2012）。

（19）东亚中国2010年12月31日的资产负债表、2010年度的利润表和现金流量表根据中华人民共和国财政部颁布的企业会计准则（2006）的规定编制，并经毕马威华振会计师事务所上海分所审计（东亚银行年度报告：2010）。

（20）管理利率风险的工具包括利率掉期和其他衍生工具。（东亚银行2009：210）

（21）银行成功实现人民币利率衍生产品交易电子化系统管理，提升做市交易能力，完成人民币利率互换交易量333亿元。（中国银行SA股2008：58）。

4. 翻译练习

银行标识语翻译

（1）Business Banking

（2）Personal Banking

（3）Credit Cards

（4）Financial Management

（5）Duty Manager

（6）Foreign Exchange Agents of Bank of China

（7）Increasing Fund for the Transport IC Card

（8）Exchange for Small Bills

（9）Take a Number

（10）Users' Guide for ATM System

（11）Mind Your Steps

（12）Form Completion Desk

（13）Suggestions

（14）Information Desk

(15) Window for the Disabled

(16) Position Closed

警务公示语翻译

(1) DUI Prohibited

(2) Beat Patrol

(3) Fingerprint Collecting

(4) Foreign Affairs Administration Section

(5) Excluding Public Holidays

(6) Slow down and Give Way to Pedestrians

(7) International Travel Information

(8) Reports Office

(9) Visa Fee for Countries on Reciprocal Treaties

(10) Form Completion Area

(11) Report to the Police While Green Light is on.

(12) Processing Fee

(13) Online Applications Accepted

(14) Arrival Date

(15) No Entry. Authorized Only.

(16) Public Relation Area

(17) Case Investigation Office

(18) Records Room

(19) International Travel Application

(20) Dangerous Articles Prohibited

二、汉译英

1. 案例

交通公示语

当前站	禁止喧哗	办公区域	IC卡查询机	请查看基准票价
上一站	禁止靠近	请节约用水	确认键	小心夹手
无障碍坡道	请爱护公共设施	检票处(地铁站)	车票无效,请使用有效车票	勿将物品放入扶梯间隙处
未开通车站	警务室	开站时间	关站时间	轨道交通出入口周边区域信息
轨道交通车站站区图	请勿挤靠	硬币兑换处	基督教堂	公交车站点
地铁	售票处	道路	请减速行驶	禁止随地吐痰

（续表）

接待处	候机室	高速公路	请保持地铁清洁	禁止通行
问询处	限速	前方施工请绕行	机动车禁止入内	不准擅入
租车服务	闭路监控电视	闲人免进	不准超车	请排队上车
行李存放处	酒后驾车	妇女儿童优先	禁止吸烟	电梯维修，请走楼梯
请任何人不得越过此线	（停车场边）限持停车证者使用	此处禁止入内	没有预约谢绝访问	访客停车场
公交车专用车道	超车道	候机楼	起飞/到达时间	有/无申报
入境检查	（机场）免税店	安全检查	老幼病残孕专座	票面余额不足
如遇不寻常状况请上报	请让老年人和残障人先上车	汽车行驶中禁止与司机交谈	允许存放，但后果自负	禁止U型转弯
前方有隧道	限速48公里/小时	自行车存放处	请携带好随身物品	先下后上，文明乘车
下车时请注意安全	检票处	晕机袋		

2. 翻译工作坊课程规划

第一，文本解读。

（1）分析汉语公示语的语言特征并对上述给出公示语进行分类，分析不同类别的公示语的语言特征是否类同；

（2）目的语读者的心理特征；

（3）结合社会因素、中英公共设施的不同、目的语公示语语言特征三个方面提出相应的翻译策略。

第二，分组翻译（六人一组）。具体要求如下：

（1）按照所提出的翻译策略，各组成员分别进行翻译；

（2）组内进行翻译、修改，拟初稿；

（3）将初稿合并，六人进行小组讨论，统一术语，纠查错误，拟定稿。

（4）各组提交定稿。

第三，翻译教学讨论。

（1）以上各组分别由代表进行报告演示，说明本组翻译策略的选择的依据；

（2）所有同学对各组所提出的翻译策略进行讨论；

（3）教师给出参考译文，结合学生译文进行评析，讲解相关翻译技巧。

3. 参考译文

Current Station	No Loud Noise	Office Area	IC Card Inquiry	Please check for basic ticket fare
Last Station	Keep Clear	Please Conserve Water	Confirmation Button	Warning: Pinch Point. Keep hands clear during operation

（续表）

Wheelchair Ramp/ Accessibility Ramp	Please Take Care of Public Properties	Ticket Check	The ticket is not valid. Please use a valid one.	Don't put objects in the escalator gap
Station not in service	Police	Open：××	Close：××	Area Map
Station Layout	Keep off the Door	Change	Church	Bus Stop
Subway	Ticket Office	Ave/St/Rd	Please Reduce Speed	No Spitting
Reception	Departure Lounge	Expwy	Keep the Subway Litter Free	No Thoroughfare
Information	Speed Limit	Construction Ahead	No Access to Vehicles/No Entry for Vehicles	No Trespassing
Car Rental	C. C. T. V(Closed Circuit Television)	Stuff Only	No Overtaking	Queue Up for the Bus
Luggage Depository	DUI(Drive Under Influence of Alcohol)	Women and Children First	No Smoking	Lift Under Repairs, Please Take the Stairs
No Persons Allowed Beyond the Line	Parking Restricted to Permit Holders	This Area Closed	Seen by Appointment Only	Visitors Parking Only
Buses Only	Overtaking Only	Terminal Building	Departure/ Arrival Time	Something/Nothing to Declare
Passport Control	Duty-free Shop	Security Check	Priority Seats for People in Need	Insufficient Fare
See Something, Say Something	Please Let Seniors and Disabled People Board First	No Talking to Driver in Moving Bus	With Permission, but at Owner's Risk	No U Turn
Tunnel Ahead	Speed Limit 48km/h	Cycle Storage	Please Take Your Belongings	Please Let the Passengers Get Off First
Watch Your Step While Getting Off	Check-in	Airsickness Bag		

4. 翻译练习

（一）校园公示语：湖北文理学院襄阳十大历史名人翻译

（1）卞和：玉石鉴赏家，春秋荆（今湖北南漳县）人，于荆山得一璞，先后献厉王、武王，皆视为石，断其双足。文王即位，卞和抱璞恸哭荆山下，王闻之，令人剖璞，果得宝玉，乃称"和氏璧"。今南漳有玉印岩。

（2）宋玉：辞赋家，战国鄢（今湖北宜城市）人，代表作有《高唐赋》、《神女赋》、《登徒子好色赋》等。"下里巴人"、"阳春白雪"、"曲高和寡"等典故出自其作品，与屈原并称"屈宋"。今宜城有宋玉冢。

（3）刘秀（前6—57）：政治家，汉南阳郡蔡阳（今湖北枣阳市）人，新朝末年，与兄起兵反莽，昆阳之战大破莽军。公元25年立东汉，为光武帝。执政间偃武修文，实施度田，世称"光武中兴"。今枣阳有白水寺。

（4）王粲（177—217）：文学家，字仲宣，东汉山阳高平（今山东邹县）人。居襄阳16年。代表作有《七哀诗》、《登楼赋》等。在"建安七子"中文学成就最著，与曹植并称"曹王"。今襄城有王粲井、王粲宅、仲宣楼。

（5）诸葛亮（181—234）：政治军事家，字孔明，东汉琅琊（今山东沂南县）人。17至27岁在隆中躬耕苦读，代表作有《出师表》、《诫子书》等。刘备"三顾茅庐"，亮献《隆中对》，后为蜀国丞相。今襄城西有古隆中。

（6）习凿齿（？—383）：史学家，字彦威，东晋襄阳人，世代为荆楚豪族，襄阳侯习郁之后，少有志气，博学通达，著有《汉晋春秋》54卷和我国最早的人物志之一《襄阳耆旧记》。今襄城南有习家池。

（7）释道安（312？—385）：佛学家，本姓卫，东晋常山（今河北冀州市）人，应习凿齿之邀到襄阳，居15年，讲授《般若经》，撰写《安录》，注释经文，统一僧人为"释"姓，确立戒规，弘扬佛教。今襄城南有谷隐寺。

（8）萧统（501—531）：编纂家，字德施，南朝梁兰陵（今江苏常州）人，生于襄阳，2岁立为太子。编纂《文选》（后称《昭明文选》）30卷，为我国现存最早的文学作品总集。今襄城有昭明台。

（9）孟浩然（689—740）：诗人，人称孟襄阳，唐襄阳人。《全唐诗》收录其诗200余首，代表作有《春晓》、《过故人庄》等。系山水田园诗派代表人物，与王维并称"王孟"。曾隐居鹿门山。今襄城南有故居涧南园。

（10）米芾（1051—1107）：书画家，字元章，号襄阳漫士，人称"米颠"，北宋襄阳人。其书法与苏轼、黄庭坚、蔡襄并称宋四大家；画创"米家山水"。传世之作有《蜀素帖》、《苕溪诗帖》、《虹县诗卷》等。今樊城有米公祠。

（二）南京旅游景点公示语翻译

（1）国民政府总统府办公楼

一楼　文书局

二楼　总统、副总统办公室　秘书长办公室

三楼　国务会议厅

（2）旅游景点指示图

总统府防空洞

国民政府行政院

清两江总督署史料展

洪秀全历史文物陈列

马厩

（3）行政院（北楼）

建于 1920 年代，"行政院"三字为国民政府主席、后任行政院长的谭延闿所题。行政院为国民政府最高行政机关，成立于 1928 年 10 月 25 日，掌理内政、外交、财经、军政、文教等事务。

行政院北楼（景区办公区）

复园（东花园）

清两江总督署史料展

陶林二公祠

马厩

（4）桐音馆

重建于清同治九年（1870 年），因雨水落在梧桐叶上啪啪有声而得名。

孙中山起居室

孙中山临时大总统办公室

总统府礼堂

游客服务中心

（5）南京博物院指示牌

历史馆

特展馆

艺术馆

数字馆

民国馆

非遗馆

小剧场

如意工坊

（三）南京总统府简介

总统府建筑群，位于南京长江路 292 号，迄今已有 600 多年历史。

明朝初年，这里曾是归德侯府和汉王府；清朝为江南总督署、两江总督署，也是江宁织造府的一部分。清康熙、乾隆皇帝下江南时，均以此为"行宫"。

太平天国时期，洪秀全在此兴建了规模宏大的天朝宫殿。后曾国藩又在此处重建两江总督署，林则徐、李鸿章、刘坤一、沈葆桢、左宗棠、张之洞、端方等清朝重臣在此就任过两江总督。

1912 年 1 月 1 日，孙中山在此就任中华民国临时大总统；以后的 15 年间，先后作为江苏总督府、副总统府等机构；1927 年国民政府成立，这里成为国民政府机关；抗日战争期间，这里先后成为日军机关和汪伪政权的办公处。

1949 年 4 月 23 日南京解放，24 日凌晨，中国人民解放军占领总统府。

新中国成立后，总统府一直作为政府机关办公场所。1998 年，江苏省人民政府决定在总统府旧址筹建南京中国近代史遗址博物馆。经过精心规划和多年的恢复建设，逐步形成今天的规模。

总统府景区占地面积约9万平方米，分三个参观区域：中区（中轴线）主要有国民政府、总统府及所属机构；西区有孙中山临时大总统办公室、秘书处、西花园、孙中山起居室以及参谋本部等；东区主要有行政院、陶林二公祠、马厩和东花园等。在三个参观区域中，又分布着总统府文物史料、孙中山与南京临时政府、太平天国、清两江总督署、国民政府行政院等十多个史料和复原陈列。

今天，总统府正以诸多保存完好的近代中西建筑遗存，国内独一无二的民国历史文化氛围，珍贵的文物和史料，风景优美的自然环境，热情地欢迎来自海内外的嘉宾。

第六章

公司简介翻译

第一节 公司简介及翻译策略

公司简介在概念上有广义和狭义之分。广义上包括公司简介（company profile/about us）、企业文化（company value）、企业历史（history）、经营管理（management）、公司领导简介（leadership）、公司成就（achievement & awards）、公司动态（news）等。狭义的公司简介主要包括公司的性质、实力和经营范围等内容。

公司企业简介从大体而言可以分为两类：一类为公司的简要内容或概览，是最常见的类型。其中有的简介文字简短，有的则篇幅较长，分类较细，内容较为详尽；另一类则近似于广告文本。篇幅不长，信息量不大，但更注重塑造公司的形象，宣传公司的服务和经营理念。

一、公司简介的语言特征

1. 选词精确

企业介绍是一家企业对外宣传，传播形象的重要材料，选词要求精确，不容模棱两可。我国的国有企业分为大、中型，在措辞时，一定不能夸大其词，应该实事求是精准、客观的描述公司规模。

2. 简洁

公司简介属于商务文体的一种，要求简洁易懂，选词避免生僻晦涩。句法和篇章结构根据不同民族的语言特点各有不同。如英文常在段首点明主旨，而汉语往往在结尾归纳总结。不论使用哪种语言描述或介绍一个公司概况，都应该以直接、简洁为原则，方便读者在短时间轻松了解公司的大概情况。

3. 正式

公司简介属于广告宣传材料，措辞和句法都应该保持较为正式的文体风格。选词方面不能使用过于口语化的词汇，句法方面也要避免过多使用简单句，应使用较为正式的语体表达。

二、公司简介的翻译策略

1. 注意中西方思维差异,适度选择归化和异化或二者相结合的翻译方法。中西思维差异可以反映在时间、位置、哲学思维等各个方面,翻译时要注意这些细节,选择符合读者审美,适合读者理解的译文。

2. 关注文化特色词,翻译时做到动态对等。由于公司简介会介绍公司所处的地理位置及历史背景灯相关信息、公司的文化经营等,不可避免地会涉及一个民族特有的文化现象。如提到公司企业文化时,会有"儒家""道家"等不同思想的介绍。英美方面会有一些国家历史或与当代文化相关联的信息。翻译时,尤其注意这些文化特色词的处理。译者可以根据原文总体把握,有目的的选择动态对等的原则进行翻译。

3. 注意英汉语言差异,文体风格做到简朴华丽各有不同。英语企业简介偏重于信息介绍,语言风格朴实。汉语企业简介经常使用评价性较强的词汇,如国内"最先进的"生产基地、"最受消费者欢迎的"产品,而且经常使用华丽的辞藻进行修饰,以期给人留下深刻的印象。

第二节　案例及习题

一、英译汉

1. 案例

Haier is the leading brand of white goods globally and the most valuable brand in China. With its 29 manufacturing plants, 8 comprehensive R&D centers, 19 overseas trading companies across the world and more than 60,000 global employees, Haier has involved into a giant multinational corporation.

Guided by the famous brand strategy determined by CEO Zhang Ruimin, Haier has adopted several strategies during different stages, namely Brand Strategy, Diversification Strategy and Internationalization Strategy. At the end of 2005, Haier came to its 4th strategic stage of global brand building. Thanks to 25 years of consistent efforts, its reputation throughout the world has been heightened significantly. In 2009, the brand value of Haier amounted to RMB 80.3 billion. Since 2002, Haier has topped the Most Valuable Brand list for seven consecutive years. Nineteen products of Haier, including refrigerator, air conditioner, washing machine, television, water heater, computer, mobile phone and home appliances integration, have been awarded as Chinese Famous Brand products. Haier refrigerator and washing machine are among the first group of Chinese World Famous Brand products awarded by the General Administration of Quality Supervision, Inspection and Quarantine of the P. R. C.

In March 2008, Haier was selected as one of the "China's Top 10 Global Brands" by *Financial Times* for the second time. In June 2008, Haier ranked 13th and 1st among Chinese companies on the list of the world's "600 Most Reputable Companies", released by *Forbes*. In July 2008, Haier ranked first in terms of overall leadership among Chinese mainland companies in *The Wall Street Journal Asia's* annual survey of "Asia's 200 Most Admired Companies" for the fifth time. Haier has become an international brand, and its prestige is rising fast with its expansion into the international market.

According to the latest data released by Euromonitor, with a market share up to 5.1 percent, Haier ranks first among the brands of white goods all over the world in term of market share and it was the first time for a Chinese company to be the number one brand in white goods industry. At the same time, the market share of Haier refrigerator and washing machine is 10.4 percent and 8.4 percent respectively, both ranking first in the industry. Moreover, Haier leads the world in intelligent home appliances integration, network household appliances, digitization, large scale integrated circuit and new materials. "Innovation driven" Haier has been committed to providing effective solutions to global consumers and achieving a win-win outcome with them.

Up to the end of 2009, Haier had applied for 9,738 patents, 2,799 of which were invention patents, ranking first among Chinese appliance enterprises. Just in 2009, Haier applied for 943 patents, 538 invention patents included, which means two invention patents were applied for each business day on average. On the base of its independent intellectual property, Haier has participated in the setting of 23 international standards, and 7 patents of them involving powder-free wash technology and technology of anti-electric wall have been issued and implemented, which indicates independent innovation of Haier has won international recognition in standards field. Haier has leaded or taken part in the preparing and revising of a total of 232 national standards, 188 of which have been issued and 10 awarded the China Standards Innovation & Contribution Award; more over, Haier has participated in the preparing of 447 industry standards and other standards. Haier is the appliance company most involved in raising international, national and industry standards.

Haier is the only Chinese enterprise to be a member of management decision-making team of International Electro-technical Commission (IEC) and was selected to be the first "Practice base for standard innovation" globally by IEC in June, 2009.

In innovation practice, Haier's exploration and implementation of Overall Every Control and Clear management mode characterized by completing the work of today to harvest today's success, market chain management and individual-order combination development pattern has attracted high attention from international management field. Up to now, commercial colleges of Harvard University, University of South California, International Institute for Management Development (IMD), European Business School and Kobe University have conducted case studies on above mentioned aspects. Nearly 30 management cases of Haier have been included into their case libraries by 12 universities in the world, with case of "Haier culture to activate the fish in shock" included into case library of commercial college of Harvard University and "market chain" management case included into EU case library.

Entering into the fifth-year in implementing its global brand building strategy, Haier, in 2010, will continue to promote its enterprise spirit of "creating resources and winning global reputation" and work style of "individual-order combination, quick decision-making", and to further promote information process recreation. As an independent operation entity of individual-order combination, Haier will strive to build a system to meet the dynamic needs of the user through business model innovation of "Just-in-time model with zero inventory" based on the combination of virtual and actual network and consistently conduct innovations for the benefits of users to create a world famous brand owned by Chinese.

2. 翻译工作坊课程规划

第一，文本解读。

（1）思考英语商务文体的语言特征，并结合语言特征分析上述公司简介的语言特征；

（2）了解海尔公司的相关背景；

（3）结合语言的正式度和公司简介的特定语言风格，以及翻译目的来确定相应的翻译策略。

第二，分组翻译（三人一组）。具体要求如下：

（1）按照所提出的翻译策略，各组成员分别进行翻译；

（2）组内进行翻译、修改，拟初稿；

（3）将初稿合并，三人进行小组讨论，统一术语，纠查错误，拟定稿。

（4）各组提交定稿。

第三，翻译教学讨论。

（1）以上各组分别由代表进行报告演示，说明本组翻译策略的选择的依据；

（2）所有同学对各组所提出的翻译策略进行讨论；

（3）教师给出参考译文，结合学生译文进行评析，讲解相关翻译技巧。

3. 参考译文

海尔集团是世界白色家电第一品牌、中国最具价值品牌。海尔在全球建立了29个制造基地，8个综合研发中心，19个海外贸易公司，全球员工总数超过6万人，已发展成为大规模的跨国企业集团。

海尔集团在首席执行官张瑞敏确立的名牌战略指导下，先后实施名牌战略、多元化战略和国际化战略。2005年底，海尔进入第四个战略阶段——全球化品牌战略阶段。创业25年的拼搏努力，使海尔品牌在世界范围的美誉度大幅提升。2009年，海尔品牌价值高达803亿元人民币。自2002年以来，海尔品牌价值连续7年蝉联中国最有价值品牌榜首。海尔品牌旗下冰箱、空调、洗衣机、电视机、热水器、电脑、手机、家居集成等19个产品被评为中国名牌,其中海尔冰箱、洗衣机还被国家质检总局评为首批中国世界名牌。

2008年3月,海尔第二次入选英国《金融时报》评选的"中国十大世界级品牌"。2008年6月,在《福布斯》"全球最具声望大企业600强"评选中,海尔排名13位,是排名最靠前的中国企业。2008年7月,在《亚洲华尔街日报》组织评选的"亚洲企业200强"中,海尔集团连续五年荣登"中国内地企业综合领导力"排行榜榜首。海尔已跻身世界级品牌行列,其影响力正随着全球市场的扩张而快速上升。

据世界著名消费市场研究机构欧洲透视(Euromonitor)发布最新数据显示,海尔在世界白色家电品牌中排名第一,全球市场占有率5.1%。这是中国白色家电首次成为全球第一品牌。同时,海尔冰箱、海尔洗衣机分别以10.4%与8.4%的全球市场占有率,在行业中均排名第一。在智能家居集成、网络家电、数字化、大规模集成电路、新材料等技术领域,海尔也处于世界领先水平。"创新驱动"型的海尔致力于向全球消费者提供满足需求的解决方案,实现企业与用户之间的双赢。

截止到2009年年底,海尔累计申请专利9 738项,其中发明专利2 799项,稳居中国家电企业榜首。仅2009年,海尔就申请专利943项,其中发明专利538项,平均每个工作日申请2项发明专利。在自主知识产权的基础上,海尔已参与23项国际标准的制定,其中无粉洗涤技术、防电墙技术等7项国际标准已经发布实施,这表明海尔自主创新技术在国际标准领域得到了认可;海尔主导和参与了232项国家标准的编制、修订,其中188项已经发布,并有10项获得了国家标准创新贡献奖;参与制定行业及其他标准447项。海尔是参与国际标准、国家标准、行业标准最多的家电企业。

海尔是唯一一个进入国际电工委员会(IEC)管理决策层的中国企业代表,2009年6月,IEC选择海尔作为全球首个"标准创新实践基地"。

在创新实践中,海尔探索实施的"日事日毕,日清日高"的"OEC"(Overall Every Control and Clear)管理模式、"市场链"管理及"人单合一"发展模式引起国际管理界高度关注。目前,已有美国哈佛大学、南加州大学、瑞士IMD国际管理学院、法国的欧洲管理学院、日本神户大学等商学院专门对此进行案例研究。海尔的近30个管理案例被世界12所大学写入案例库,其中,"海尔文化激活休克鱼"管理案例被纳入哈佛大学商学院案例库,海尔"市场链"管理被纳入欧盟案例库。

2010年,海尔实施全球化品牌战略进入第五年。海尔将继续发扬"创造资源、美誉全球"的企业精神和"人单合一、速决速胜"的工作作风,深入推进信息化流程再造,以人单合一的自主经营体为支点,通过"虚实网结合的零库存下的即需即供"商业模式创新,努力打造满足用户动态需求的体系,一如既往地为用户不断创新,创出中华民族自己的世界名牌!

4. 英译汉翻译练习

(1)   **Xiangyang Economic Development Zone**

Xiangyang Economic Development Zone is located in Xiangfan City in the north-west of Hubei. Adjacent to the base of Dongfeng Motor Corporation in Xiangyang, the zone takes up a planned area of 334 hectares.

Taking full advantage of being the close neighbor of the base of Dongfeng Motor Corporation and the national base of grain, cotton and edible oil, the zone adheres to highlighting its characteristics of industrial agglomeration and forms a leading industry focusing on auto spare parts, textile and clothing, food processing and trade logistics.

Up to now, the zone had introduced more than 150 enterprises into its parks, which include more than 20 large-scaled ones.

A number of well-known enterprises has settled and invested in its industrial parks, such as Thailand's Chia Tai Group, Shandong Flower Group, COFCO, Chengdu Hope Group, The United States Harvest Group, Hubei Wing Wah Group and Hubei Xiao-cotton Group.

Shenzhen Industrial Park in Hubei is a well-designed high standard comprehensive park built by Xiangfan City and Xiangyang district through their city-district cooperation. It is an ideal vehicle for the transference of industries from the east coast.

Xiangyang Economic Development Zone

Address: No. 119 Diamond Avenue, Fancheng District, Xiangfan City, Hubei

Zip Code: # # # # #

Tel: # # # # #

Fax: # # # # #

(2) **Xiangfan Hi-tech Industry Development Zone**

Xiangfan Hi-tech Industry Development Zone is located in Xiangfan, a famous historical and cultural city in northwest of Hubei. Approved by the State Council as a national-level development zone in the November of 1992, the zone takes up a planned total area of 100 square kilometers.

The zone takes implementation of the Torch Plan and attaches great importance on the development of high-tech industry.

The zone now is composed of three major parks, namely the Hi-tech Industrial Park, the Auto Industrial Park and Shenzhen Industrial Park.

All together, the zone has introduced more than 1,800 various enterprises from more than 20 countries and regions, among which there are world top 500 investing enterprises such as PSA Peugeot Citroen, US Danathe, US Cummins and Japan Nissan.

The Hi-tech Industry Development zone has production capacity of automotive vehicle for Teana sedan, "Dongfeng Sundance Kid" light truck, Dongfeng station wagon and Dongfeng Special Vehicle. It also owns a complete industrial chain of car engine, axle, seat angle adjusting devices, bearings, electrical, instrumentation and other key auto spare parts. The total number of supporting companies is up to more than 160.

Meanwhile, the zone has the Asia's largest and best equipped car proving ground and the National Automotive Test Center.

While promoting its special auto industry, the Hi-tech Industry Development Zone is actively expanding the industrial area of national defense equipment, electromechanical integration, and new materials.

Products from the zone, such as rescue aircraft bouncing seats, solid-propellant rockets and missiles，special optical glass，synthetic green insulators，motor soft starter products，and automotive adhesive agent，have gained a good reputation from the same industry.

The energy-saving equipment manufacturing with a total investment of 10 billion will make the zone a national innovative energy-saving equipment manufacturing industrial base and a demonstrative zone of national low-carbon economic industry.

The Hi-tech zone is now planning to take electronic information and biological medicine as the focus of future industrial development and to promote a new round of massive investment and development.

Xiangfan National Hi-Tech Development Zone

Address：Office Building of Administration Committee of Development Zone，Car City Avenue，Xiangfan，Hubei

Zip Code：＃＃＃＃＃

Tel：＃＃＃＃＃

Fax：＃＃＃＃＃

二、汉译英

1. 案例

上海志远翻译服务有限公司

公司简介：

　　成立于1996年的志远翻译社是一家全球语言服务提供商，提供包括笔译、口译、软件本地化及网站国际化等在内的多语言翻译服务。依托本地各领域专家及工程师所组成的资源与人才网络，致力于为各行业客户提供优质服务。

　　如今，志远翻译社已成为美国翻译协会会员、中国翻译协翻译委员服务会成员单位以及江苏省高院涉外民事商事司法法文书委托翻译机构。伴随其全球化进程，志远翻译社已在苏州，昆山、上海、北京和北美建立运营和分支机构，拥有长期稳定的合作伙伴与客户资源，在国内同行业中处于领先地位。

行业经验：

　　在十几年的运营中，志远翻译社成功地完成了数十万件翻译项目，涵盖了从法律、金融、机械、制造、能源、汽车到电子、高新技术、IT、软件、媒体、出版及旅游等广泛领域。以法律为例，翻译了包括大量法律法规，合同文本、上市文件、反倾销诉讼文件、公司章程、法学论文等在内的资料。这些资料经过使用，已得到质量上的验证和认可，可作为模板和参考资料，供新项目随时调取使用。

专业实力：

　　译员遍及世界各地，他们将自身的语言能力与必要的文化背景及专业知识相结合，为客户提供优质精准的翻译服务。为确保质量，志远翻译社将所有工作纳入其严格的质量保证流程中，以期完美满足客户需求。

我们的译员：

为各自领域内的专家；

具备专业背景并获得认证，能充分领会所译内容；

为经验丰富、技艺非凡的母语专家；

具备多学科、多任务操作能力；

熟悉如欧洲大陆，中国，日本，韩国及阿拉伯等东西方国家和地区的全部主要语言；

为精心遴选的译员；

通过 ATA 内部合格译员、DTP 排版人员及项目加之已久经验的自由译员为后盾，能为客户提供从任意语言到任意语言如母语般，忠实于原文的多语言翻译服务，使 ATA 无论从小到单页文件抑或大到多语言项目都能够做到游刃有余。

解决方案：

凭借在翻译服务与软件上的专业实力，志远翻译社可向客户提供全球化 (Globalization)，国际化（Internalization），本地化（Localization）和翻译（Translation）等 GILT 外包服务，为客户提供包括咨询、创意、创作、支持工具开发和 DTP 排版等服务在内的多语言解决方案。

质量保证：

ATA 明确规定了质量保证流程，对任务的各个环节进行评价与跟踪，务求向客户提供给合格译文。

翻译管理：

（1）翻译流程：

志远翻译拥有非常完善的标准化项目管理流程。我们的翻译服务流程业已经过 ISO9001 认证，配合自行研发的基于互联网的可视化项目管理系统（TMS），最大程度地协调多译员多流程操作，极大地提升了项目质量和成本绩效、缩短了项目周期。

（2）翻译工具

ATA 使用当前主流的翻译工具如 Trados、SDLX、Déjà vu 和 Wordfast 等进行项目翻译工作，以保证专业术语，产品名称以及其他重复性内容的统一性，并且提高翻译速度，缩短项目周期，协助客户利用效率创造价值。

（3）翻译记忆

翻译记忆机制（Translation Memory System），可将以往翻译过的、原文字及其对应的目标文字存储在数据库中。当我们为您处理后续以及新资料的翻译时，CAT 工具可以随时帮我们检索相应的资源，保证术语的统一。

在新建项目中，通过对比源文字与之前 TM 中的源文字，TMS 体现出两大主要用途：

根据 TM 自动翻译新建项目中的源文字；

对 TM 中新建项目源文字相似的部分给出翻译建议，便于译员可酌情更改。

所做更改都会添加进 TM 中，使 TM 处于不断更新提炼，从而加快翻译速度。

（4）翻译术语

在编辑、翻译与交流过程中，需要可靠、易懂、好用的信息，而这些信息要准确、清晰和标准化，尤其是做到术语的统一。面对信息内容创作与传递日益增长的需求，有必要创建、存储及更新术语资源。

制作来源语和目标语对照的术语表,可供您在自行处理语言项目时参考使用。这是我们提供的附加值服务,通常它是免费的。

证书认证:

毋庸置疑,在翻译领域的高度专业是我们的核心竞争力。我们的翻译流程经过英国国家质量保证局(NQA)审核注册,已通过 ISO 9001:2000 国际质量体系认证,致远翻译社因而成为中国大陆率先通过 ISO 认证的翻译公司之一。

联系我们:

全国统一客服电话:＃＃＃＃＃＃＃＃

地址:上海愚园路 168 号环球世界大厦 A 栋 8 层(200040)

2. 翻译工作坊课程规划

第一,文本解读。

(1) 公司简介属于商务文体,结合商务汉语的语言特征分析上述公司简介的语言特征;

(2) 案例为翻译公司的公司简介,了解翻译公司的运作模式和情况。

(3) 结合语言的正式度、商务文体的语用价值,公司简介的特定语言风格确定相应的翻译策略。

第二,分组翻译(三人一组)。具体要求如下:

(1) 按照所提出的翻译策略,各组成员分别进行翻译;

(2) 组内进行翻译、修改,拟初稿;

(3) 将初稿合并,三人进行小组讨论,统一术语,纠查错误,拟定稿。

(4) 各组提交定稿。

第三,翻译教学讨论。

(1) 以上各组分别由代表进行报告演示,说明本组翻译策略的选择的依据;

(2) 所有同学对各组所提出的翻译策略进行讨论;

(3) 教师给出参考译文,结合学生译文进行评析,讲解相关翻译技巧。

3. 参考译文

ABOUT US

Founded in 1996，Arthur Translation Agency（ATA）is a family of companies providing global language services of the highest standard including translation, interpretation，software localization and website globalization in many languages in combination with a unique network of resources and capabilities contributed by local technicians and engineers in a wide diversity of industries，ATA can afford quality services to the customers from all sections of business.

Today ATA has enjoyed continual growth with its global offices in Suzhou，Kunshan, Shanghai，Beijing and North America supported by many long-standing partners and suppliers，and ranks among China's leading providers in the sector for multilingual communication. Meanwhile，ATA has been accepted for memberships by both American Translators Association and the Translator's Association of China，and furthermore appointed by the Higher People's Court of Jiangsu Province as the Certified Translation Service Provider for its judicial documents in relation to foreign civil and commercial matters.

EXPERIENCE

With more than a decade of experience, ATA has successfully accomplished hundreds of thousands of legal & finance, mechanical & manufacturing, energy & automotive, electronics& hi-tech, IT & software, media & publishing, travel &tourism translation cases. As for legal translations, our translation project reference includes large volume of laws and codes, contracts and agreements, listing documents, anti-dumping lawsuit files, articles of association and jurisprudent essays. Those proven cases are available for being used as templates and references to provide all-the-time access for new projects.

EXPERTISE

Located around the world, our translators contribute essential cultural and subject matter expertise in combination with language skills to produce translations of the highest accuracy and quality. As a further guarantee of quality, all our work is carried out in accordance with ATA's stringent linguistic QA processes. It is their job to ensure that the translation conforms fully to the expectations of the target audience.

Our translators:

are specialists in their chosen field.

fully understand and are qualified in the subject matter they translate.

are experienced linguists who always translate into their native tongue.

are fully able to multi-task and work in more than one discipline.

work regularly in all the major western and eastern European languages, Chinese, Japanese, Korean and Arabic.

are supported by a carefully selected panel of freelancers.

With our in-house qualified translators, DTP staff and project managers plus a network of tried and tested freelancers as back-up, customers can be assured of faithful translation of content from a language into another language that appears as though it was written in the mother tongue, and ATA is thus enabled and scalable to cope with a full spectrum of projects ranging from a single page up to the largest of multilingual projects.

SOLUTIONS

With expertise in translation services and software, ATA is able to offer one-stop solutions for Globalization, Internationalization, Localization and Translation (GILT) outsourcing services. ATA is an established and reliable partner for multilingual consultancy, originality, production, support tools development DTP and otherwise.

QUALITY ASSURANCE

QA processes are clearly defined and each step of every assignment is scored and tracked to ensure that every translation is fully validated before delivery to our customers.

TRANSLATION MANAGEMENT

（1）Translation Process

ATA develops a well-functioned and standardized project management system which enables precise control over the quality and progress of translation. By our ISO9001 certified translation process with our proprietary Internet based TMS ATA's translators are coordinated in a multi-process operation to the maximum which extent enormously promoted the quality, cut the cost and shortened lifecycle of project.

（2）Translation Tools

The primary CAT tools we use are:

> Trados
>
> SDLX
>
> Déjà vu
>
> Wordfast

With ATA any information can be delivered into any language quickly, efficiently and consistently at shorter lifecycle and low cost.

（3）Translation Memory

Translation memory systems （TMS） have established themselves as the most successful and reliable type, one that stores previously translated segments of text together with their target-language equivalents as language pairs for the purpose of reuse and consistency.

The TMS compares the source text for a new translation with the stored, previously translated source text. In doing so it applies to two fundamental principles:

Automatic translation of text using previous translations from the TM;

Proposal of suggested translations for text that is similar to previous source text where manual editing at translator's options.

Any modification will be added to the TM so as to keep it constantly updated and continually refined to boost translation speed.

（4）Terminology

The editing, translation and communication of reliable, comprehensible and user-friendly information requires precise, unambiguous, standardized and above all consistent terminology. Increasingly high demands on the production and presentation of information content make it a necessity to create, store and update terminological resources.

In the course of processing a project, ATA will tailor make a terminology table with the source and target languages as pairs on request of our customer, who can use it as reference when a linguistic project should be internally dealt with. Most an end, it is provided free of charge as a value-added service.

CERTIFICATION

It's no doubt that highly specialized translation constitutes our core competitiveness. Up to now, ATA's translation process has been assessed and registered by the National

Quality Assurance Ltd. (NQA) against the provision of ISO9001:2000. ATA therefore became one of the earliest ISO9001 certified translation companies in the Chinese mainland.

CONTACT US

Toll-free Hotline：＃＃＃＃＃

ADRESS

Shanghai Arthur Translation Agency Co., Ltd.

4. 汉译英翻译练习

（1）　　　　　　　　**襄樊裕泰铜铅合金钢带制造有限责任公司简介**

襄樊裕泰铜铅合金钢带制造有限责任公司，成立于 1995 年 8 月，是一家专业生产铜铅合金滑动轴承材料的高新技术企业。

公司现有员工 198 人，专业技术人员 59 人，其中中高级以上职称 36 人；拥有十二条网带传送连续烧结炉生产线，合金钢带年生产能力达 5 000 吨，铜铅合金粉末年生产能力 1 500 吨。

2001 年公司通过 ISO9000 质量体系论证，2002 年被认定为湖北省高新技术企业。2003 年公司科技人员研制的《纳米镍铜铅合金滑动轴承材料》通过省科技厅鉴定，被国家科技部批准为国家重点新产品推广计划，公司正在逐步组织生产。2004 年荣获国家火炬计划襄樊汽车动力与部件生产基地骨干企业。

公司生产的铜铅合金材料，具有耐高速、耐高载、耐疲劳强度高等特点，在机械性能等方面充分显示了其优越性，能够满足各种载荷发动机的要求，其综合性能达到国内领先水平，并且可替代进口产品。产品广泛应用于汽车、工程机械、家用电器、机床等行业。目前，公司生产的产品已在配套主机东风公司、康明斯 cummins（东风康明斯）三个系列、斯泰尔两个系列、潍柴和 CA488、FD493、CY4105、CA6102、YC6105、YC6108、WX6110、YC6112、YC6113 发动机上的曲轴瓦、连杆瓦、连杆小头衬套、齿轮衬套都已装机配套使用，并与多家摩擦件厂家配套。国内多家大型的发动机制造厂家已大批量选用我公司生产的钢带制造的产品，受到广大用户的一致好评和欢迎。

公司自成立以来，始终坚持"质量第一、服务至上"的原则，狠抓质量管理和技术创新工作，产品已被列为"湖北省科技成果重点推广计划"，并先后荣获襄樊市"湖北省科技成果奖"、"优秀科技企业"、"襄樊市科技进步一等奖"、"襄樊市民营经济 50 强"和先进单位等光荣称号。随着公司生产经营稳步发展和扩大，我们相信，凭着年轻裕泰人的智慧和科学管理方法，我们将期待着中国的每一根轴都支撑在裕泰铜铅合金钢带上，并将跨出国门走向世界。热情的裕泰人竭诚欢迎客商前来洽谈、合作，并携手共同创造美好的明天。

地址：湖北省襄樊市汽车产业开发区车城大道 38 号

电话、传真：＃＃＃＃＃

（2）　　　　　　　　**襄阳光彩国际产业园招商手册**

一、专案背景

襄阳，原名襄樊，2010 年，经国务院批准，更名为襄阳。全市面积 1.97 万平方公里，人口591万,其中市区人口141万。襄阳位于中国中部,居长江最大支流汉江的中游,南襄盆地南部,至今已有2800多年的历史,是国家历史文化名城,湖北省省域副中心城市,湖北省第二大城市,湖北西部支点城市,是鄂、豫、陕、渝四省接壤地区30万平方公里范围内最大的中心城市。襄阳是我国华中、华北、西南Y型交通网络的中心,是全国高速公路主骨架上的重要节点,是全国铁路运输重要枢纽之一,已形成了一条汉江、两座机场、三条铁路和四通八达的高速公路,水、陆、公、空的立体交通网络,实现了与武汉、郑州、西安、重庆、成都等周边1000公里左右的城市朝发夕至的"一日经济圈"。

襄阳市是全国36个明星工业城市之一,是中央、省属三线军工企事业集中的城市,全市工业已发展形成以轻工、纺织、机械、汽车制造、电子、医药、建材、冶金、化工、食品为主要产业支柱的工业体系,尤以汽车产业的发展闻名于世。襄阳市全省战略地位突出,省委、省政府对襄阳的发展寄予厚望,要求加快"产业襄阳、都市襄阳、文化襄阳、绿色襄阳"建设步伐,在"十二五"末建设成为城区面积200平方公里、城区人口200万的特大型城市,GDP要突破4000亿元,冲刺5000亿,在全省经济中的比重达到15%左右。

襄阳自然环境优美,名胜古迹众多,旅游资源丰富。共有自然旅游资源和人文旅游资源两大景系,49种景类,404处(点)景型。襄阳是三国故事的源头和三国文化的发祥地,以三国文化为主要特色。闻名中外、脍炙人口、家喻户晓的古典名著《三国演义》120回的故事中有31回发生在襄阳。襄阳作为湖北省"一江两山三城"旅游开发的中轴和重要门户,已成为武当山、神农架和三国文化旅游热线的中心城市,中西部地区旅游经济的集散地。

二、开发商简介

襄阳光彩国际产业园是湖北百盟集团襄阳彩诚投资实业有限公司投资20亿元人民币开发建设的大型园区。该公司是一家专业从事城市综合体、现代工业集中区、专业市场集中区、现代物流产业园等投资开发的综合性公司。公司自2009年5月成立以来,通过不断努力和开拓实践,已经依托华中光彩大市场为龙头,逐步建成了一个集中央商业区、商贸物流区、商务配套区和工业制造区相结合的新型综合产业开发区,形成了前店后厂、前商后仓、产供销一体化产业、城市化的发展格局。

公司现有38家控股实体子公司,在襄阳地区投资近100亿元,先后开发中国光彩事业襄阳工业园、襄阳光彩台商产业园、襄阳光彩国际产业园、光彩国际农业产业园、襄阳三国旅游文化园、光彩田宇再生资源有限公司、宜城光彩大市场、宜城光彩工业园、谷城光彩综合产业园和南漳光彩综合产业园等项目。

公司按照"自建平台、自招客商、自主经营、自求发展"四自模式建设的涵盖工业、仓储、物流、商业和配套国际小区"四位一体"的大型现代化产业园区,在中西部地区首创"低成本进驻、低成本管理、低成本运营、低成本发展"四低模式,使入园企业能够进的来、留得住和持续发展,得到了社会各界广泛的认可和大力推举。

三、项目建设内容

1. 专案概述

襄阳光彩国际产业园,是襄阳"十二五"规划期间,襄阳市政府在稳步实施"四个襄阳"的发展战略规划情况下,有意委托襄阳彩诚投资实业有限公司新建的一座大型综合性产业园,产业园位于湖北省襄阳市高新区,规划总占地2000亩,计划总投资3亿元,涵盖汽车零部件生产、电子信息、新能源、材料、国际功能服务等多个项目内容。

2. 项目地址

襄阳市高新区,毗邻襄阳光彩台商产业园和东风二汽基地

3. 项目建设内容

(1) 汽车零部件产业区:

包括发动机系统、底盘、汽车制动系统、车身、电气设备(发电机、蓄电池)。本项目区入驻企业主要以生产、加工、销售汽车配件为主。为整车企业新车型研发的互动和对接提供有力支撑。

(2) 电子信息工业区:

为汽车电子、消费电子、光电子、软件及服务外包、信息集成、信息服务、网上交易平台和网上公告平台等企业提供发展平台。

(3) 机械制造产业区:

引入生产高科技机械、电子基件及军工生产所需的成套技术设备的大中型企业,从根本上实现项目区的工业化。

(4) 新能源,新材料产业区:

为从事研究有机硅新材料、光学新材料、光伏新材料三大领域等非常规企业提供发展平台。在电子信息材料、先进金属材料、电池材料、磁性材料、新型高分子材料、高性能陶瓷材料和复合材料等方面引进高端企业入驻。

(5) 国际化功能配套区:

为更好地服务于入驻的外资企业,做好外商的后勤保障工作,项目区将建设大型的国际小区,建设中西式餐厅,高档会所、国际教育,培训机构,购物广场,会议接待中心,高尔夫球场、休闲娱乐项目等内容,让入驻的每家企业都能体会到"家"的温暖,从根本上解决企业的后顾之忧。

四、政策优势

襄阳光彩国际产业园为使园区尽快建成投产,首创"低成本进驻、低成本管理、低成本运营、低成本发展"四低模式,让入园企业能够低成本进的来、留得住和持续双赢发展,为入驻企业快速长久发展提供保障。

入园企业的发展就是我们园区的发展,入园企业的成功就是我们园区的成功。具体政策如下:

1. 企业生产电价费用下降:

享受大集团客户用电政策。

2. 员工成本下降:

襄阳人口 590 万,劳动力资源丰富,工资待遇和福利费用较低。大中专高校林立,职业技术学校培养的各类专业人才队伍庞大,就地用人成本较低。

3. 地方税收下降:

入驻企业享受两免三减半优惠政策,即前两年税收 100% 奖励,后三年按 50% 奖励,采用先征后返的政策。

4. 工程建设投入成本下降:

园区统一建立工程规划建设中心,为企业提供厂房规划、图纸设计、基础设施建设、厂房建设、配套设施建设、环境绿化及其养护等方面提供统一支持,有力减轻企业在工程建设方

面的大资金投入和大精力付出。

5. 厂房购买成本下降：

采用成本＋利润的阳光透明式销售政策，让更多的客商进的来，留得住、能发展。

｛（土地成本＋配套费用）＋公摊成本＋税收费用＋建安成本（根据厂房建设标准、跨度、高度、设施等核算）｝＊30％利润＝入园企业总投入

6. 对内管理成本下降：

园区统一建立后勤服务中心，为企业提供专家科研基地、职工宿舍、商务酒店、娱乐中心、商业中心、商务中心、展示中心、仓储中心、电子交易平台、会务中心、保安保洁、礼仪接待、人才培训等多项综合服务。

7. 对外减少项目报批环节：

园区统一建立行政服务中心，配合企业协调政府各大职能部门，减去不必要的应酬和负担，设立工商、银行、税务、法律等一系列窗口，代办各项证照服务。

8. 财务投入成本下降：

园区统一建立融资担保中心，为企业提供提担保、反担保支持，提供厂房按揭、流动资金贷款、项目贷款、贸易融资、抵押贷款等8大资本运营服务，极力打造入园企业"零成本购置厂房"发展模式，让中小企业将有限的资金优先应用于生产和销售。

9. 物流成本下降：

襄阳是中国几何地理中心，航空、铁路、高速公路、汉江水运交通便利，物流成本本身相对较低。园区统一建立物流中心，专门为入园企业提供物流运输服务和仓储基地，有效降低入园企业物流成本。

10. 产品销售成本降低：

园区统一建立产品销售展示中心，建立独立产品展示中心和管道销售网络，让企业产品有展示平台，致力于打造产供销一体化平台，组建专班人员协助企业打通全国销售管道，不仅让企业在生产环节较低成本，还在销售方面给予最大支持和协助。

（3）　　　　　　　　　　**苏宁电器公司简介**

苏宁电器1990年创立于江苏南京，是中国3C（家电、电脑、通讯）家电连锁零售企业的领先者，是国家商务部重点培育的"全国15家大型商业企业集团"之一。截至2009年，苏宁电器在中国30个省、直辖市、自治区，300多个城市拥有1 000家连锁店，80多个物流配送中心、2 000多个售后网点，经营面积500万平方米，员工12万名，年销售规模突破1 000亿元。品牌价值455.38亿元，蝉联中国商业连锁第一品牌。名列中国上规模民企前三，中国企业500强第54位，入选《福布斯》亚洲企业50强、《福布斯》全球2 000大企业中国零售企业第一。

2004年7月，苏宁电器（002024）在深圳证券交易所上市。凭借优良的业绩，苏宁电器得到了投资市场的高度认可，是全球家电连锁零售业市场价值最高的企业之一。

围绕市场需求，按照专业化、标准化的原则，苏宁电器将电器连锁店面划分为旗舰店、社区店、专业店、专门店4大类、18种形态，旗舰店已发展到第七代。苏宁电器采取"租、建、购、并"四位一体、同步开发的模式，保持稳健、快速的发展态势，每年新开200家连锁店，同时不断加大自建旗舰店的开发，以店面标准化为基础，通过自建开发、订单委托开发等方式，

在全国数十个一、二级市场推进自建旗舰店开发。预计到 2020 年,网络规模将突破 3 000 家,销售规模突破 3 500 亿元。

整合社会资源、合作共赢。满足顾客需要、至真至诚。苏宁电器坚持市场导向、顾客核心,与全球近 10 000 家知名家电供应商建立了紧密的合作关系,通过高层互访、B2B、联合促销,双向人才培训等形式,打造价值共创、利益共享的高效供应链。

与此同时,坚持创新经营,拓展服务品类,苏宁电器承诺"品牌、价格、服务"一步到位,通过 B2C、联名卡、会员制营销等方式,为消费者提供质优价廉的家电商品,并多次召开行业峰会与论坛,与国内外知名供应商、专家学者、社会专业机构共同探讨行业发展趋势与合作策略,促进家电产品的普及与推广,推动中国家电行业提升与发展。目前,苏宁电器经营的商品包括空调、冰洗、彩电、音像、小家电、通讯、电脑、数码、八个品类(包括自主产品),上千个品牌,20 多万个规格型号。

服务是苏宁的唯一产品,顾客满意是苏宁服务的终极目标。苏宁电器立志服务品牌定位,连锁店、物流、售后、客服四大终端为顾客提供涵盖售前、售中、售后一体化的阳光服务。

连锁店服务方面,苏宁电器以客户体验为导向,不断创新店面环境与布局,制定了系列店面服务原则,率先推出 5S 服务模式,会员专区、VIP 导购实现一站式购物。根据顾客多样化需求,提供产品推荐、上门设计、延保承诺、家电顾问等服务。

物流是苏宁电器的核心竞争力之一。苏宁电器建立了区域配送中心、城市配送中心、转配点三级物流网络,依托 WMS、TMS 等先进信息系统,实现了长途配送、短途调拨与零售配送到户一体化运作,平均配送半径 80~300 公里日最大配送能力 17 万台套,实现 24 小时送货到户。

苏宁电器相继在杭州、北京、南京等地开发建设了现代化物流基地,上海、天津、沈阳、成都、长春、无锡、合肥、徐州等地物流基地建设也全面铺开。预计到 2015 年,完成全国 60 个物流基地的布局。通过专业化、机械化、信息化的运作,苏宁电器物流基地可支持 50~200 亿元的年商品销售规模,零售配送半径最大可达 150 公里,同时还承担、地区售后服务中心、地区呼叫中心、地区培训中心等功能。

"专业自营"是苏宁电器售后服务的特点,目前,苏宁电器全国拥有 1 800 多个售后网点、30 家高端技术服务中心,15 000 名服务人员、500 名高技能电器技师,提供安装、维修、保养等各项服务,服务品类涉及彩电、冰洗、小家电、通讯、IT 五大品类、上百个品牌,拥有多项作业技术与国家发明专利,成为业内首个国家职业技能鉴定资质单位。

客户服务方面,苏宁电器建立了业内首个以呼叫中心为平台、以 CRM 为管理目标的客户服务体系。2007 年,苏宁电器率先建立了业内最大的南京呼叫中心——座席数约 1 000 人,拥有 1 000 多条电话线路,全国日最大信息量 10 万条,实现了全国统一受理与回访,全国统一服务热线 4008-365-365 全天 24 小时真诚守候。

信息化是零售业的核心竞争力。苏宁电器视信息化为企业神经系统,建立了集数据、语音、视频、监控于一体的信息网络系统,有效支撑了全国 300 多个城市、数千个店面、物流、售后、客服终端运作和十多万人的一体化管理,信息化建设先后入选中国商业科技 100 强、中国企业信息化 500 强(第 44 位)。依托苏宁 SAP/ERP 系统,B2B、B2C、OA、SOA、HR、BI、WMS、TMS、CRM、Call Center 等信息应用系统,实现了"供应商、内部员工、消费者"三位一体"的全流程信息集中管理。此外,苏宁电器先后携手与 IBM、微软、SAP、思科等国际知名

IT 企业开展信息系统建设战略合作,打造国际化智慧型企业。

百年苏宁,人才为本。人力资源是苏宁电器的核心竞争力,苏宁电器将人力资源视为企业长久发展的战略资本,建立了系统化的招聘选拔、培训培养、考核激励与发展规划体系。秉承人品优先、能力适度、敬业为本、团队第一的用人理念,坚持自主培养,内部提拔的人才培养方针,苏宁电器先后实施了 1200 工程、总经理梯队、采购经理梯队、店长梯队、督导梯队、销售突击队、蓝领工程等 10 多项人才梯队计划,倡导员工与企业共同成长、长远发展。展望未来,苏宁电器将立足国内与国际两个市场同步开发,以经营创新和管理提升为基础,保持稳健快速的发展步伐。到 2010 年底,电器连锁店总数突破1 200 家,销售规模突破1 500 亿,实现网络规模、品牌效益、管理与服务等全方位的行业领先,进入世界 500 强;到 2020 年,电器连锁店总数将达 3 000 家,销售规模达 3 500 亿,同时完成 3 00 个电器旗舰店、60 个物流基地的建设,进入世界一流企业的行列,成为"中国的沃尔玛"。服务是苏宁的唯一产品,苏宁电器将矢志不移,持之以恒,为打造中国最优秀的连锁服务品牌不懈努力!

第七章

公文翻译

第一节 公文文件的语言特点

公务文书是法定机关与组织在公务活动中,按照特定的体式、经过一定的处理程序形成和使用的书面材料,又称公务文件。公文文件用来传达政策、处理公务、协调关系,保证各项公务的高效进行。公文文件在内容上可分为:命令、决定、公告、通告、通知、通报、议案、报告、请示、批复、意见、函、纪要、决议、公报十五种。公文一般由份号、密级和保密期限、紧急程度、发文机关标志、发文字号、签发人、标题、主送机关、正文、附件说明、发文机关署名、成文日期、印章、附注、附件、抄送机关、印发机关和印发日期、页码等组成。

公务文件在日常工作中起着重要的作用,公文写作具有规范性、正式性、简洁性、严谨性四个特点。

1. 规范性

公文文件要求在形式、格式上要符合规范。根据具体内容的不同,公文文件的形式和格式也不同,在公文撰写过程中要遵循特定的形式和格式。

2. 正式性

公文是政府机关、企事业单位传达信息指令的专业工具,是一种公开正式的交流方式,因而文字组织和形式上要求具有高度的正式性。

3. 简洁平实

公文文件要求语言简明扼要、观点鲜明、平实庄重。公文是机关、企事业单位用来指导、沟通、传递信息、规范行为、公务联系的重要工具,不仅在现行工作中具有凭据记载作用,对于过去的事情,它又成为各级党政机关公务活动的历史记录。公文是重要的史料依据,需要归档保存,因而公文写作尤其要简约平实,庄重得体。

4. 准确严谨

公文是单位间进行商洽、询问、回答或交流的基础,洽谈完毕后有时要与有关企业、部门或单位签订合同、协议书等。因而公文文件的内容要求观点严谨、鲜明,表达准确严谨。

例:请示和批复

＃＃＃大学公共管理学院文件

＃＃＃＃＃公管院发〔2014〕05 号　　　　　　　　　　签发人:＃＃＃

关于公共管理学院建立心理健康实验室的

请　示

＃＃＃大学教务处:

由于心理健康在师生中的作用不断加强,为辅导和疏导学生就学和就业中的压力。为了提高我院的综合竞争力和培养科研氛围,建立心理健康实验室符合当代社会发展的趋势,日益成为高等教育不可缺少的一部分。

以上申请妥否,请批复。

附件:1. 建立心理健康实验室的可行性分析
　　　2. 建立心理健康实验室的费用预算
　　　3. 心理健康实验室的组织结构和日常运行

公共管理学院(章)

二〇一三年六月一日

主题词:＃＃＃**大学发展规划办公室**　　　　**心理健康实验室**　　　　**批复**

抄送:＃＃＃**大学教务处**　＃＃＃**大学财务处**

＃＃＃大学公共管理学院印制　　　　　　　　　　2013 年 6 月 1 日印发

(共印 20 份)

＃＃＃大学发展规划办公室文件

＃＃大学发展规划办发〔2014〕05 号　　　　　　　　签发人:＃＃

＃＃＃大学教务处关于同意公共管理学院

建立心理健康实验室的批复

公共管理学院:

《关于公共管理学院建立心理健康实验室的请示》＃＃＃大学公管院发〔2014〕05 号文收悉。为增强学生心理健康与承受压力的能力,提高学生综合素质,提升公共管理学院的综合竞争力,同意公共管理学院建立心理健康实验室的请示。建立实验室的效用用以实际的原则,并定期心理健康报告及运行情况报学校审查,建立进程及成果报学校审核。

特此批复。

＃＃＃大学教务处

二〇一三年六月二日

主题词:＃＃＃**大学教务处**　　　**实验室**　　　**批复**

抄送:公共管理学院院长　**公共管理学院教务科**　**公共管理学院党总支**

＃＃＃大学发展规划办公室印制　　　　　　　　2013 年 6 月 2 日印发

第二节　公文文件的翻译原则

公文作为一种专门用途文体，有其特殊的功能和语言特征，这决定了公文翻译在遵循翻译的一般规则的同时又具有其独特的翻译标准和特点。前文提到，公文具有传递、洽谈、沟通交流的工具性作用，在语言和格式上具有高度的正式性、规范性、简洁性和严谨性，在翻译的时候，译者不仅要关注公文的功能作用，还要重视公文独特的语言风格。此外，公文蕴藏着一个国家深厚的文化、社会及历史内涵，因而仅仅考虑功能和语言特点还远远不够。翻译的时候要结合社会、历史、文化等多方面因素进行理解，对源语透彻分析，通过对比英汉公文文体的差异，采用顺应原则给出符合受众接受度的译文。

"语言顺应论"（顺应 adaptation，又译为适应）原本是生物进化论中的一个概念，当被作为一种视角引入语用学研究，便出现了"语言顺应论"。顺应理论由比利时著名语言学家、国际语用学会秘书长维索尔伦（Verschueren）在 2000 年提出，其主要观点是：使用语言的过程就是不断选择语言的过程，人们之所以能够在使用语言过程中做出选择是因为语言具有变异性、商讨性和顺应性。要对语言现象做出语用解释，必须考虑四个方面：语境关系顺应、语言结构顺应、动态顺应和顺应过程中的意识程度。

1. 语境关系顺应（即语境关联成分 contextual correlates of adaptability）

在公文翻译中，我们需要考虑的语境关系主要有语言语境和交际语境。在语境因素中，思维意识的运作、认知机制以及译者的目的和接受能力对译者的语言选择具有突出影响。翻译时译者要考虑翻译的交际目的，顺应读者的语言环境，可以采用归化的翻译方法进行翻译。如：中文公文中经常引用"兹"来表达文体的正式度，"兹定于……"，译者可采用顺应原则，用"hereby"（It hereby ... ）来翻译。

例：

免职通知

经董事会决定，免去王海先生担任的董事长办公室主任职务，现予公布。

董事长办公室

译文：

Notice of dismissal

It is hereby proclaimed that the board directors have decided to dismiss Wang Hai from the post of chief of the president's office.

The President's office

某些行政类公文主要目的是文件的强制执行，对相关各方具有法律约束力，具有可强制执行性。此类公文翻译更重视对原文内容和风格的忠实程度，极为强调"严谨"、"准确"和"简明"。该例中译者顺应目标受众的认知规律，使用了英语受众所熟识和接受的公文格式和语言。

2. 语言结构顺应（即结构对象 structural objects of adaptability）

翻译公文文件时，要注意中英语言结构的差异。中文句式简短，而英语公文采用长句，并且多用名词、动名词成分进行修饰。基于这一特点，汉英翻译时，要顺应英文语言结构，使英文读者更好地接受译文。

例： 对于犯罪情节轻微不需要判处刑罚的，可以免于刑事处分，但可以根据条件的不同情况，予以训诫或者责令具结悔过、赔礼道歉、赔偿损失，或者由主管部门予以行政处分。

译文： Where the circumstances of a person's crime are minor and do not require sentencing for punishment, an exemption from criminal sanctions may be granted him, but he may, according to the different circumstances of each case, be reprimanded or ordered to make a statement of repentance or formal apology, or make compensation for losses, or be subjected to administrative sanctions by the competent department.

根据顺应原则，译者在翻译时采用了长句，并且使用了大量的名称和名称结构来表达，如 an exemption from，sentencing for punishment 等。

例： 如合营公司与买受人签订的买卖合同进行了修改，如果代理人未对该修改适当地通知合营公司，合营公司因此发生的损害和经济损失应由代理人负责。

译文： The Agent shall be responsible for damages and economic losses incurred by the Joint Venture Company solely due to the failure by the Agent to properly inform the Joint Venture Company of any amendments to the sales contract entered into by the Agent on behalf of the Joint Venture Company with a purchaser.

3. 动态顺应（动态性 dynamics of adaptability）

汉英公文翻译过程也是个不断选择语言的过程，是译者为促成与目标受众达成认知一致而对原语的语境和语言结构之间做出动态顺应的过程。

例： 对下岗失业人员自谋职业和自主创业，在有条件的地方设立专门窗口，实行工商登记、税务办理、劳动保障事务代理等"一条龙"服务。

译文： Wherever the conditions are right, a special office should be set up to provide a "coordinated process" service covering industrial and commercial registration, taxation procedures and labor protection matters, to laid-off and unemployed persons who have set up their own businesses.

"龙"在中国是吉祥神圣的象征，而在西方却代表邪恶。原文"一条龙"应采取顺应策略将原文"一条龙"服务所代表的"流水线型成套服务"含义译出即"coordinated process" service，实现为译文读者服务的动态顺应原则，如译为"one dragon service"就会失去交际目的，无法正确传达原文的内涵意义。

4. 顺应过程中的意识程度（即意识突显性 salience of adaptability）

语言顺应过程意识突显是指语言使用中表现出来的有一定语用功能特性的自反意识（或元语用意识）。语言顺应过程意识突显程度取决于意义生成过程中交际者的认知心理状态以及在语言选择过程中做出的语言顺应程度。因而语言顺应过程意识突显程度要受语境关系顺应、结构客体顺应、动态顺应三个因素的影响和制约。这就是说，翻译时候要综合考虑前三个适应，以完成语言顺应过程意识突显，即要考虑翻译目的、道德观念、价值观念和社会规范等方面。

例：我们愿同非洲国家一道努力，抓住历史机遇，促进共同发展。

译文：We in China are ready to work with African countries in an effort to seize the development.

英语译文将"愿"调整翻译为"ready to"，并且将"我们"清晰界定为"We in China"，并且将原文的并列动宾结构划分成其他的结构，这显然是译者为了突显这篇公文的主旨，即表明中国立场、加强中非国家间的相互理解，促进双方的互利合作。该例体现了译文受语境顺应、动态顺应及结构顺应的综合制约，英文译文体现出"自我意识"的突显。

第三节　案例及习题

一、英译汉

1. 案例

Judgment No. 1476 (25 November 2009)：Acevedo et. al. V. The Secretary-General of the United Nations

SUSPENSION OF GRANTING OF PERMANENT APPOINTMENTS—CONVERSION OF CONTRACTUAL STATUS FOR STAFF ON FIXED. TERM APPOINTMENTS TO PERMANENT APPOINTMENTS—STAFF SHALL BE APPOINTED BY THE SECRETARY. GENERAL UNDER REGULATIONS ESTABLISHED BY THE GENERAL ASSEMBLY. —CONSIDERABLE LATITUDE OF DISCRETION ENJOYED BY THE SECRETARY-GENERAL IN MATTERS OF APPOINTMENT, PROMOTION AND CONVERSIONS.

The Applicants were staff members of the United Nations serving on fixed-term appointments，with an entry on duty date prior to 1995. Secretary-General's bulletin ST/SGB/280，issued on 9 November 1995，informed all staff members of the Secretary-General'S decision to suspend the granting of permanent and probationary appointments，effective 13 November 1995. On 9 September 2004，the Secretary-General submitted his definitive proposals on new contractual arrangements，including a number of transitional measures which would ensure the protection of acquired rights of staff in service when the amended rules and regulations would come into force. In its resolution 59/226 of 23 December 2004，the General Assembly took note of the Secretary • General's proposals，and decided to revert to the issue at its sixtieth session，in 2005.

Between 10 November 2003 and 9 March 2004，the Applicants submitted requests to the Secretary-General for review of the decision to "keep in force the freeze on the granting of permanent appointments". The Organization replied to all such requests that the issue was under review, and that the Secretary—General had approved a one-time review of all staff who may have met the requirements to be considered for conversion to a permanent appointment. Should the Applicants meet the criteria for such conversion, they would be considered appropriately by the Staff Management Coordination Committee (SMCC).

Following this reply, the Applicants filed separate appeals "the Joint Appeals Board (JAB)" (联合申诉委员会). The Organization and the Applicants agreed on 16 June 2006 that the appeal be submitted directly to the Tribunal pursuant to article 7 (1) of its Statute. On 17 October 2006, the Applicants filed an application with the Tribunal.

In setting out the legal framework, the Tribunal noted that Article 101 (1) of the Charter of the United Nations provides that staff shall be appointed by the Secretary-General under regulations established by the General Assembly. Accordingly, staff regulation 4. 5(b) provides that the Secretary-General shall prescribe which staff members are eligible for permanent appointments. In 1982, the General Assembly decided in resolution 37/126 that staff members of fixed-term appointment upon completion of five years of continuing good service shall be given reasonable consideration for a career appointment, this decision was implemented as of 1 January 1993 in staff rule 104. 12.

The Tribunal observed that it had long recognized the considerable latitude of discretion enjoyed by the Secretary-General in matters of appointment, promotion and conversions (see Judgments No. 362 Williamson (1986) and No. 958 Draz (2000)). The Tribunal noted that the General Assembly, by resolution 57/305 of 1 May 2003, had requested the Secretary-General to continue current contractual arrangements, which required maintaining the suspension on granting permanent appointments and maintaining status quo conferred by existing mandates. The Tribunal stated that the Secretary-General was thus entitled to refuse consideration of the Applicants for conversion of their contractual status, based on ST/SGB/280/Amend. 1, and in light of all circumstances, including the subsequent General Assembly resolutions on the matter.

The Tribunal rejected the application in its entirety.

2. 翻译工作坊课程规划

第一,文本解读。

(1) 介绍联合国司法系统,并对联合国判决文件有一定的认识;

(2) 分析法律公文文体的语言特征,把握正式、准确、专业的原则;

(3) 结合法律文体、公文文体的语言特征及所学翻译理论提出相应的翻译策略。

第二,分组翻译(六人一组)。具体要求如下:

(1) 按照所提出的翻译策略,各组成员分别进行翻译;

(2) 组内进行翻译、修改,拟初稿;

(3) 将初稿合并,六人进行小组讨论,统一术语,纠查错误,拟定稿。

(4) 各组提交定稿。

第三,翻译教学讨论。

（1）以上各组分别由代表进行报告演示，说明本组翻译策略的选择的依据；

（2）所有同学对各组所提出的翻译策略进行讨论；

（3）教师给出参考译文，结合学生译文进行评析，讲解相关翻译技巧。

3. 参考译文

1476 号判决(2009 年 11 月 25 日)：阿塞维多等人诉联合国秘书长

暂停准予终身任职——定期任职的员工的合同身份向终身任职身份的转化——联合国秘书长根据大会规定条例委任员工——联合国秘书长在委任、晋升和转化事宜上享有相当范围的自由裁量权。

申请人是 1995 年以前登记入职并服务于联合国的定期任职员工。于 1995 年 11 月 9 日发布并于 1995 年 11 月 13 日生效的 ST、SGB、280 号联合国秘书长公告告知所有员工，联合国秘书长决定暂停准予终身任职和试用任职。2004 年 9 月 9 日，联合国秘书长提交了其关于新合同安排的最终提议，该提议包括一些过渡性措施，如果修订后的规则和条例生效，这些过渡性措施会确保对在职员工的既得权利进行保护。大会在其 2004 年 12 月 23 日第 59/226 号决议中采纳了联合国秘书长的提议，并决定于 2005 年第 16 届会议上重提该问题。

在 2003 年 11 月 10 日至 2004 年 3 月 9 日期间，申请人向秘书长提交申请要求对"继续保持暂停准予终身任职"这一决定进行复审。该组织对所有这样的申请作出答复称该问题正在审查当中，而且秘书长已同意对可能满足转变成终身任职员工考虑条件的所有员工进行一次性审查。如果申请人符合此类转换的条件，那么工作人员和管理当局协调委员会会对他们予以正当考虑。

在此回复之后，申请人们各自向联合申诉委员会提起了上诉。2006 年 6 月 16 日，该组织和申请人达成一致，根据法庭章程的 7(1)章将该上诉直接交由法庭。2006 年 10 月 17 日，申请人向法庭提交了申请。

为了陈列法律框架，法庭指出，联合国宪章第 101(1)章规定秘书长须根据大会制定的规章对员工进行委任。相应地，员工条例 4.5(b)中规定秘书长应规定哪些员工具有被终身任职的资格。1982 年，大会在 37/126 项决议中决定，对于持续五年在工作中表现良好的定期任职的员工，应该对其终身任职予以合理的考虑；该决定自 1993 年 1 月 1 日起在员工细则 104.12 中开始执行。

法庭表示早就认识到了秘书长在任职、晋升和职位转换这些方面享有相当大的自由裁量权(参照 362 号判决威廉姆森(1986)和 958 号判决德拉兹(2000))。法庭指出，大会依据 2003 年 5 月 1 日的 57/305 项决议要求秘书长延续当前的合同安排，这就要求维持暂停准予终身任职这一决定，以及维持现有授命所产生的现状。基于 ST/SGB/280/修正案.1 并考虑到所有情况，包括随后大会在这个问题上的决议，法庭规定，秘书长因此有权拒绝考虑转变申请人的合同身份。

法庭驳回了全部申请内容。

4. 英译汉(汉译英)翻译练习

（1）　　　　　　　　　海事公文

PANAMA MARITIME AUTHORITY MERCHANT MARINE, CIRCULAR MMC－265	Pan Canal Building Albrock，Panama City Republic of Panama Tel：(507)501－5000 segumar@segumar.com

To：　Ship owners/Operators，Company Security Officers，Legal
Representatives of Panamanian Flagged Vessles，Panamanian Merchant
Marine Consulates and Recognized Organizations(ROs)

Subject：Maritime Labour Convention，2006(MLC，2006)—Occupational Groups (DEFINITIONS)

Reference：Maritime Labour Convention，2006(MLC，2006)

（2）　　　　　　　《非洲投资者报告》节选

Investors' entry strategy

Notwithstanding the evidence of the survey of long term survival of joint ventures and some of their advantages，manufacturing and service firms interviewed in 2010 reported a definitive preference for investing in SSA through new wholly-foreign owned subsidiaries (Figures 2. 2a and 2. 2b). Seventy-six per cent of subsidiaries of TNCs were established as Greenfield investments，in the form of establishing new facilities. Wholly-owned foreign private firms followed a similar Investment path，with 17 per cent in the survey sample having invested in new joint ventures.

There was little evidence of an active market for buying local firms as an entry mode，more were purchased from existing foreign investors. Only 30 manufacturing firms，or three per cent of the sample，involved privatization of previously state-owned assets. These patterns of investment were repeated in the services sector.

This was quite distinct from other regions of the world，where mergers and acquisition of existing establishments were the normal mode of foreign investment.

Origin of foreign investors

Investor origin may contain information relevant for understanding firm performance. For example，differential performance may be related to the concept of appropriate technology，with technology from the South closer and more suitable to local conditions and，therefore，easier to adopt and adapt in Africa. On the other hand，it is possible that more sophisticated technology，such as that originating from North，is needed. In addition，African countries differ in their characteristics，with，for example，some having greater absorption capacity than others.

At the country level two European economies with long historical ties with Africa, the United Kingdom and France are both displaced by India as the largest single source of foreign firms investing in manufacturing with 17 per cent of the total sample (Figure 2.4a). The United Kingdom and France with 11 and 8 per cent of foreign firms in the survey, respectively, were the second and fourth most important source countries. China was third with nine per cent of the sample. In box 2.4 survey findings on Chinese manufacturing in Africa are presented. Intra-regional investment from within sub-Saharan Africa (excluding South Africa) accounted for 13 per cent of the sample.

In the services sector there was much greater diversity in countries of origin. France supplied the greatest number of investors (17 per cent), while India was ranked second with 12 per cent and Kenya was third. (Figure 2.4b)

Type of foreign investors

Another characteristic that may affect productivity performance is whether a foreign firm is a TNC, which may imply strong organization backing and access to superior technology or an FE, which tends to be relatively small and have less organizational capital (Figures 2.5). This proved to be a significant source differential firm performance.

The survey revealed a vast majority of investors in the manufacturing sector were Fes. Only approximately one-third of firms were TNCs. Most investors in manufacturing, thus, seemed to come from developing countries and were to a greater extent FEs rather than TNCs. In services, however, the distribution was considerably more even, with more than half of firms FEs.

(3)　　　　　促令日本投降之波茨坦公告

Proclamation Defining Terms for Japanese Surrender Issued, at Potsdam, July 26, 1945

1. We—the President of the United States, the President of the National Government of the Republic of China, and the Prime Minister of Great Britain, representing the hundreds of millions of our countrymen, have conferred and agree that Japan shall be given an opportunity to end this war.

2. The prodigious land, sea and air forces of the United States, the British Empire and of China, many times reinforced by their armies and air fleets from the west, are poised to strike the final blows upon Japan. This military power is sustained and inspired by the determination of all the Allied Nations to prosecute the war against Japan until she ceases to resist.

3. The result of the futile and senseless German resistance to the might of the aroused free peoples of the world stands forth in awful clarity as an example to the people of Japan. The might that now converges on Japan is immeasurably greater than that which, when applied to the resisting Nazis, necessarily laid waste to the lands, the industry and the

method of life of the whole German people. The full application of our military power, backed by our resolve, will mean the inevitable and complete destruction of the Japanese armed forces and just as inevitably the utter devastation of the Japanese homeland.

4. The time has come for Japan to decide whether she will continue to be controlled by those self-willed militaristic advisers whose unintelligent calculations have brought the Empire of Japan to the threshold of annihilation, or whether she will follow the path of reason.

5. Following are our terms. We will not deviate from them. There are no alternatives. We shall brook no delay.

6. There must be eliminated for all time the authority and influence of those who have deceived and misled the people of Japan into embarking on world conquest, for we insist that a new order of peace, security and justice will be impossible until irresponsible militarism is driven from the world.

7. Until such a new order is established and until there is convincing proof that Japan's war-making power is destroyed, points in Japanese territory to be designated by the Allies shall be occupied to secure the achievement of the basic objectives we are here setting forth.

8. The terms of the Cairo Declaration shall be carried out and Japanese sovereignty shall be limited to the islands of Honshu, Hokkaido, Kyushu, Shikoku and such minor islands as we determine.

9. The Japanese military forces, after being completely disarmed, shall be permitted to return to their homes with the opportunity to lead peaceful and productive lives.

10. We do not intend that the Japanese shall be enslaved as a race or destroyed as a nation, but stern justice shall be meted out to all war criminals, including those who have visited cruelties upon our prisoners. The Japanese Government shall remove all obstacles to the revival and strengthening of democratic tendencies among the Japanese people. Freedom of speech, of religion, and of thought, as well as respect for the fundamental human rights shall be established.

11. Japan shall be permitted to maintain such industries as will sustain her economy and permit the exaction of just reparations in kind, but not those which would enable her to re-arm for war. To this end, access to, as distinguished from control of, raw materials shall be permitted. Eventual Japanese participation in world trade relations shall be permitted.

12. The occupying forces of the Allies shall be withdrawn from Japan as soon as these objectives have been accomplished and there has been established in accordance with the freely expressed will of the Japanese people a peacefully inclined and responsible government.

13. We call upon the government of Japan to proclaim now the unconditional surrender of all Japanese armed forces, and to provide proper and adequate assurances of

their good faith in such action. The alternative for Japan is prompt and utter destruction.

二、汉译英

1. 案例

国家税务总局关于发布《企业重组业务企业所得税管理办法》的公告
国家税务总局公告 2010 年第 4 号

2010 年 7 月 26 日

现将《企业重组业务企业所得税管理办法》予以发布，自 2010 年 1 月 1 日起施行。

本办法发布时企业已经完成重组业务的，如适用《财政部 国家税务总局关于企业重组业务企业所得税处理若干问题的通知》（财税〔2009〕59 号）特殊税务处理，企业没有按照本办法要求准备相关资料的，应补备相关资料；需要税务机关确认的，按照本办法要求补充确认。2008、2009 年度企业重组业务尚未进行税务处理的，可按本办法处理。

特此公告。

2. 翻译工作坊课程规划

第一，文本解读。

（1）公告属于周知性公文，与通告、布告具有同等功能和作用，公告有其具体的时效和使用范围。公告的事项和内容分类较多，领域宽泛，因而公告的语言特征除了具备公文文体的语言特征外，还受公告内容的影响；

（2）了解税务方面的知识；

（3）结合公告的语言特征及税务方面的术语提出相应的翻译策略。

第二，分组翻译（三人一组）。具体要求如下：

（1）按照所提出的翻译策略，各组成员分别进行翻译；

（2）组内进行翻译、修改，拟初稿；

（3）将初稿合并，三人进行小组讨论，统一术语，纠查错误，拟定稿。

（4）各组提交定稿。

第三，翻译教学讨论。

（1）以上各组分别由代表进行报告演示，说明本组翻译策略的选择的依据；

（2）所有同学对各组所提出的翻译策略进行讨论；

（3）教师给出参考译文，结合学生译文进行评析，讲解相关翻译技巧。

3. 参考译文

Announcement of the State Administration of Taxation on Promulgation of the Administrative Measures for Enterprise Income Tax on Enterprises' Restructuring Business

Announcement of the State Administration of Taxation [2010] No. 4

July 26，2010

The Administrative Measures for Enterprise Income Tax on Enterprises' Restructuring Business is hereby promulgated，which shall come into effect on January 1,

2010.

Where the enterprise has already completed the restructuring business upon the promulgation of these Measures, and if the special taxation treatment provided in the Circular of the Ministry of Finance and the State Administration of Taxation on Issues Concerning the Enterprise Income Tax on Enterprises' Restructuring Business (Cai Shui [2009] No. 59) applies but such enterprise fails to prepare relevant materials in accordance with the requirements of these Measures, then such enterprises shall file relevant materials for supplement; in case that the confirmation of taxation authorities is required, such confirmation shall be supplemented in accordance with the requirements of these Measures. Where the 2008 or 2009 restructuring business of an enterprise has not yet been subject to taxation treatment, the relevant taxation shall be handled in accordance with these Measures.

It is hereby notified the above.

4. 汉译英翻译练习

（1）   禁烟令

近年来,通过各方共同努力,公共场所禁烟工作取得积极进展。但也要看到,在公共场所吸烟的现象仍较普遍,特别是少数领导干部在公共场所吸烟,不仅危害公共环境和公众健康,而且损害党政机关和领导干部形象,造成不良影响。

共产党官员应带头不在政府办公室、学校、医院、体育和文化场所,以及公共交通工具内吸烟。共产党官员也应在公共场所制止他人抽烟以在全社会形成禁烟控烟的良好氛围。违反规定的领导干部要给予批评教育,造成恶劣影响的,要依纪依法严肃处理。

（2）

选举代理人委任通知

《选举程序(行政长官选举)规例》第 12、14 及 15 条
2002 年行政长官选举
选举日期:2002 年 3 月 24 日
第一部分 委任(由候选人填写)

1. 本人是上述选举的候选人,现委任下列人士在上述选举担任本人之选举代理人:

中文姓名(正楷):

英文姓名(大楷):

香港身份证号码:

联络电话号码:

地址:

2. 本人明白,该选举代理人可以代表本人进行一切本人身为候选人可合法进行与上述选举有关的事情,惟下列事情除外:——

(a) 做出《行政长官选举条例》第 16(7)条或《选举程序(行政长官选举)规例》第 4(1)

(b)条所提述的声明；

（b）作为获提名的候选人而在提名表格上签署；

（c）作为候选人而在退选通知书上签署；

（d）委任选举代理人；

（e）委任选举开支代理人；

（f）在不损害《选举程序(行政长官选举)规例》第13条的原则下，代候选人招致选举开支；及

（g）撤销选举代理人或选举开支代理人的委任。

3. 本人亦明白，本人可能须根据《选举(舞弊及非法行为)条例》第29(1)条，为本人的选举代理人的行动负责。惟该条例第29(2)条亦指出在某些情况下，候选人可就其代理人的行动请求宽免。

4. 本人可随时将一份填妥并由本人签署的指定表格送交选举主任，以撤销此选举代理人的委任。

候选人姓名：

身份证明文件号码：

签署： 日期：

第二部分 接受委任(由选举代理人填写)

5. 本人的个人资料乃如上述第一段所列。本人现接受此通知第一部分所述之委任：

选举代理人姓名(正楷)：

签署： 日期：

第三部分 证明(由见证人填写)

6. 本人声明此通知第一部分及第二部分乃分别由候选人及选举代理人于本人见证下签署。

7. 本人个人资料如下：——

中文姓名(正楷)：

英文姓名(大楷)：

身份证明文件号码：

地址：

签署： 日期：

选举代理人委任通知填写说明

1. 此通知内提及的选举日期是指首三轮投票的日期。根据《选举程序(行政长官选举)规例》第17(3)条，如需进行第四轮或其后任何一轮投票，便会于翌日进行，如有需要，则日复一日地进行，直至有候选人当选为止。此通知适用于任何一轮投票。

2. 每一位候选人只可委任一名选举代理人。只有年满18岁的香港身份证持有人方可被委任为选举代理人。然而，候选人应确保并无委任任何选举主任、助理选举主任，或任何已获总选举事务主任委任协助进行投票或点票的人士(通常为政府公职人员)为其选举代理人。

3. 填妥的委任通知指定表格，可由专人送递、邮递或图文传真方式送交选举主任。委任通知送交选举主任后，该项委任方正式生效。

4. 除了少数例外的事项外(请参阅表格第一部分第 2 项),获正式委任的选举代理人有权于选举期内处理一切原本可由做出委任的候选人亲自处理的必要事务,亦可于候选人缺席的任何时候,代表候选人采取任何与竞选有关的行动。这些由选举代理人采取的行动,效力与候选人亲自采取的行动无异。

5. 此通知第一部分应由候选人填写(包括有关选举代理人的姓名及地址)及签署。第二部份应由选举代理人填写及签署。签署第一部分及第二部分时,均须有一位见证人在场。见证人可以是任何年满 18 岁并持有身份证明文件的人士。见证人应填写及签署此通知第三部分。

6. 选举主任会向所有其他候选人送交载有选举代理人详情的通知。他亦会将该通知展示于办事处外的显眼处。

7. 你须注意下列有关填报个人资料的说明——

(a)资料用途

此通知内的个人及其他有关的资料,会供选举事务处及选举主任作有关选举的用途。

(b)资料转介

此通知内的资料可能会提供给获授权的部门或机构处理,用作与选举有关的用途。另外,选举主任会向其他候选人送交选举代理人详情的通知。

(c)索阅个人资料

任何人有权根据《个人资料(私隐)条例》内所载的条款要求索阅及修订他所提供的个人资料。

(d)查询

查询有关此通知收集的个人资料(包括索阅及修正个人资料),应向总选举事务主任(地址:香港湾仔港湾道 25 号海港中心 10 楼)提出。

选举管理委员会
2001 年 12 月

(3) **派遣函**①

兹证明申请人×××出生于×年×月×日,性别×,从×××年×月×日起在本公司工作,任本公司×××职务,月薪人民币××××元。公司派遣×××赴埃及开罗参加Interbuild 2007 建筑展及埃中贸易投资洽谈会,机票、三晚酒店等费用由埃及政府提供。我公司保证其在埃及期间遵守当地法律,并在商务活动结束后按期回国,继续在我公司任原职。如×××未征得主办方许可未按期回国,我单位愿承担相关责任及法律纠纷所引起的费用。

×××××××××有限公司(盖章)
负责人签字:
××/××/2007

---

① http://wenku. baidu. com/view/a78cd20ef78a6529647d5378. html? from＝search

第八章

外贸函电翻译

第一节　外贸函电的语言特点

随着对外贸易的快速发展,中国正与越来越多的国家进行经济合作和文化交流。外贸函电是洽谈和合作的有效手段之一,在国际贸易中发挥着重要的作用。外贸函电属于商务应用文,具有约定、提供信息、提供凭证三个功能,其语言特点有:

1. 完整

一篇外贸函电要求包含提供给读者的全部必要信息并且包含对读者所提所有问题的答复。例如,当买方因接受卖方报盘而回函,必须陈述其接受报盘的详细条件或是接受报盘的凭证,如报盘单,信函及广告等。

2. 具体

外贸函电的陈述要具体确定,一般不使用模糊、意义宽泛和抽象的词汇。例如时间表达上,不能使用"昨天""明天"等不具体的词汇,而应写清具体的年月日。

3. 清楚

清楚原则主要是为了避免相互误解。在措辞时,首先在脑海中要有一个具体的观点。

例:As to the steamer sailing from Shanghai to Los Angeles, we have bimonthly direct services.

其中 bimonthly 有两层含义,即"一个月两次"和"每两个月一次",在上文中,作者并没有把自己的意图表达清楚,应该改写为:

We have two direct sailings every month from Shanghai to Los Angeles.

或者:

We have a direct sailing from Shanghai to Los Angeles every two months.

4. 简洁

简洁性原则是外贸函电的一个重要语言特征。简洁的函电可以节约发函者和读者的时间。但需要注意的是,简洁的同时也要完整、具体和清楚。

例: a long period of time 改为 a long time

at this time 改为 now

come to a decision 改为 decide

due to the fact that 改为 because 等等。

5. 礼貌

为了给潜在客户留下诚实、热情、专业的印象,外贸函电要求发函者遵循礼貌原则。外贸信函多采用礼貌客气的措辞,充分体谅对方,注意对方的要求、愿望和感情,为双方的合作营造一个友好的气氛。这有助于减少贸易纠纷或索赔申诉,从而促进交易的达成。英文中可能会使用虚拟语气、被动语态、疑问句等方法表达婉转、礼貌的态度。试比较以下例子:

例(1) You made a very careless mistake during the course of shipment.

A very careless mistake was made during the course of shipment.

例(2) We inform you that we are unable to deliver the machines on time.

We are extremely sorry that we could not deliever the machines on time.

5. 体谅

体谅原则体现了作者对读者态度上的充分考虑,或者说作者写作时是站在读者的立场上考虑问题或者遣词造句。试比较以下例子:

例(1) We allow a 5% discount for cash payment.

You earn a 5% discount when you pay cash.

例(2) May I express my thanks for the account you recently opened with our store.

Thank you for the account you opened at Johnson's.

第二节 外贸函电的翻译原则

1. 忠实、准确、统一的原则

本原则要求译者忠实原文,意思准确表达,做到中英文统一。

2. "半文言体"表达方式

外贸函电英汉互译时,要注意把握恰当的文体特征,使译文得体。外贸函电中的常用一些套语:

例: We thank you for all past favor, and we are always at your service.

谢谢贵方以往的惠顾,并盼总能为您效劳。

例：We are pleased to inform you that we have commenced a business as a commission agent.

欣告我方已展开经营代销业务。

汉语外贸函电中的常用词汇是介于文言与口语词汇之间的"半文言体"，如"欣告"、"欣寄"、"我方"、"贵方"、"非……"、"惠顾"、"告知"等等，这些词汇的使用可以使译文既易懂又庄重。

3. 动态美兼静态美

英语词法和句法体系有别于汉语，如英语中名词、介词占优势，所以在选择表述动作意义的方式时常常是静态表述方式多于动态表述方式。这样行文显得更为精练和多样化。而汉语重动态描写，有多用动词的固有习惯，常常大量使用兼动式和连动式，在选择表述动作意义的方式时常常是动态表述方式多于静态表述方式。动态美体现在科学论证上讲究逻辑严密，静态美体现对科学结论真实性的表达方式上，即表述力求客观，行文追求简洁通畅。翻译的时候要动静结合，遵循中英两种语言的语言特点，把握语言美，更好地为读者服务。

例：Having had your name and address from the Commercial Counsellor's Office of the Embassy of the People's Republic of China in Australia, we now avail ourselves of this opportunity to write to you and see if we can establish business relations by a start of some practical transactions.

从中华人民共和国驻澳大利亚大使馆商务参赞处获悉贵公司名称和地址，现借此机会与贵公司通信，意在达成一些交易，并以此建立业务关系。

英文中"a start of some practical transactions"为名词短语，译文巧妙反映了汉语的动态美，转而译为动词结构"达成一些交易"。

第三节 案例及习题

一、英译汉

1. 案例

Dear Sirs,

Messrs. Armstrong & Smith of Sheffield inform us that you are exporters of cotton bed-sheets and pillowcases. We would like you to send us details of your various ranges, including sizes, colours and prices, and also samples of the different qualities of the materials used.

We are large dealers in textiles and believe there is a promising market in our area for moderately priced goods of the kind mentioned.

When replying, please state your terms of payment and discount you would allow on purchases of not less than 100 dozen of individual items. Prices quoted should include insurance and freight to Liverpool.

Yours faithfully,

...

A reply to the above letter:

Dear Sirs,

We are very pleased to receive your inquiry of 15th January and are enclosing our illustrated catalogue and price list giving the details you asked for. Also by separate post we are sending you some samples and feel confident that when you have examined them you will agree that the goods are both excellent in quality and reasonable in price.

On regular purchases in quantities of not less than 100 dozen of individual items, we would allow you a discount of 2%. Payment is to be made by irrevocable L/C at sight.

Because of their softness and durability, our cotton bed-sheets and pillowcases are rapidly becoming popular; and after studying our prices, you will not be surprised to learn that we are finding it difficult to meet the demand. But if your order not later than the end of February, we would ensure prompt shipment.

We invite your attention to our other products such as table clothes and table napkins, details of which you will find in the catalogue, and look forward to receving your first order.

Yours faithfully,

...

2. 翻译工作坊课程规划

第一,文本解读。

(1) 对比分析外贸函电的中英语言特征,指出上文中的英文函电的语言特点;

(2) 结合中英外贸函电的语言特点、文体特征及翻译原则给出适当的翻译策略。

第二,分组翻译(六人一组)。具体要求如下:

(1) 按照所提出的翻译策略,各组成员分别进行翻译;

(2) 组内进行翻译、修改,拟初稿;

(3) 将初稿合并,六人进行小组讨论,统一术语,纠查错误,拟定稿。

(4) 各组提交定稿。

第三,翻译教学讨论。

(1) 以上各组分别由代表进行报告演示,说明本组翻译策略选择的依据;

(2) 所有同学对各组所提出的翻译策略进行讨论;

(3) 教师给出参考译文,结合学生译文进行评析,讲解相关翻译技巧。

3. 参考译文

敬启者:

承雪菲耳、阿姆史特朗、史密斯公司介绍,得知你方是经营棉质床单和枕套的出口公司,为此,拟请告知你方经营品种的尺寸、颜色和价格等详细情况,并请惠寄各种不同用料的样品。

我行是经营纺织品的主要经销商,如上述这类商品价格公道,相信在这里定会获得畅销。

复信时，请说明支付条款，并请告知各类品种购量达 100 打时的折扣。此外，请报利物浦到岸价。

　　　　　　　　　　　　　　　　　　　　　　　　　　　　　　　　……敬上

对上述信件的回信：

敬启者：

　　欣悉你 1 月 15 日询盘来函。现随函付寄我公司的插图目录和价目表，上面列有你方所需的各项细节。另函寄你方一些样品，我相信你们检验该项样品后，定会同意我们产品价廉物美的意见。

　　如各类产品购量达 100 打时，我们通常给 2% 的折扣，凭不可撤销即期信用证支付。

　　我们的棉质床单和枕套，由于柔软耐用，已成为畅销品种。相信你们研究我们的价格后，定会认为这些产品供不应求是不足为怪了。但是如果你方能在 2 月底以前订货，我方保证即期装运。

　　另一方面，敬请关注我公司所经营的台布、餐巾等其他各种产品，所附目录列有该项产品的详细情况。盼即订购。

　　　　　　　　　　　　　　　　　　　　　　　　　　　　　　　　……敬上

4. 英译汉翻译练习

　　（1）　　　　　　　　　　**Letter for Amending the L/C**

Dear Sirs，

　　We have received your L/C No. 3639 issued by the Chartered Bank，London for the amount of £12,345 covering 15,000 Dozen Stretch Nylon Socks. On perusal，we find that trans-shipment and partial shipment are not allowed.

　　As direct steamers to your port are few and far between，we have ship via Hong Kong more often than not. As to partial shipment，it would be to mutual benefit because we could ship immediately whatever we have on hand instead of waiting for the whole lot to be completed. Therefore，we are cabling this afternoon，asking you to amend the L/C to read "Partial shipments and trans-shipment allowed".

　　We shall appreciate it very much if you will see to it that amendment is cabled without delay，as our goods have been packed ready for shipment for quite some time.

　　　　　　　　　　　　　　　　　　　　　　　　　　　Yours faithfully，

　　　　　　　　　　　　　　　　　　　　　　　　　　　...

　　（2）　　　　　　　　　　**Letter for Insurance Information**

Dear Sirs，

　　Answering you letter of June 25 in regard to insurance，we would like to inform you of the following：

　　（1）All Risks：Generally we cover insurance WPA & War Risk in the absence of definite instructions from our clients. If you desire to cover All Risks，we can provide such coverage at a slightly higher premium.

（2）Breakage：Breakage is a special risk，for which can extra premium will have to be charged. The present rate is about … ％. Claims are payable only for that part of the loss，that is over 5％.

（3）Value to be insured：We note that you wish us to insure shipments to you for 10％ above invoice value，which is having our due attention.

We trust the above information will serve your purpose and await your further news.

Yours truly，
…

二、汉译英

1. 案例

装船指示：

敬启者：

6月5日电悉，你方已接受我方订货，购买2 000台IBM－99型计算机以及彩色显示器、主板和驱动器各300件。不日即寄你方订货确认书。

因此笔交易是按广州到岸价成交，你方必须在8月底货运抵广州。

因这些计算机及部件容易震坏，必须用适于海运的木箱包装，能经受得起磕碰。明亮金属部件应涂上滑油，以防途中受潮，而且在气候多变的情况下，这种滑油不致溶化流失。

相信你方对上述说明会完全明白，希望用户能对交货完全满意。

……敬上

2. 翻译工作坊课程规划

第一，文本解读。

（1）指出上文中的汉语函电的语言特点和专业词汇；

（2）结合中英外贸函电的语言特点、文体特征及翻译原则给出适当的翻译策略。

第二，分组翻译（六人一组）。具体要求如下：

（1）按照所提出的翻译策略，各组成员分别进行翻译；

（2）组内进行翻译、修改，拟初稿；

（3）将初稿合并，六人进行小组讨论，统一术语，纠查错误，拟定稿。

（4）各组提交定稿。

第三，翻译教学讨论。

（1）以上各组分别由代表进行报告演示，说明本组翻译策略的选择的依据；

（2）所有同学对各组所提出的翻译策略进行讨论；

（3）教师给出参考译文，结合学生译文进行评析，讲解相关翻译技巧。

3. 参考译文

Shipment Instruction

Dear Sirs,

We are in receipt of your telegram of 5th June, from which we understand that you have booked your order for 2,000 sets of IBM - 99 computers and respective 300 pieces of color monitors, main boards and drivers.

Since the purchase is made on CIF basis, you are to send the goods to Guangzhou by the end of August.

As these goods are susceptible to shock, they must be packed in seaworthy wooden cases capable of withstanding rough handling. The right metal parts should be protected from water and dampness in transit by a coating of slushing compound that will keep out dampness, but will not liquefy and run off under changing weather conditions.

We trust that the above instructions are clear to you and that the shipment will give the users entire satisfaction.

Yours faithfully,

...

4. 汉译英翻译练习

（1）　催促卖方装船函

敬启者：

我方已给你方发了不少信电，但迄今未获你方有关标题货交货日期方面的消息，请予注意。

前信已告你方，我方用户急需这些货物，并要我们保证早日交货。

在此情况下，第 2450 号信用证再次延期是明显办不到的。我们有责任想提醒你方注意，此信用证 8 月 10 日到期。

有关各方均望你方能马上办理交货事宜。我方希望接到你方电报装船通知，不能再次拖延。

······敬上

（2）　要求分批装运和信用证展期

敬启者：

由于我地强烈的地震袭击厂房，你方 22 号订单 3 500 匹细布不可能一次交货了，深表歉意。

为此，我昨日电告你方，请允许分批交货，即 1 500 匹在合同期内交付，其余 2 000 匹在 9 月份交货，希望你方能同意将信用证展期至 10 月 15 日。虽然这是不可抗力造成的，我们为此亦很抱歉，现在正竭尽全力恢复工厂生产。

对我们的处境请予谅解，并盼答应我们的要求。

······敬上

第九章

报刊翻译

第一节　报刊的语言特征

信息化时代就是信息产生价值的时代。随着计算机技术的发展，报刊也从传统的纸质文本发展到电子报纸和电子期刊。大量的国际国内报刊涌现在人们的生活中，成为阅读的热点。这迫切要求对这些信息的翻译也要跟上时代的步伐。报刊的目的性、时效性、事实性和不同语言和文化的差异性使得报刊具有独特的语言特征：

一、词汇特征

1. 简洁有力

报刊要求提供的信息真实可信、生动形象，因而能够吸引读者，便于传播。但要广大读者能够省时省力地看懂，报刊经常使用缩写词或缩略词和简短小词，遣词造句力求简洁有力。

2. 外来词、新词的大量使用

经常掺用外来语是报刊词汇使用的一大特点。因为报刊具有时效性，陈述中会提及外国的或新近出现的事物，一方面引起读者的兴趣与注意，一方面可以更贴切地表达某词语的内涵。

例：The shipping company, starting from scratch in 1952, has blossomed into the doyen of the maritime freight industry.

这家船务公司于 1952 年白手起家，至今已发展壮大，成为海上货运业的龙头老大。

Doyen 是法语，原意是"资格最老的元老"，转义为"龙头老大"。

随着科技的进步，新事物、新思想、新经验会时有发生。旧的词汇已无法承载新的概念和思想，新的表达方式便应运而生。新词的构成可以有：旧词衍生新义（如 gay 一词原意为"快乐的"，后衍生为"同性恋者；同性恋的"）、新事物产生新词（如 DNA 即脱氧核糖核酸，euro 欧元，bachelor mother 未婚母亲）、旧词派生新词（auto-alarm 自动报警器，computalk

计算机对话，cybercafe 网吧）、类比生成新词（颜色类别：black list 黑名单，blue-collar workers 蓝领；地点类比：landscape 类比出 cityscape 市景）。

二、句法特征

1. 简洁

报刊的简洁性表现在多方面。首先，简单句多于复合句。为了节约版面，便于读者阅读和理解，报刊的撰写要求尽可能在一个句子中包含较多的信息，不得不打破简单的句型结构，或采用合并句子的方法，将原先两句或两句以上的句子才能表达的事实合并成一个句子，所以句子结构显得松散。第二，省略句较为常见，如连接词 that 经常省略。第三，大量使用前置定语来修饰名词，这可以使句子结构紧凑严密，简洁利落。第四，起句常用名词结构，使句子简洁易懂，语句结构清晰。

2. 灵活

报刊的内容有时较为枯燥，有时为了吸引读者的注意力和兴趣，常常采用灵活的句法使读者阅读起来不感到乏味。第一，起句形式灵活多样，名词作为主语开头的较为常见，但除此之外，介词短语起句、非限定动词起句法、独立结构起句法等多种表达法均出现在报刊中。第二，直接引语和间接引用灵活使用。第三，各种句式的灵活使用，如静态句、欧式长句以及被动句等句式的混合使用。

三、修辞特征

修辞手段的大量使用使报刊更简练、形象，并富有趣味性。常用的修辞手段主要包括比喻、双关、夸张和借用典故成语等。

第二节　报刊的翻译策略

1. 互文性视角

互文性（Intertextuality）理论是当代西方后现代主义思潮中产生的一种文本理论。该理论的创始人，法国的符号学家朱莉娅·克里斯蒂娃认为"每一个文本都是用马赛克般的引文拼嵌起来的，每一个文本都是对其他文本的吸收和转化。"这就是说任何文本都不可能脱离其他文本存在，每个文本的意义都产生于它跟其他文本的相互作用中。互文性理论体现了文本之间的继承和发展关系。报刊的翻译应注意互文性视角。译者应多关注原文的语篇风格、作者风格，力求使译文的风格做到恰如其分。

2. 主位推进模式

主位概念最早由布拉格学派创始人之一马泰休斯（V. Mathesius：1947）提出。他把位于句首的在交际中引出话题的称为主位（Theme），是已知信息，其他成分是述位（Rheme），是新信息,句子的主位结构和信息之间存在一定的对应关系。在一个语篇中,主述位不只是在句子中起到组织语句出发点的作用,还通过句与句之间的反复衔接成为实现语篇衔接和连贯的主要手段之一。因此,主位的选择决定了语篇的发展方向,主位的翻译也就特别重要。英汉两种语言在表达上可能有主述位同一,主述位不同一,在翻译中要视实际情况、译语语言习惯来进行主述位的调整。

例:Italian aid worker Clementina Cantoni, who was held hostage for more than three weeks in Afghanistan, has been released, the Afghan Interior Ministry said Thursday.

译文一:意大利女人质克莱门蒂娜·坎托尼,在阿富汗被绑架 24 天后获释,阿富汗内政部发言人星期四说。

译文二:阿富汗内政部发言人星期四表示:在阿富汗被绑架 24 天后,意大利女人质克莱门蒂娜·坎托尼已安全获释。

译文一是按照原文的主位、述位进行翻译的,这样的译文语言不符合汉语规范,读起来也让人觉得有些拗口。与之比较,译文二以"发言人……表示……"为起始点的话题主位推进为框架的语篇模式,更符合汉语语言主谓语的"话题-说明"关系。很明显,此句译文的主位结构与原文相比做了很大的调整,这是由汉语语言的特点所决定的。

3. 语域理论

语域是语言使用者认为适用于某一具体场合的语言。韩礼德认为,语域是由语言特征组成的,与语言情景特征有相互联系,具体体现出话语范围、话语方式和话语基调的特点。话语范围是指某种社会行为,反映出语言使用者的目的;话语方式是指语言的表达方式,分为口头语言和书面语言;话语基调是指交际双方的关系。

语域的变化幅度常以语言不同的正式程度和非正式程度(levels of formality/informality)来描述。Martin Joos(1962)提出五个等级,即最正式体(frozen)、正式体(formal)、商议体(consultative)、随意体(casual)、非正式体(intimate)。在翻译报刊时,译者应注意这些特征和语言功能,从而保证译文语域选择的正确性,以免出笑话甚至政治性的错误。

例:The two leaders stated that both countries would develop good-neighborly and friendly relations on the basis of mutual respect for sovereignty and territorial integrity, non-aggression, non-interference in each other's internal affairs, equality and mutual benefit and peaceful co-existence.

两位领导人声明,两国将在互相尊重主权和领土完整,互不侵犯,互不干涉内政,平等互利与和平共处的基础上发展睦邻友好关系。

该例信息量很大。其话语范围是一则政治时事新闻,正式程度很高;话语方式是书卷语体的新闻;话语基调是反映相互之间的政治关系。译文也是这种扩展形式,体现了句法的语域标志,虽然受到正式程度句法语域的制约,使用了较多的嵌入结构,但并没有影响新闻英语表达简洁、意义清晰的要则,而且更充分显示出政治时事新闻的交际功能。

第三节　案例及习题

一、英译汉

1. 案例

A question of standards

(From *The Economist Global Agenda*)

More suggestions of bad behaviour by tobacco companies. Maybe

ANOTHER round has just been fought in the battle between tobacco companies and those who regard them as spawn of the devil. In a paper just published in the *Lancet*, with the provocative title "Secret science: tobacco industry research on smoking behaviour and cigarette toxicity", David Hammond, of Waterloo University in Canada and Neil Collishaw and Cynthia Callard, two members of Physicians for a Smoke-Free Canada, a lobby group, criticise the behaviour of British American Tobacco (BAT). They say the firm considered manipulating some of its products in order to make them low-tar in the eyes of officialdom while they actually delivered high tar and nicotine levels to smokers.

It was and is no secret, as BAT points out, that people smoke low-tar cigarettes differently from high-tar ones. The reason is that they want a decent dose of the nicotine which tobacco smoke contains. They therefore pull a larger volume of air through the cigarette when they draw on a low-tar rather than a high-tar variety. The extra volume makes up for the lower concentration of the drug.

But a burning cigarette is a complex thing, and that extra volume has some unexpected consequences. In particular, a bigger draw is generally a faster draw. That pulls a higher proportion of the air inhaled through the burning tobacco, rather than through the paper sides of the cigarette. This, in turn, means more smoke per unit volume, and thus more tar and nicotine. The nature of the nicotine may change, too, with more of it being in a form that is easy for the body to absorb.

According to Dr Hammond and his colleagues, a series of studies conducted by BAT's researchers between 1972 and 1994 quantified much of this. The standardised way of analysing cigarette smoke, as laid down by the International Organisation for Standardisation, which regulates everything from computer code to greenhouse gases, uses a machine to make 35-millilitre puffs, drawn for two seconds once a minute. The firm's researchers, by contrast, found that real smokers draw 50—70 ml per puff, and do so twice a minute. Dr Hammonds's conclusion is drawn from the huge body of documents disgorged by the tobacco industry as part of various legal settlements that have taken place in the past few years, mainly as a result of disputes with the authorities in the United States.

Dr Hammond suggests, however, the firm went beyond merely investigating how people smoked. A series of internal documents from the late 1970s and early 1980s shows that BAT at least thought about applying this knowledge to cigarette design. A research report from 1979 puts it thus: "There are three major design features which can be used either individually or in combination to manipulate delivery levels: filtration, paper permeability, and filter-tip ventilation." A conference paper from 1983 says, "The challenge would be to reduce the mainstream nicotine determined by standard smoking-machine measurement while increasing the amount that would actually be absorbed by the smoker". Another conference paper, from 1984, says: "We should strive to achieve this effect without appearing to have a cigarette that cheats the league table. Ideally it should appear to be no different from a normal cigarette... It should also be capable of delivering up to 100% more than its machine delivery."

None of the documents discovered by the three researchers shows that BAT actually did redesign its cigarettes in this way, and the firm denies that it did. However, BAT's own data show that some of its cigarettes delivered far more nicotine and tar to machines which had the characteristics of real smokers than to those which ran on ISO standards. In the most extreme example, in a test carried out in 1987, the "real smoking" machine drew 86% more nicotine and 114% more tar from Player's Extra Light than the ISO machine detected, although smoke intake was only 27% higher.

Regardless of how this came about, the irony is that low-tar brands may have ended up causing more health problems than high-tar ones. As one of BAT's medical consultants put it as early as 1978, "Perhaps the most important determinant of the risk to health or to a particular aspect of health is the extent to which smoke is inhaled by smokers. If so, then deeply inhaled smoke from low-tar-delivery cigarettes might be more harmful than uninhaled smoke from high-tar cigarettes." The firm, meanwhile, points out that the ISO test has been regarded as unreliable since 1967, and says its scientists have been part of a panel that is working on a new ISO standard.

2. 翻译工作坊课程规划

第一,文本解读。

(1) 分析报刊的语言特征,具体罗列出来,给出每个特征的例子;

(2) 总结目的语读者的特点;

(3) 结合互文性、语域理论及主位推进模式三个方面提出相应的翻译方法。

第二,分组翻译(六人一组)。具体要求如下:

(1) 按照所提出的翻译策略,各组成员分别进行翻译;

(2) 组内进行翻译、修改,拟初稿;

(3) 将初稿合并,六人进行小组讨论,统一术语,纠查错误,拟定稿。

（4）各组提交定稿。

第三，翻译教学讨论。

（1）以上各组分别由代表进行报告演示，说明本组翻译策略的选择的依据；

（2）所有同学对各组所提出的翻译策略进行讨论；

（3）教师给出参考译文，结合学生译文进行评析，讲解相关翻译技巧。

3. 参考译文

一个关乎标准的问题

（源自《经济学人》杂志）

也许，烟草公司对那些不良行为应多提点建议。

烟草公司与那些视其为"魔鬼之子"的人之间刚刚又进行了新一轮的交锋。新近出版的《柳叶刀》刊登了一篇题目颇具煽动性的论文《秘密科研——烟草业开展对吸烟行为和香烟毒性的研究》，作者是加拿大沃特鲁大学的戴维·哈蒙德以及加拿大一个名为"无烟加拿大医师"游说团的两名成员尼尔·科里肖和辛西娅·加拉德。他们对英美烟草公司的行为提出了批评，称该公司拟对某些烟草产品进行处理，企图让监督部门误以为其焦油含量低，而实际上这些产品仍会使得烟民吸收高浓度的焦油和尼古丁。

正如英美烟草公司所指出，人们吸低焦油含量香烟的感觉不同于高焦油含量香烟，这在过去和现在都不是什么秘密。这是因为他们需要烟草中含有适量尼古丁，抽低焦油品种的香烟时所吸入的空气含量也因此比抽高焦油品种的香烟时高，（译者注：也就是说，尼古丁含量过高，烟就很难吸，不容易抽得动。）而这高出来的空气含量也弥补了瘾性物质（尼古丁）的不足。

不过，一支点燃的卷烟可是一个复杂的玩意儿，并且空气量增加也会带来意想不到的结果，特别是当我们大口吸烟时往往会很快抽完一支烟，此时所吸入的空气更多来自于燃烧的烟草而非卷烟纸侧。因而，这就意味着每多吸一口空气，就会多吸一口焦油和尼古丁。多数尼古丁都以一种易被人体吸收的形式存在，因此尼古丁的性质也可能发生改变。

据哈蒙德医生及其同事们称，英美烟草公司的研究员已于1972年到1994年间通过一系列研究，对上述大部分问题进行了定量检测。卷烟烟尘分析的标准方法，是由国际标准化组织（ISO）（该组织可对包括计算机代码和温室气体在内的所有问题作出规定）制定的，此法利用一台机器喷发出35毫升的烟雾，受试者每分钟吸一次、每次持续2秒即可吸完。以此为对照，英美公司研究员发现，真正的烟民每分钟2次即可吸完50至70毫升烟雾。哈蒙德医生是从烟草业提供的大量文献中得出这一结论的。过去几年烟草业与美国当局一直僵持不下，遂签署了各类法律协议。作为其中的一项内容，烟草业被迫拱手交出这些文献。

不过哈蒙德医生表示，英美公司所调查的不仅仅是人们的吸烟方式。英美公司20世纪70年代末、80年代初的一系列内部文献表明，该公司至少曾考虑过将这一知识用于卷烟设计。1979年的一份研究报告上这样说道："可分别或联合应用与设计有关的三个要素，即过滤、烟卷包装纸的通透性以及过滤嘴的通气效果，来控制焦油和尼古丁的释放水平。"1983年一份会议论文也提到，"关键在于，要在提高吸烟者尼古丁实际吸收量的同时，减少可被标准检测方法测定到的含量。"1984年另一份会议论文说："我们应当努力达到这一效果并能在检测中蒙混过关。理想化的结果是，这种香烟看上去应与一般香烟无任何差异……并且释放的尼古丁及焦油量要比机器释放的高出 100％。”

三名研究人员发现的文献中没有一篇表明英美公司确曾采用这种方法对其生产的卷烟进行了改良，而且该公司也矢口否认这么干过。英美公司内部资料显示，其生产的某些卷烟向机器（具有实际吸烟者特征）释放的尼古丁和焦油量远远超出国际标准化组织（ISO）标准。最为极端的例子是，在 1987 年进行的一项实验中，“真吸烟”机器从“玩家之光”（Player's Extra Light）牌卷烟中吸收的尼古丁和焦油量比国际标准化组织（ISO）仪器实际检测到的量分别高出 86％ 和 114％，而烟雾摄入量仅高 27％。

不管事实真相是怎样的，具有讽刺意味的是，低焦油卷烟竟然比高焦油卷烟可能更有损于健康。正如一名英美公司医学顾问 1978 年所言，“也许，吸烟者吸烟时的深浅度是危及健康或者健康某一特定方面的最重要决定性因素。若果真如此，从低焦油卷烟中深深吸入的烟对人的危害可能比高焦油卷烟中未被吸入的烟更大。”与此同时，英美公司指出，自 1967 年以来，国际标准化组织（ISO）的试验一直都被认为是不可靠的。并且言称其公司的科学家们已加入某评估委员会，正在研究制定新的国际标准化组织（ISO）标准。

4. 英译汉翻译练习

（1）　　　　　　　　　**Rejoice for Utopia is nigh！**

ONE hundred years ago an American immigrant invented science fiction.

Okay, that's not true. Not even close. People have been building fantastic narratives out of scientific gobbledygook since the days of the Greeks. Lucian of Samosata imagined a trip to the moon over 17 centuries before Jules Verne took a whack at it. And decades before 1911 Verne and H. G. Wells wrote the stories that established the contours of the genre: fantastic voyages in space and time, alien encounters, technology run amok, and so forth. The term "science fiction" wouldn't even be invented until 1929.

But the genre as a coherent field of literary endeavour—as the thing that takes up a whole wall at your local Barnes & Noble or Waterstone's—might not have come to be if it weren't for a failed inventor-turned-publisher with aesthetic ambitions. Naive, utopian and romantic, a man named Hugo Gernsback ended up establishing a new strand of science fiction, one that helped shape (and was shaped by) the American century.

Gernsback had come to America in 1904 with the common immigrant dream of striking it rich. He planned to revolutionise battery technology, but when that didn't pan out he turned to scientific-magazine publishing. He started out with mail-order catalogues for his imported radio-equipment business, but, as the years went on, his efforts took a more explicitly literary turn. Amazing Stories, which he founded in 1926, has a fair claim to being the first magazine dedicated solely to what he called "scientifiction". It would go on to help define the genre, publishing the debuts of some of its greatest authors. The ever-expanding community of science-fiction readers and fans was so grateful it named its highest honour after him; there isn't an science-fiction writer from Asimov to Zelazny who hasn't coveted a Hugo trophy.

But in 1911 all that lay in the future—a topic which, to be fair, was something Gernsback was pretty interested in. As a young man of 27, he was witnessing a new century and a newly revitalised country all at once. America's can-do spirit involved a gleeful embrace of technology (the trans-continental railroad! The wizard of Menlo Park: Thomas Edison! Henry Ford's Model T!). New inventions, discoveries and achievements seemed to be rolling off the brand-new assembly line every day, and the factual articles of *Modern Electrics*, Gernsback's magazine (its name a kind of romantic statement itself), were hardly capacious enough to contain the sense of possibility. And so he turned, diffidently, to fiction.

Ralph124C 41+: A Romance of the Year 2660, a novel serialised in 12 parts in *Modern Electrics*, is arguably the first major work of American science fiction. It was avidly read, in later reprints in the 1920s, by the adolescents who would become the first generation of great science-fiction writers. Gernsback's story was important and influential, but not without flaws. Jack Williamson, the late, great "dean of science fiction", conceded upon rereading the book seven decades later that "though Gernsback was not concerned with literary art", the story was more enjoyable than he had expected.

Williamson was being charitable. *Ralph124C 41+* is a bad book. Actually, that's also charitable. It is, in fact, a terrible book, full of creaky plot concepts, wooden dialogue, flimsy characters and subtle undertones of racism. (The romance between the titular Ralph and a gal named Alice is almost ruined by an evil Martian kidnapper, who flouts the laws preventing inter-racial marriage—laws which, the book implies, aren't such a bad idea.) It is worth noting that "Ralph" was produced at almost the same time as *Birth of a Nation*.

But all that's a sideshow to the book's appeal: its real "romance" isn't between Ralph and Alice, who are kind of drippy anyway, but between science-loving humanity and the bright, shining future created for them by technological innovation. Like much of the most captivating science fiction, "Ralph" suggests a future that combines the entirely plausible and the insanely far-fetched. This is the main reason the book is so significant (if not quite readable) today. The first real invention suggested in the novel is the Telephot, which, it emerges, is basically Skype mixed with a dash of Chatroulette (the latter by accident: a crossed wire connects Ralph with his love interest, a sign of the novel's structural sagginess). And then there's the Newspaper, essentially an iPad that runs on microfilm; and one of Ralph's inventions, Permagatol, a gas that helps retrieve people from the jaws of death.

Permagatol may seem like nonsense now, but who knows? Gernsback, in his introduction to the 1925 edition, made a reasonable point that catches at the heart of every science-fiction fan. "The author appreciates that many of the predictions and statements appear to verge upon the fantastic," he writes, but he adds that that's what readers thought when they read about Jules Verne's submarine in *Twenty Thousand Leagues*

Under the Sea. If anything, Verne had too modest an imagination, Gernsback added; science was progressing so quickly that "it seems fair to assume that the conception herein described will, 750 years hence, be found to have fallen far short of the actual progress made in the interim." Remember Telephot, ye Skypers, and rejoice, for Utopia is nigh!

It's no coincidence that this gee-whiz, awestruck and optimistic faith in technology is portrayed in the novel as American. A character admiringly remarks, 750 years after Gernsback's time, that "You Americans still lead the world ... Upon my word, the old saying that 'nothing is impossible in America' still holds good." Gernsback's European predecessors were less sanguine about what the future held, with science fiction that tended towards the dystopian (think about Wells's *The Time Machine*, with its Morlocks, or, for that matter, Mary Shelley's *Frankenstein* with its out-of-control technology). But Gernsback's Ralph, however, says confidently that "Today it is not brute force that counts, but scientific knowledge."

Within several years, of course, the Great War would show just how scientific mass destruction could be; but in that brief, shining moment, Gernsback, that heir of Ford and Edison, could spin a dream of better living through technology that seemed to breathe particularly American air. It's a strain that's had remarkable resilience through the century; Gernsback's DNA can be seen in Heinlein and in Asimov and in Avatar (well, the good guys in Avatar, anyway).

So happy birthday, Ralph. You won't be born for roughly 625 years, but that's no paradox a good work of science fiction can't resolve.

(2)　　　　　　**To see a world in a grain of sand**

That quarry's nature, reported this week in the Proceedings of the National Academy of Sciences, is not a complete surprise. A larger virus, called Mimivirus, which lives in freshwater amoebas, turned up in 2003 and a few other, similar, viruses have been found since then. But CroV is by far the biggest to come out of the sea.

Those who like their categories cut and dried may wonder whether viruses are alive or not. Wise biologists do not struggle too much with such questions. Viruses have genes, can reproduce and are subject to the evolutionary pressures imposed by natural selection. That is enough for biology to claim them. As for CroV, those 544 genes (composed of 730,000 base pairs, the DNA letters in which the language of the genes is written) mean its genome is bigger than those of several bacteria—creatures which everyone agrees are alive.

The problem with categorical thinking in biology is that evolution does not work like that. It actually works by whatever works working. If an organism can successfully subcontract part of the business of metabolism to another while retaining the rest itself, rather than off loading the whole lot as most viruses do, then there are no rules to stop it happening.

CroV seems to do just that. Besides the genes that relate to protein synthesis it has others which encode DNA repair mechanisms and still others which are involved with protein recycling and signalling within cells. This is not mere hijacking. It is tantamount to a complete personality transplant for the infected cell.

About a third of CroV's genes are similar to Mimivirus genes, suggesting they share a distant ancestor. On the other hand, two-thirds are not. A significant chunk of them seem to have been copied from bacteria. But the majorities are unique, and previously unknown to science. A whole new chapter of life, in other words, has been opened.

This discovery, then—and the earlier one of C. roenbergensis itself—speak volumes, albeit in a microscopic language, about biodiversity. Two centuries after Carl Linnaeus invented the system now used to describe it, and a century after Charles Darwin worked out what causes it, the ability of that diversity to surprise is still staggering.

二、汉译英

1. 案例

全球最大的棉花消费国中国，已就印度几天之前出台的棉花出口禁令提出正式抗议。与此同时，有迹象显示，印度正在对这项禁令做出重新考虑。

印度总理曼莫汉·辛格（Manmohan Singh）紧急要求数位内阁成员重新评估这项禁令。此前，印度农业部长表示，棉花出口禁令有损棉农利益。

印度总理办公室的一份声明称，评估结果将于今日公布。

总理办公室的一位官员说，相关内阁成员很可能会取消这项禁令。

该官员向英国《金融时报》表示："确实存在取消禁令的实际可能性，而且可能性很大。"

不过，这一政策逆转并非板上钉钉。印度政府正在综合考虑对华关系、印度棉农利益及它对印度强大的纺织业的担心，以求寻找到平衡点。

在棉价经历了两年时间的大起大落之后，这种政策面的突变正在进一步加大棉花市场的波动性。

去年，供应短缺曾推动棉价涨至每磅2美元以上，创下纪录高点。当时的短缺在一定程度上就是由印度出台的一项出口禁令造成的。没想到的是，在棉纺厂纷纷对采购合同违约之后，棉价后来回落至每磅不到1美元的水平。

包括嘉吉（Cargill）、来宝集团（Noble Group）和嘉能可（Glencore）在内的棉花贸易商由此遭受到巨大损失。

在印度出台两年之内的第二项出口禁令之后，棉价今年已有所上涨。

3月5日，印度又出台了本文开头提到的那项禁令，且立即生效实施。此举旨在保障印度国内纺织企业得到充足的棉花供应。印度是全球第二大棉花生产国。

过去一年，中国大举购买棉花来建立政府储备，以求支撑国内农场棉花价格、缓冲价格波动。

美国农业部（USDA）估计，截至今年1月底，中国已从国外购买了多达500万包棉花来充实储备；若加上国内采购量，中国在本作物年度要占到全球棉花消费总量的15%。

2. 翻译工作坊课程规划

第一,文本解读。

(1) 分析汉语报刊的语言特征,罗列出来,并给出每个特征的例子。

(2) 与英文报刊的语言特点进行对比;

(3) 结合互文性、语域理论及主位推进模式三个方面提出相应的翻译方法。

第二,分组翻译(六人一组)。具体要求如下:

(1) 按照所提出的翻译策略,各组成员分别进行翻译;

(2) 组内进行翻译、修改,拟初稿;

(3) 将初稿合并,六人进行小组讨论,统一术语,纠查错误,拟定稿。

(4) 各组提交定稿。

第三,翻译教学讨论。

(1) 以上各组分别由代表进行报告演示,说明本组翻译策略选择的依据;

(2) 所有同学对各组所提出的翻译策略进行讨论;

(3) 教师给出参考译文,结合学生译文进行评析,讲解相关翻译技巧。

3. 参考译文

China, the biggest consumer of cotton, has lodged a formal protest against India's ban on cotton exports amid signs that India is rethinking the ban that was implemented a few days ago.

Manmohan Singh, India's Prime Minister urgently requested a group of cabinet members to review the ban after the country's agriculture minister said that the curbs on the fibre would hurt farmers.

The outcome of the review would be made public today, a statement from the prime minister's office said.

An official in the prime minister's office said cabinet members were likely to lift the ban.

"There is a realistic, high chance that the ban will be lifted," the official told the *Financial Times*.

The U-turn is, however, not certain as New Delhi balances its relationship with Beijing and the interests of its farmers with the concerns of its powerful textile industry.

The abrupt policy changes are adding further volatility to the cotton market after two years of sharp swings in prices.

Cotton rose to an all-time high of more than $2 a pound last year amid a shortage in part created by an export ban by India, only to fall afterwards to less than $1 after cotton mills defaulted on contracts.

Cotton traders including Cargill, Noble Group and Glencore suffered big losses as a result.

Cotton prices have risen this year after India banned exports for the second time in two years.

India, the second-largest producer of cotton, instituted the ban with immediate effect on March 5, in a move aimed at ensuring sufficient supply of cotton for domestic textile companies.

India's move came after China had aggressively bought bales over the past year for a government reserve as a way of supporting domestic farm prices and buffering against price volatility.

By late January, China had bought as many as 5m bales of foreign cotton for the reserve which, along with its domestic purchases, made up 15 per cent of global cotton consumption in the current crop year, the US Department of Agriculture estimated.

4. 汉译英翻译练习

（1）

美欧日将中国稀土出口控制诉诸 WTO

美国、欧盟（EU）和日本已联手向世界贸易组织（WTO）提起诉讼，希望打破中国对全球稀土供应的控制。稀土是多种高技术加工中必不可少的矿物质。

美国总统巴拉克·奥巴马昨天宣布了提出上述诉讼的消息。这起由全球领先富裕经济体发起的非同寻常的联合诉讼表明，西方国家领导人认为就稀土贸易行为与中国政府进行磋商，在政治和经济上已势在必行。

奥巴马表示，美国并不希望与中国发生对抗，但在必要时会他毫不犹豫地诉诸法律。"我们更希望进行对话……但如果我们的工人和企业受到不公正贸易行为的伤害，我会在必要时采取行动。"

奥巴马已把保护美国制造商不受他所谓不公平竞争的伤害，列为今年美国政府经济政策的核心内容之一。

为了反击米特·罗姆尼（Mitt Romney）等共和党人有关美国政府对中国过于软弱的指责，奥巴马重申，他向世贸组织提起诉讼的案件数量是上届政府的近两倍。在今年 11 月的总统选举中，罗姆尼很可能成为他的竞争对手。

中国稀土产量占全球产量的 90％以上。稀土是从武器到黑莓（Blackberry）等大量产品生产所必需的 17 种化学元素。2010 年，中国在一场外交纠纷之后暂停向日本出口稀土，从此，该国在全球稀土供应中的主导地位引起了外界的警觉。

大宗商品生产国的出口限制，是当今世界贸易中最具争议的问题之一。许多批评人士指责，这种旨在为国内生产商提供廉价原材料的做法是不公平的。今年 1 月份，欧盟和美国在向 WTO 提起的针对中国限制其他工业原材料出口的诉讼中，取得了终审胜诉。WTO 这一裁定结果为此次稀土诉讼打下了铺垫。如果中国在 60 天内不能与相关各方通过磋商达成协议，欧盟、美国和日本可以要求 WTO 成立一个专家组对此案做出裁决，其结果很可能是对中国实施贸易制裁。

中国政府驳斥了上诉指控，表示中国将继续"依据世贸规则对稀土出口实行有效的管理"。中国外交部表示，中方希望"其他拥有稀土资源的国家也积极开发稀土资源，共同承担全球稀土供应的责任"。

中国官方通讯社新华社表示,这一举动可能伤害到全球第一大和第二大经济体之间的经济关系。

过去,起伏不定的价格走势已迫使中国以外的生产商离开了市场。20世纪60年代至80年代,全球最大的稀土矿是在美国加州。该矿于2002年关闭,但2010年又恢复了生产。

欧盟、美国和日本之所以采取一致行动,可能是希望避免遭到中国的报复,就像中国在2010年中断对日稀土出口那样。

去年,随着中国以外地区产能的扩大,全球稀土价格已大幅下降。

美国官员表示,交由WTO裁决将防止中国今后再度试图控制稀土出口。

欧盟贸易专员卡洛·德古赫特(Karel De Gucht)失望地表示,在1月份的WTO原材料出口裁定中败诉后,中国并未采取措施化解外界对其稀土政策的担忧。他表示,"这让我们别无选择,只能再次向中国的出口制度发起挑战。"

(2)

中国的富人们缺了些什么?

中国青年报和新浪网联合开展的一项调查发现,中国富人的社会形象较差。

该项于上周开展的民意调查显示,在3990名受访者中,有70%的人认为富人道德低下,不值得尊重。仅有4%的人对富人持正面印象。

调查表明,中国富人身上最缺乏的三大品质是社会责任感、自律精神和爱心。

据《中国经济时报》统计数据,我国年收入至少5万美元的富裕人口数量以每年15%的速度增长,目前已达150万人。

该调查发现,受访者对富人的发家方式最为质疑。

中国传媒大学的一名研究生说:"有些富人是通过受贿等不法手段来积聚财富的。"

即便如此,调查发现,一些合法致富、有社会责任感及有爱心的富豪还是深受人们尊敬的。

调查显示,约60%的人认为具备这些品质的富人值得尊敬。

在投票调查中,港、澳、台地区及国外的富豪得到的票数远多于大陆富豪。

香港房地产大亨李嘉诚最受尊重,其次是比尔·盖茨,大陆房地产大亨王石和篮球巨星姚明。

北京体育大学的一名学生说:"中国大陆的富豪对慈善事业的贡献太少,得到的太多。"

中国人民大学的喻国民教授认为中国企业家们要有长远的眼光和战略投资意识。"企业的社会责任不是单纯的慈善,它还是联系企业、政府和公众的纽带。"

第十章

会议发言辞及演讲翻译

第一节 会议发言辞及演讲的文体特征

发言辞或演讲辞是指在特定的场合,特定的时间以口语为载体向听众表达自己的观点和感情,进行宣传与鼓动,使其接受自己观点的一种文体。演说者为了使自己主题鲜明,语言生动,在演说辞中会大量使用各种修辞手段来实现其语用意义,拨动听众心弦。

1. 大众性

会议发言辞及演讲是一种社会活动,演讲的对象是广大听(观)众,少则几个、几十个,多则成千上万。演讲作为一种宣传形式,具有鲜明的大众性。

2. 可视听性

发言人要像演员一样,运用面部、身势、手势,以至一切可以理解的动作,使他的讲话艺术化,既有视觉形象,又有听觉效果。

3. 主题集中

由于受时间、场地、对象等的限制,演讲不可能太长,一般为一到两个小时。因此,每一场演讲通常集中解决一个问题。

4. 时间性强

时间性首先表现在发言辞及演讲的时代色彩十分强烈,反映民众的呼声,促进历史的发展。其次,演讲的时间性还表现在演讲过程中的及时性、瞬时性和临场性。有时发言人会观察听众的反应,并根据反应随时调整自己演讲的内容和形式。

5. 逻辑思维与形象思维统一

讲究逻辑性,重在晓之以理,以理服人。同时,演讲还需具备一定的文艺性,在恰当的时候动之以情,使听众受到感染,是逻辑思维与形象思维的和谐统一。

6. 思想内容与艺术形式相结合

内容与形式是不可分割的,发言辞或演讲的内容必须具备正确的思想,用典型的事实,论证科学的知识。此外还要有严整而完美的结构,即内容的组织、安排的形式和方法。

第二节　会议发言辞及演讲的翻译原则

一、语篇指向性分析

正确的理解是翻译的必要功课之一。进行科学的语篇分析是理解会议发言辞和演讲文本的有效手段之一。在系统功能语言学框架下,语篇是"指任何不完全受句子语法约束的在一定语境下表示完整意义的自然语言"。语篇产生于语境,语篇指向性涉及以下四个基本层面:时间(time)、地点(place)、参与者关系(participant relations)、事实(factuality)。会议发言辞及演讲的语篇指向性一般比较明确,当语篇的指向性不明确时,就需要受话人或读者去想象、去联想,然而,由于读者对事物的接受能力存在差异,生活阅历不尽一致,想象力的强弱不一,学养的高低也不同,对语篇的指向性理解和感受各不相同,因而一篇演讲或发言辞的指向性的看法也就不一样。在翻译的时候,首先要对原文进行必要的语篇指向性分析,明确篇章的指向性,再确定正确的翻译方法。

二、文本功能分析

根据纽马克的文本分类方法,文本语言具有表达功能、信息功能及呼唤功能。译者在翻译时,要对文本的功能进行分类,然后采取相应的翻译方法。

1. 表达功能　文本—语义翻译

表达功能主要体现在说话者用话语表达思想感情,这类文本强调原作者的权威性,翻译时要遵循忠实原文的原则。表达功能在于传递源文本生产者的情感,就必然趋向于忽视文本接受者的反应,一般翻译时采用语义翻译,忠实体现原文内容和形式。如:

中国虽然取得了举世瞩目的成就,但仍然是世界上最大的发展中国家,经济社会发展面临巨大的人口、资源、环境压力,发展中不平衡、不协调、不可持续问题依然突出,实现现代化和全体人民共同富裕还有很长的路要走。

China has made remarkable achievements in development, but it remains the largest developing country in the world. Population, resources and the environment have put great pressure on our economic and social development, and there is lack of adequate balance, coordination and sustainability in our development. China has a long way to go before it can achieve modernization and common prosperity for all its people.

原文具有高度正式性,从文本类型分析来看,属于表达功能文本,因而,译者主要采用了语义翻译方法,如"举世瞩目的成就"(remarkable achievements)、"还有很长的路要走"(has a long way to go)。

2. 信息功能和呼唤功能　文本—交际翻译

　　文本的信息功能主要指一个话题的全部信息,信息性文本的核心内容是内容的真实性,作者的语言是次要的,在翻译时,译者在语言应用上可不以原作为标准,而以目标语读者的语言层次为标准,力求通顺易懂。

　　呼唤功能文本强调以读者为中心,目的是让读者去思考和感受。翻译的时候,应把目的语读者放在首要位置,发挥目的语优势,不拘泥于原文的表达方式,使译文语言尽量达到与原作语言同样的效果。

第三节　案例及习题

一、英译汉

1. 案例

Secretary-General's Message on World Tourism Day

I am delighted that the UN World Tourism Organization is celebrating this year's World Tourism Day under the theme "Tourism and Biodiversity". Despite repeated global pledges to protect the planet's species and habitats—and the goods and services they provide—the variety of life on Earth continues to decline at an unprecedented rate. Human activities are the cause. This year—the International Year of Biodiversity—provides a timely opportunity to focus on the urgency of safeguarding biodiversity for the wealth, health and well-being of people in all regions of the world.

Tourism and biodiversity are closely intertwined. Millions of people travel each year to experience nature's splendor. The income generated by sustainable tourism can provide important support for nature conservation, as well as for economic development. Furthermore, sustainable tourism can help to raise awareness among tourists and local communities of the importance of biodiversity to our everyday lives.

Through initiatives such as its "Sustainable Tourism—Eliminating Poverty" project, and its collaboration with the UN family, national tourism authorities and the private sector, the World Tourism Organization is helping to highlight the links between tourism, poverty alleviation and biodiversity. The tourism community is becoming increasingly aware of its responsibility. And indeed there is much the sector can contribute to protecting biodiversity, including by integrating simple measures such as managing tour groups to minimize disturbance to wildlife or buying supplies only from sustainable sources.

On this World Tourism Day, I commend the tourism community for its growing recognition of the importance of conserving the diversity of life on Earth, and I urge all partners to strengthen their commitment to sustainability.

2. 翻译工作坊课程规划

第一，文本解读。

（1）分析汉语演讲辞的语言特征；

（2）语篇指向性分析和文本功能类型分析，并列举出来；

（3）根据不同文本功能类型选择正确的翻译方法。

第二，分组翻译（六人一组）。具体要求如下：

（1）按照所提出的翻译策略，各组成员分别进行翻译；

（2）组内进行翻译、修改，拟初稿；

（3）将初稿合并，六人进行小组讨论，统一术语，纠查错误，拟定稿。

（4）各组提交定稿。

第三，翻译教学讨论。

（1）以上各组分别由代表进行报告演示，说明本组翻译策略选择的依据；

（2）所有同学对各组所提出的翻译策略进行讨论；

（3）教师给出参考译文，结合学生译文进行评析，讲解相关翻译技巧。

3. 参考译文

联合国秘书长潘基文 2010 世界旅游日致辞

我高兴地看到，联合国世界旅游组织在"旅游与生物多样性"的主题下纪念今年的世界旅游日。尽管一再做出全球承诺，要保护地球上的物种和生境——及其提供的货物和服务——但生物种类继续以史无前例的速度减少。其根源在于人类的活动。今年——国际生物多样性年——提供了一个适时的机会来集中注意为世界各地人民的财富、健康和福祉保护生物多样性的紧迫性。

旅游与生物多样性密切相连。每年有千百万人为领略壮丽的自然风光而旅游。可持续旅游业产生的收入可以为保护自然和发展经济提供重要的支持。此外，可持续旅游业还有助于游客和地方社区更多地认识到生物多样性在日常生活中的重要作用。

世界旅游组织通过诸如"可持续旅游业——消除贫穷"项目这样的举措以及同联合国系统、各国旅游主管部门和私人部门的合作，正在帮助突出宣传旅游、扶贫和生物多样性之间的联系。旅游界正日益意识到自己的责任。这个行业确实可以为保护生物多样性做出很大贡献，包括为此实行一些简单的措施，例如通过对旅游团的管理来尽量减少对野生物的干扰，或仅从可持续来源购买用品。

值此世界旅游日之际，我对旅游界日益认识到保护地球生物多样性的重要意义表示赞赏，并促请所有合作伙伴加强对可持续性的承诺。

4. 英译汉翻译练习

（1）2013 年奥巴马就职演讲

Vice President Biden, Mr. Chief Justice, Members of the United States Congress, distinguished guests, and fellow citizens:

Each time we gather to inaugurate a president, we bear witness to the enduring strength of our Constitution. We affirm the promise of our democracy. We recall that what binds this nation together is not the colors of our skin or the tenets of our faith or the origins of our names. What makes us exceptional-what makes us American-is our allegiance to an idea, articulated in a declaration made more than two centuries ago:

"We hold these truths to be self-evident, that all men are created equal, that they are endowed by their Creator with certain unalienable rights, that among these are Life, Liberty, and the pursuit of Happiness."

Today we continue a never-ending journey, to bridge the meaning of those words with the realities of our time. For history tells us that while these truths may be self-evident, they have never been self-executing; that while freedom is a gift from God, it must be secured by His people here on Earth. The patriots of 1776 did not fight to replace the tyranny of a king with the privileges of a few or the rule of a mob. They gave to us a Republic, a government of, and by, and for the people, entrusting each generation to keep safe our founding creed.

For more than two hundred years, we have.

Through blood drawn by lash and blood drawn by sword, we learned that no union founded on the principles of liberty and equality could survive half-slave and half-free. We made ourselves anew, and vowed to move forward together.

Together, we determined that a modern economy requires railroads and highways to speed travel and commerce; schools and colleges to train our workers.

Together, we discovered that a free market only thrives when there are rules to ensure competition and fair play.

Together, we resolved that a great nation must care for the vulnerable, and protect its people from life's worst hazards and misfortune.

Through it all, we have never relinquished our skepticism of central authority, nor have we succumbed to the fiction that all society's ills can be cured through government alone. Our celebration of initiative and enterprise; our insistence on hard work and personal responsibility, these are constants in our character.

But we have always understood that when times change, so must we; that fidelity to our founding principles requires new responses to new challenges; that preserving our individual freedoms ultimately requires collective action. For the American people can no more meet the demands of today's world by acting alone than American soldiers could have met the forces of fascism or communism with muskets and militias. No single person can train all the math and science teachers we'll need to equip our children for the future, or build the roads and networks and research labs that will bring new jobs and businesses to our shores. Now, more than ever, we must do these things together, as one nation, and one people.

This generation of Americans has been tested by crises that steeled our resolve and proved our resilience. A decade of war is now ending. An economic recovery has begun. America's possibilities are limitless, for we possess all the qualities that this world without boundaries demands: youth and drive; diversity and openness; an endless capacity for risk and a gift for reinvention. My fellow Americans, we are made for this moment, and we will seize it-so long as we seize it together.

For we, the people, understand that our country cannot succeed when a shrinking few do very well and a growing many barely make it. We believe that America's prosperity must rest upon the broad shoulders of a rising middle class. We know that America thrives when every person can find independence and pride in their work; when the wages of honest labor liberate families from the brink of hardship. We are true to our creed when a little girl born into the bleakest poverty knows that she has the same chance to succeed as anybody else, because she is an American, she is free, and she is equal, not just in the eyes of God but also in our own.

We understand that outworn programs are inadequate to the needs of our time. We must harness new ideas and technology to remake our government, revamp our tax code, reform our schools, and empower our citizens with the skills they need to work harder, learn more, and reach higher. But while the means will change, our purpose endures: a nation that rewards the effort and determination of every single American. That is what this moment requires. That is what will give real meaning to our creed.

We, the people, still believe that every citizen deserves a basic measure of security and dignity. We must make the hard choices to reduce the cost of health care and the size of our deficit. But we reject the belief that America must choose between caring for the generation that built this country and investing in the generation that will build its future. For we remember the lessons of our past, when twilight years were spent in poverty, and parents of a child with a disability had nowhere to turn. We do not believe that in this country, freedom is reserved for the lucky, or happiness for the few. We recognize that no matter how responsibly we live our lives, any one of us, at any time, may face a job loss, or a sudden illness, or a home swept away in a terrible storm. The commitments we make to each other-through Medicare, and Medicaid, and Social Security-these things do not sap our initiative; they strengthen us. They do not make us a nation of takers; they free us to take the risks that make this country great.

We, the people, still believe that our obligations as Americans are not just to ourselves, but to all posterity. We will respond to the threat of climate change, knowing that the failure to do so would betray our children and future generations. Some may still deny the overwhelming judgment of science, but none can avoid the devastating impact of raging fires, and crippling drought, and more powerful storms. The path towards sustainable energy sources will be long and sometimes difficult. But America cannot resist this transition; we must lead it. We cannot cede to other nations the technology that will power new jobs and new industries—we must claim its promise. That is how we will maintain our economic vitality and our national treasure—our forests and waterways; our croplands and snowcapped peaks. That is how we will preserve our planet, commanded to our care by God. That's what will lend meaning to the creed our fathers once declared.

We, the people, still believe that enduring security and lasting peace do not require perpetual war. Our brave men and women in uniform, tempered by the flames of battle, are unmatched in skill and courage. Our citizens, seared by the memory of those we have lost, know too well the price that is paid for liberty. The knowledge of their sacrifice will keep us forever vigilant against those who would do us harm. But we are also heirs to those who won the peace and not just the war, who turned sworn enemies into the surest of friends, and we must carry those lessons into this time as well.

We will defend our people and uphold our values through strength of arms and rule of law. We will show the courage to try and resolve our differences with other nations peacefully—not because we are naïve about the dangers we face, but because engagement can more durably lift suspicion and fear. America will remain the anchor of strong alliances in every corner of the globe; and we will renew those institutions that extend our capacity to manage crisis abroad, for no one has a greater stake in a peaceful world than its most powerful nation. We will support democracy from Asia to Africa; from the Americas to the Middle East, because our interests and our conscience compel us to act on behalf of those who long for freedom. And we must be a source of hope to the poor, the sick, the marginalized, the victims of prejudice—not out of mere charity, but because peace in our time requires the constant advance of those principles that our common creed describes: tolerance and opportunity; human dignity and justice.

We, the people, declare today that the most evident of truths—that all of us are created equal—is the star that guides us still; just as it guided our forebears through Seneca Falls, and Selma, and Stonewall; just as it guided all those men and women, sung and unsung, who left footprints along this great Mall, to hear a preacher say that we cannot walk alone; to hear a King proclaim that our individual freedom is inextricably bound to the freedom of every soul on Earth.

It is now our generation's task to carry on what those pioneers began. For our journey is not complete until our wives, our mothers, and daughters can earn a living equal to their efforts. Our journey is not complete until our gay brothers and sisters are treated like anyone else under the law—for if we are truly created equal, then surely the love we commit to one another must be equal as well. Our journey is not complete until no citizen is forced to wait for hours to exercise the right to vote. Our journey is not complete until we find a better way to welcome the striving, hopeful immigrants who still see America as a land of opportunity; until bright young students and engineers are enlisted in our workforce rather than expelled from our country. Our journey is not complete until all our children, from the streets of Detroit to the hills of Appalachia to the quiet lanes of Newtown, know that they are cared for, and cherished, and always safe from harm.

That is our generation's task—to make these words, these rights, these values—of Life, and Liberty, and the Pursuit of Happiness—real for every American. Being true to our founding documents does not require us to agree on every contour of life; it does not mean we will all define liberty in exactly the same way, or follow the same precise path to happiness. Progress does not compel us to settle centuries—long debates about the role of government for all time—but it does require us to act in our time.

For now decisions are upon us, and we cannot afford delay. We cannot mistake absolutism for principle, or substitute spectacle for politics, or treat name—calling as reasoned debate. We must act, knowing that our work will be imperfect. We must act, knowing that today's victories will be only partial, and that it will be up to those who stand here in four years, and forty years, and four hundred years hence to advance the timeless spirit once conferred to us in a spare Philadelphia hall.

My fellow Americans, the oath I have sworn before you today, like the one recited by others who serve in this Capitol, was an oath to God and country, not party or faction—and we must faithfully execute that pledge during the duration of our service. But the words I spoke today are not so different from the oath that is taken each time a soldier signs up for duty, or an immigrant realizes her dream. My oath is not so different from the pledge we all make to the flag that waves above and that fills our hearts with pride.

They are the words of citizens, and they represent our greatest hope.

You and I, as citizens, have the power to set this country's course.

You and I, as citizens, have the obligation to shape the debates of our time—not only with the votes we cast, but with the voices we lift in defense of our most ancient values and enduring ideals.

Let each of us now embrace, with solemn duty and awesome joy, what is our lasting birthright. With common effort and common purpose, with passion and dedication, let us answer the call of history, and carry into an uncertain future that precious light of freedom.

Thank you, God Bless you, and may He forever bless these United States of America.

(2) 美国加州前州长阿诺德·施瓦辛格在清华大学的演讲

It is wonderful to be here at this university. What a special place. I just looked around a little bit here, it's a gorgeous, gorgeous place. I want to congratulate you for going to this magnificent university here.

Now, the last time I was here in China was five years ago, and then I was promoting my movies. They had a movie festival here, the Arnold Schwarzenegger Movie Festival. I remember they showed all my movies for a week—which was a rarity, may I remind you—

and they also showed the movies on television. But we also were here to promote Special Olympics, which is an organization that helps people with mental disabilities, so I was here for both reasons.

But this time I'm here as the governor of the great state of California. I'm here representing the people of California, and we're here on a trade mission to see how we can do more business with China and to help each other, because both California is a very fast growing state, and China is a very fast growing country, and there are a lot of things that we can do for one another.

But I didn't want to miss the opportunity to come here today and to talk with the young people; as a matter of fact, to the brightest young people of China. And this is why it is so great to be here at the Tsinghua University, and I'm honored that I was invited here.

Now, I read a little bit about the history of Tsinghua, and I learned that actually this school originally prepared students to attend universities in America. Now, I also know that since the attack on our World Trade Centers it has become more and more difficult to go to the universities in America because you need to fill out all kinds of paperwork now and you have to get visas, and it's very complicated, and you have to wait a much longer period of time to go over there. But let me tell you, things are improving already. I've heard that it's easing up, the restrictions, and it's easier to get a visa. My young Chinese friends, I want to tell you that in case no one from America has ever invited you, let me do this right now personally. I want to warmly invite all of you here to come to the United States, and especially to come to California, because that's the happening place. California is the best place.

Please come and visit us, we will welcome you. I invite you all to come there and to travel, to meet the American people, and to come there and study in our universities, and some day hopefully you will come and do business over there, or maybe you'll want to move over there. Whatever your goal is, you're always welcome. America, after all, let's not forget, is the land of opportunity. And it's not only the land of opportunity for Austrians like me, but for Chinese people as well. Remember that.

I know that beginning with this century, China is also becoming a land of opportunity. It's a fast growing place, and as the students of this great university and the citizens of a rising China, I think that you have a great future also here in this country. And today I want to talk to you a little bit about the dreams, about the dreams of your future, and dreams for this country. I want to talk to you a little bit about dreams, because it seems to me that I'm somewhat of an expert in dreams, because I had a lot of my dreams become a reality. So let me just briefly tell you my story, and tell you a little bit about how I started with my career. I think that this story kind of relates a little bit also to you, and also to China.

I started way back as a weightlifter. I always liked the idea of lifting weights and being a bodybuilder. From the first moment when I gripped a barbell and held it around the bar and lifted the steel up over my head, I felt this exhilaration, and I knew then that this is something that I'm going to do; that I was in love with that, and this is going to be something that I'm going to do. I'm going to pursue the sport of weightlifting and bodybuilding.

Now, I remember the first real workout that I had. Eight miles away from my home village in Austria there was a gymnasium, and I rode to that gymnasium with a bicycle. And there I trained for half an hour, because they said that after half an hour you should stop because otherwise your body will get really sore. But after half an hour I looked at my body, and nothing had happened. So I said, "I'd better work out for another half hour." So I lifted some more. My strength didn't improve, I didn't see the muscles pop out or anything like that, so I trained for another half an hour. And then after another half hour I trained another half hour, and all together I trained two and a half hours.

Well, let me tell you something. After two and a half hours—even though they told me that I should not train that much or I would get really sore—I left the gymnasium, I rode my bicycle home. And after the first mile I got numb, and I couldn't feel anymore the handle of the bicycle, and I fell off the bike and I fell into the ditch on the side of the road. So I got up again and I tried it again. Another few yards, I fell off the bicycle again. And I tried it three, four more times, and I just couldn't ride my bicycle because my body was so numb and my legs felt like noodles.

Well, let me tell you something. The next morning when I got up, my body was so sore that I couldn't even lift my arms to comb my hair. I had to have my mother comb my hair, and you know how embarrassing that is. But you know something? I learned a very important lesson, that pain means progress. Pain is progress. Each time my muscles were sore from a workout I knew that they were growing and they were getting stronger.

I think there is a real life lesson in that. After two or three years of discipline and determination and working out hard, I actually changed my body, and I changed my strength. And that told me something; that if I could change my body that much, and if I could change the strength of my body that much, then I could also change anything else. I could change my habits, I could change my intelligence, I could change my attitude, my mind, my future, my life. And this is exactly what I have done. I think that that lesson applies to people, and it also applies to countries. You can change, China can change, everyone in the world can change.

My parents, of course, I have to tell you, didn't understand my dreams at all. They were always wondering, they said, "What is he doing? When are you going to get a job, a real job? When are you going to make money?" And all of those questions I got. And they said, "I hope we didn't raise a bum, someone that doesn't make money and just wants to live in a gymnasium and think about their bodies." Well, I endured all of this negative thinking, and the more negative the thinking got, and the more negative the questions got, the stronger and the more positive I became, the stronger I became inside.

So of course some of your families maybe think the same way, and this is why I'm mentioning that. Some of your families maybe don't believe in your dreams. But let me tell you something, my young friends. Keep your dreams. No matter what, keep your dreams. Don't give up on them, even when you are temporarily defeated or denied. Keep your dreams.

I remember the first time I went to the United States and I was competing in a competition, the World Championships in Bodybuilding. I lost. I came in second, and I was devastated. I was crushed. I felt like a loser, a major loser, let me tell you. I cried, as a matter of fact, because I felt like I disappointed my friends and I disappointed myself. But the next day I got my act together, I shifted gears, and I said, "I'm going to learn from that lesson. I'm going to stay here in America. I'm not going to go back to Europe. I'm going to stay in America and I'm going to train with the American champions, I'm going to train the American way. I'm going to eat the American food, I'm going to train with the American machines and the principles. And a year later, in America, I became the World Champion in Bodybuilding. So I think this is a very, very important lesson.

And from then on, I continued. My career took off, and everything that I wanted to do I accomplished. First it was to become a champion in bodybuilding. Later on I became a movie star, to do all the great movies, the Conan movies and the Terminator movies and all this. Then I became the governor of the great state of California, of the sixth largest economy in the world. All of this happened because of my dreams, even though other people told me that those dreams were bogus and they were crazy, but I held onto my dreams.

And people would always say, no matter what, even in bodybuilding they said I would never make it. And later on in the movies, in Hollywood they said I would not make it. They said, "You will never make it. You have a German accent. No one in Hollywood has ever made it with a German accent. Yeah, maybe you can play some Nazi roles or something like that, but you cannot become a leading star with an accent. Plus your body, you're overdeveloped, you have all these muscles. They did Hercules movies 20 years ago, that's outdated. Now it's Woody Allen. Woody Allen is in, his body is in. " And those were the messages. "And Al Pacino, the skinny guy, he is in. But not your body, it's too big. And your name, Schwarzenegger, it will never fit on a movie poster. Forget it. Forget it, you will never make it. Go back to bodybuilding. "

Well, the rest is history. After Terminator 3, I became the highest paid movie star in Hollywood. And let me tell you something, it continued on. Even when I ran for governor people said, "Arnold, you will never make it. You will never become governor of California. What do you know about government?" Well, the fact is, I knew exactly as much about government as the rest of the people knew in California, which is that government is out of touch, and it's out of sync with the people, and it needed a shakeup.

So I didn't listen to all those people that said I would never make it. I continued campaigning, I listened to my dreams, and the rest also is history. I became governor.

So always it just carried me on, those dreams. So bodybuilding gave me the confidence, movies gave me the money, and pubic service and being a governor gave me a purpose larger than myself. And that is the brief story of my dreams and a brief story of my early life, and how my dreams made me successful.

A person, of course, should not be stingy with their dreams. So I, of course, don't just think and dream about myself, but I also have dreams for you, and dreams for China. So let me just talk a little bit about that. China's economy has become an engine of human progress, lifting millions of people out of poverty. This is a moral and economic good for China and for the rest of the world. I often read that China's economy is likely to become the largest in the world over the next 50 years, and I think this is terrific. This does not mean, of course, that America will get poorer; it just means that China will get richer, and the United States will benefit from China's progress as much as the U. S. benefited from the rise of Western Europe after World War II.

Some in my country fear that China's research and development will overtake America's, but I believe that America and the world will benefit from China's scientific and technological advances. I think we will benefit from that. If China makes advances in stem cell research, the rest of the world will benefit from that. If China discovers an energy breakthrough, this is good for the rest of the world, such as the benefit of a free market.

Some fear that China will buy up American companies, but that fear also existed in the '80s, when America feared that Japan was going to buy up American companies. So what? It was just good, and to the benefit of America. We should welcome China's investment in American companies, just as we welcome the billions of dollars that China has invested in U. S. treasury bonds. This shows that China has faith in America, and American investment in China shows that we have faith in you. So I believe that China and U. S. economic relations will become even closer in the years ahead. Certainly I realize that we do not agree on everything, but who does? Certainly I realize that China has major hurdles to overcome, but it is not for me to say how China should overcome those hurdles and achieve its dreams.

But I can tell you, however, what has given America such energy and strength over the last 200 years and perhaps there are some insights in this for China. America is a nation that believes in the power of the individual, and what the individual can accomplish, no matter the color, no matter the religion, no matter the ethnic background of the individual.

Recently, as you probably have read, Rosa Parks, a former seamstress married to a barber, married to a hairdresser, died, and she lay in honor in the Rotunda of the U. S. Capitol in Washington. People from around America came to say farewell to her and to thank her for changing our history and for changing our society. Now, what did this 92-year-old black woman do that deserved such great honor? What did she do? Well, in 1955, the days of racial segregation, she had refused to give up her seat on the bus to a white man. She had refused. Her simple refusal to move to the back of the bus put into motion events that led to my country's great civil rights movement. The small protest of a woman that maybe weighed less than 100 lbs. brought down a racist system. As you can see, the individual can make a difference.

Let me tell you about another individual, Ken Behring, a millionaire California businessman who found his passion in giving wheelchairs to poor and physically disabled people all around the globe, including China. He says that he has met people who have spent years in rooms with no window, just lying there and staring up at the ceiling, never seeing the outside world unless someone was willing to pick up that person and take them outside to show them the world. He says that it's no wonder so many of those physically disabled people dream about being a bird. Mr. Behring says that most of us think that a wheelchair would be a confinement, but to millions of people it is not a confinement, it is freedom, freedom to move and to go to school, freedom to vote, freedom to get a job, and freedom for hope for the future. He has given freedom and wheelchairs to 400,000 people around the world. The individual can make a difference.

My mother-in-law, Eunice Kennedy Shriver—I always like to mention her, because it gets me on the good side of her—she, for instance, started an organization called Special Olympics. She stared Special Olympics which is for people with mental disabilities. And of course when she started that organization she was told by the experts, "Don't do it. You cannot take people with mental disabilities out of mental institutions and have them participate in sports events. They will drown in the swimming pools. They will kill each other out there, they will hurt each other. Don't do it. "But Eunice Kennedy Shriver had a dream and a passion, and today millions of people compete in Special Olympics around the world, including right here in China. This is why I was here five years ago. Five years ago you had 50,000 participants in the Special Olympics. Today, five years later, you have 500,000 participants in Special Olympics. 500,000 people are getting a chance to participate in sports programs, getting a chance to have health care, have a chance to be treated equally, with respect and with tolerance. So Eunice Kennedy Shriver exemplifies that the individual can make a difference.

And I think what I'm trying to say to you is that each and every one of you can make a difference. So as you study and as you become smarter, and as you become richer, think about that, that there are millions of people that need your help. Now, you maybe ask yourself the question, what can I do? Well, let me tell you. Even though you maybe have no money or anything, you can go out and help a child that has not yet learned yet how to read. You maybe can go out and help a person that is physically handicapped, to lift them up and to take them outside so they can see the world. There are so many different things that you can do. You maybe can take a person that is mentally disabled, to take them to a soccer game. There are all kinds of things that the individual can do to reach out and to help.

Imagine what could be accomplished if the dreams of China's 1. 3 billion individuals could be unleashed. Imagine what could happen. Each of you here has the power of the individual within you, you have the power of your dreams within you, and these are tremendous powers. You're young, you're educated, and you are the very best China has to offer. My young Chinese friends, I believe in your dreams. I believe that you can achieve them, and I believe you can make a difference, a big difference. All you have to do is just make the commitment. All you have to do is create the action and commit, and say, "Let's do it." Go out and do it. I'm asking you. Do it for yourself, do it for China, and do it for the good of the world. Thank you very much for listening.

Thank you.

二、汉译英

1. 案例

来苏格兰(做 TED 讲演)的前夜,我被邀请去上海做"中国达人秀"决赛的评委。在装有八万现场观众的演播厅里,在台上的表演嘉宾居然是(来自苏格兰的,因参加英国达人秀走红的)苏珊大妈(Susan Boyle)。我告诉她,"我明天就要启程去苏格兰。"她唱得很动听,还对观众说了几句中文,她并没有说简单的"你好"或者"谢谢",她说的是——"送你葱"(Song Ni Cong)。为什么? 这句话其实来源于中国版的"苏珊大妈"——一位五十岁的以卖菜为生,却对西方歌剧有出奇爱好的上海中年妇女(蔡洪平)。这位中国的苏珊大妈并不懂英文,法语或意大利文,所以她将歌剧中的词汇都换做中文中的蔬菜名,并且演唱出来。在她口中,歌剧《图兰朵》的最后一句便是"Song Ni Cong"。当真正的英国苏珊大妈唱出这一句"中文的"《图兰朵》时,全场的八万观众也一起高声歌唱,场面的确有些滑稽。

我想苏珊大妈(Susan Boyle)和这位上海的卖菜农妇的确属于人群中的少数。她们是最不可能在演艺界成功的,而她们的勇气和才华让她们成功了,这个节目和舞台给予了她们一个实现个人梦想的机会。这样看来,与众不同好像没有那么难。从不同的方面审视,我们每个人都是不同的。但是我想,与众不同是一件好事,因为你代表了不一样的观点,你拥有了做改变的机会。

我这一代中国人很幸运地目睹并且参与了中国在过去二三十年中经历的巨变。记得1990 年,当我刚大学毕业时,我申请了当时北京的第一家五星级酒店——长城喜来登酒店销售部门的工作。这家酒店现在仍在北京。当我被一位日本籍经理面试了一个半小时之后,他问到,"杨小姐,你有什么想问我的吗?"我屏住呼吸,问道,"是的,你能告诉我,具体我需要销售些什么吗?"当时的我,对五星级酒店的销售部门没有任何概念,事实上,那是我第一次进到一家五星级酒店。

我当时也在参加另一场"面试",中国国家电视台的首次公开试镜,与我一起参与选拔的还有另外 1000 名大学女毕业生。节目制作人说,他们希望找到一位甜美、无辜、漂亮的新鲜面孔。轮到我的时候，我问道"为什么在电视屏幕上，女性总应该表现出甜美漂亮，甚至是服从性的一面？为什么她们不能有她们自己的想法和声音？"我觉得我的问题甚至有点冒犯到了他。但实际上，他们对我的表现印象深刻。我进入了第二轮选拔、第三轮、第四轮，直至最后的第七场选拔，我是唯一一个走到最后的试镜者。我从此走上了国家电视台黄金时段的荧幕。你可能不相信，但在当时，我所主持的电视节目是中国第一个，不让主持人念已经审核过的稿件的节目（掌声）。我每周需要面对两亿到三亿左右的电视观众。

几年以后，我决定来美国哥伦比亚大学继续深造，之后也开始运营自己的媒体公司，这也是我在职业生涯初始时所没有预料到的。我的公司做很多不同的业务，在过去这些年里，我访谈过一千多人。经常有年轻人对我说，"杨澜，你改变了我的人生"，我对此感到非常自豪。我也幸运地目睹了整个国家的转变：我参与了北京申奥和上海世博会。我看到中国在拥抱这个世界，而世界也进一步的接受中国。但有时我也在想，今天的年轻人的生活是什么样的？他们（与我们相比）有什么不同？他们将带给中国，甚至整个世界的未来一些怎样的变化？

我想通过社交媒体来谈一谈中国的年轻人们。首先，他们是谁，他们是什么样子？这是一位叫郭美美的女孩儿，20岁，年轻漂亮。她在中国版的Twitter——新浪微博上，炫耀她所拥有的奢侈品，衣服、包和车。她甚至宣称她是中国红十字会的工作人员。她没有意识到她的行为触及了中国民众极为敏感的神经，这引发了一场全民大讨论，民众开始质疑红十字会的公信力。中国红十字会为了平息这场争议甚至举办了一场记者会来澄清，直至今日，对于"郭美美事件"的调查仍在继续，但我们所知道的事实是，她谎报了她的头衔，可能是因为她的虚荣心，希望把自己和慈善机构联系起来。所有那些奢侈品都是她的男朋友给她买的，而那位"男朋友"的确曾经是红十字会的工作人员。这解释起来很复杂，总之，公众对他们的解释仍然不满意，这仍然是在风口浪尖的一件事。这件事体现出（中国社会）对长期不透明的政府机关的不信任，同时也表现出社交媒体（微博）巨大的社会影响力。

微博在2010年得到了爆炸性的增长，微博的访问用户增长了一倍，用户的访问时间是2009年的三倍。新浪（sina.com），一个最主要的微博平台，拥有1.4亿的微博用户，而腾讯拥有两亿用户。（在中国）最有名的微博主——不是我——是一位电影明星，她拥有近九百五十万"粉丝"。接近80%的微博用户是年轻人，三十岁以下。因为传统媒体还在政府的强力控制之下，社交媒体提供了一个开放的平台进行了一些（民众观点的）分流。因为这样分流的渠道并不多，从这个平台上爆发出的能量往往非常强烈，有时候甚至过于强烈。

通过微博，我们可以更好地了解到中国的年轻一代。首先，他们中的大多数都出生在八零九零年代，在独生子女的生育政策的大背景下长大。因为偏好男孩的家庭会选择性的堕胎，现在（中国）的年轻男性的数量多过年轻女性三千万，这可能带来社会的不稳定（危险），但是我们知道，在这个全球化的社会中，他们可能可以去其他国家找女朋友。大多数人都拥有良好的教育。这一代中国人中的文盲率已经低于1%。在城市中，80%的孩子可以上大学，但他们将要面对的是一个有接近7%的人口都是老年人的社会，这个数字在2030年会增长到15%。在这个国家，传统是让年轻人从经济上和医疗上来支持老年人，这意味着，一对年轻的夫妻将需要支持四个平均年龄是73岁的老人。

所以对于年轻人而言，生活并不是容易。本科毕业生也不再是紧缺资源。在城市中，本科生的月起薪通常是400美元（2 500人民币），而公寓的平均月租金却是500美元。所以他们的解决方式是合租——挤在有限的空间中以节省开支,他们叫自己"蚁族"。对于那些准备好结婚并希望购买一套公寓的中国年轻夫妇而言,他们发现他们必须要不间断的工作30到40年才可以负担得起一套公寓。对于同样的美国年轻夫妇而言,他们只需要五年时间。

在近两亿的涌入城市的农民工中,他们中的60%都是年轻人。他们发现自己被夹在了城市和农村中,大多数人不愿意回到农村,但他们在城市也找不到归属感。他们工作更长的时间却获得更少的薪水和社会福利。他们也更容易面临失业,受到通货膨胀、银行利率、人民币升值的影响,甚至美国和欧盟对于中国制造产品的抵制也会影响到他们。去年,在中国南方的一个制造工厂里,有十三位年轻的工人选择了结束自己的生命,一个接一个,像一场传染病。他们轻生的原因各有不同,但整个事件提醒了中国社会和政府,需要更多地关注这些在精神上和生理上都与外界脱节的年轻农民工人。

对于那些回到农村的年轻人,他们所经历的城市生活,所学到的知识,技巧和建立的社会网络,让他们通常更受欢迎。特别是在互联网的帮助下,他们更有可能获得工作,提升农村的农业水平和发展新的商业机会。在过去的一些年中,一些沿海的城镇甚至出现了劳动力短缺。

这些图片展现出整体的社会背景。第一张图片是恩格斯系数(食品支出占总消费支出的比例),可以看到在过去的十年中,食物和生活必需品在家庭消费中的比例有所下降(37%),然后在过去的两年中,这项指数上升到39%,说明近两年中生活成本的攀升。基尼系数早已越过了危险的0.4,到达0.5——这甚至高过了美国——体现出极大的贫富差距,所以我们才看到整个社会的失衡。同时,"仇富心态"也开始在整个社会蔓延,任何与腐败和走后门相关的政府或商业丑闻都会引发社会危机和不稳定。

通过微博上很火的话题,我们可以看到年轻人的关注点。社会公正和政府的公信力是他们首要需求的。在过去的十年中,急速的城市化让民众读到太多强制私人住户拆迁的新闻,这引发了年轻一代的愤怒和不理解。有时候,被拆迁的住户以自杀和自焚的方式来抗议(强制拆迁行为)。当这些事件越来越常在互联网上被揭露出来,人们期待政府可以采取一些更积极的制止行动。

好消息是,今年早些时候,人民代表大会通过了一项关于房屋征用和拆迁的新法规,将征用和拆迁的权利从当地政府移交到了法庭。相同的,很多其他与公共安全相关的问题也在互联网上被热烈讨论。我们听到有太多空气污染、水污染、有毒食品的报道。你甚至都想不到,我们还有假牛肉。人们用一种特殊的材料加入鸡肉和鱼肉中,然后以牛肉的价格进行出售。最近,人们对食用油也很担忧,大量的餐馆被发现在使用"地沟油"。所有这些事件引发了互联网上民众观点的大爆发。幸运的是,我们看到了政府正在更积极和更及时地对这些民众的质疑给予回应。

一方面,年轻人越来越积极地参与到公共事务中;另一方面,他们也在寻找或者说迷失与个人生活的价值和定位。中国很快就要超过美国,成为世界上第一大奢侈品消费国——这还不包括中国人在国外的消费。但你知道吗,超过半数中国的奢侈品消费者的(年)收入都低于两千美元。他们其实并不富裕,他们用那些奢侈品牌的服装和包体现身份和社会地位。这是一位在电视节目上公然表明,自己宁愿在宝马车里哭也不坐在自行车后笑的年轻女孩。当然,我们也有更多的年轻人,喜欢微笑,不管是在宝马还是在自行车上。

在下一幅图中,你看到的是现在非常流行的"裸婚",这并不代表这"裸露出席婚礼",这体现的是年轻人愿意接受结婚不买房，不买车，不买钻戒，甚至不办婚宴的这个现实，作为对纯朴的真爱的致敬。但同时，人们也在通过社交媒体做一些善事。这幅图片里，这辆车上装有 500 只被"绑架"来，准备被送去屠宰的狗，这辆车被网友们发现后，人们开始通过微博关注事态的进展，并且通过捐钱，捐食物和做义工来试图拦截该车。在几个小时的周旋后，这 500 条狗获救并被放生。有更多的人在通过微博寻找丢失的孩子。一位父亲将他失散的儿子的照片发布到微博上，在几千条"转发"之后，他的儿子被找到，家庭的团聚也在微博上被报道出来。

"幸福（感）"是近两年中国的流行词汇。幸福感不仅仅与个人体验和价值观相关，更多的，它与环境息息相关。人们在思考：我们是否要牺牲环境来提升 GDP？我们要怎样进行社会和政治体制的改革来应对经济的发展，保持稳定性和可持续性发展？同时，这个系统的自我修正能力是否足够强大，是否能够让生活在其中的人民接受在前进过程中的各种压力和困难？我想这些都是中国人民需要回答的问题，而中国的年轻一代将在改变这个国家的过程中也改变自己。

谢谢大家。

2. 翻译工作坊课程规划

第一，文本解读。
（1）分析英语演讲辞的语言特征；
（2）语篇指向性分析和文本功能类型分析，并列举出来；
（3）根据不同文本功能类型选择正确的翻译方法。
第二，分组翻译（六人一组）。具体要求如下：
（1）按照所提出的翻译策略，各组成员分别进行翻译；
（2）组内进行翻译、修改，拟初稿；
（3）将初稿合并，六人进行小组讨论，统一术语，纠查错误，拟定稿。
（4）各组提交定稿。
第三，翻译教学讨论。
（1）以上各组分别由代表进行报告演示，说明本组翻译策略选择的依据；
（2）所有同学对各组所提出的翻译策略进行讨论；
（3）教师给出参考译文，结合学生译文进行评析，讲解相关翻译技巧。

3. 参考译文

The night before I was heading for Scotland, I was invited to host the final of "China's Got Talent" show in Shanghai with the 80,000 live audiences in the stadium. Guess who was the performing guest? Susan Boyle. And I told her, "I'm going to Scotland the next day." She sang beautifully, and she even managed to say a few words in Chinese. So it's not like "hello" or "thank you," that ordinary stuff. It means "green onion for free." Why did she say that? Because it was a line from our Chinese parallel Susan Boyle—a 50-some-year-old woman, a vegetable vendor in Shanghai, who loves singing Western opera, but she didn't understand any English or French or Italian, so she managed to fill in the lyrics with vegetable names in Chinese. (Laughter) And the last sentence of Nessun Dorma that she was singing in the stadium was "green onion for free." So as Susan Boyle was saying that, 80,000 live audiences sang together. That was hilarious.

So I guess both Susan Boyle and this vegetable vendor in Shanghai belonged to otherness. They were the least expected to be successful in the business called entertainment, yet their courage and talent brought them through. And a show and a platform gave them the stage to realize their dreams. Well, being different is not that difficult. We are all different from different perspectives. But I think being different is good, because you present a different point of view. You may have the chance to make a difference.

My generation has been very fortunate to witness and participate in the historic transformation of China that has made so many changes in the past 20, 30 years. I remember that in the year of 1990, when I was graduating from college, I was applying for a job in the sales department of the first five-star hotel in Beijing, Great Wall Sheraton—it's still there. So after being interrogated by this Japanese manager for a half an hour, he finally said, "So, Miss Yang, do you have any questions to ask me?" I summoned my courage and poise and said, "Yes, but could you let me know, what actually do you sell?" I didn't have a clue what a sales department was about in a five-star hotel. That was the first day I set my foot in a five-star hotel.

Around the same time, I was going through an audition—the first ever open audition by national television in China—with another thousand college girls. The producer told us they were looking for some sweet, innocent and beautiful fresh face. So when it was my turn, I stood up and said, "Why do women's personalities on television always have to be beautiful, sweet, innocent and, you know, supportive? Why can't they have their own ideas and their own voice?" I thought I kind of offended them. But actually, they were impressed by my words. And so I was in the second round of competition, and then the third and the fourth. After seven rounds of competition, I was the last one to survive it. So I was on a national television prime-time show. And believe it or not, that was the first show on Chinese television that allowed its hosts to speak out of their own minds without reading an approved script. (Applause) And my weekly audience at that time was between 200 to 300 million people.

Well after a few years, I decided to go to the U. S. and Columbia University to pursue my postgraduate studies, and then started my own media company, which was unthought of during the years that I started my career. So we do a lot of things. I've interviewed more than a thousand people in the past. And sometimes I have young people approaching me say, "Lan, you changed my life," and I feel proud of that. But then we are also so fortunate to witness the transformation of the whole country. I was in Beijing's bidding for the Olympic Games. I was representing the Shanghai Expo. I saw China embracing the world and vice versa. But then sometimes I'm thinking, what are today's young generations up to? How are they different and what are the differences they are going to make to shape the future of China, or at large, the world?

So today I want to talk about young people through the platform of social media. First of all, who are they? What do they look like? Well this is a girl called Guo Meimei—20 years old, beautiful. She showed off her expensive bags, clothes and car on her microblog, which is the Chinese version of Twitter. And she claimed to be the general manager of Red Cross at the Chamber of Commerce. She didn't realize that she stepped on a sensitive nerve and aroused national questioning, almost a turmoil, against the credibility of Red Cross. The controversy was so heated that the Red Cross had to open a press conference to clarify it, and the investigation is going on. So far, as of today, we know that she herself made up that title—probably because she feels proud to be associated with charity. All those expensive items were given to her as gifts by her boyfriend, who used to be a board member in a subdivision of Red Cross at Chamber of Commerce. It's very complicated to explain. But anyway, the public still doesn't buy it. It is still boiling. It shows us a general mistrust of government or government-backed institutions, which lacked transparency in the past. And also it showed us the power and the impact of social media as microblog.

Microblog boomed in the year of 2010, with visitors doubled and time spent on it tripled. Sina. com, a major news portal, alone has more than 140 million microbloggers. On Tencent, 200 million. The most popular blogger—it's not me—it's a movie star, and she has more than 9.5 million followers, or fans. About 80 percent of those microbloggers are young people, under 30 years old. And because, as you know, the traditional media is still heavily controlled by the government, social media offers an opening to let the steam out a little bit. But because you don't have many other openings, the heat coming out of this opening is sometimes very strong, active and even violent.

So through microblogging, we are able to understand Chinese youth even better. So how are they different? First of all, most of them were born in the 80s and 90s, under the one-child policy. And because of selected abortion by families who favored boys to girls, now we have ended up with 30 million more young men than women. That could pose a potential danger to the society, but who knows; we're in a globalized world, so they can look for girlfriends from other countries. Most of them have fairly good education. The illiteracy rate in China among this generation is under one percent. In cities, 80 percent of kids go to college. But they are facing an aging China with a population above 65 years old coming up with seven-point-some percent this year, and about to be 15 percent by the year of 2030. And you know we have the tradition that younger generations support the elders financially, and taking care of them when they're sick. So it means young couples will have to support four parents who have a life expectancy of 73 years old.

So making a living is not that easy for young people. College graduates are not in short supply. In urban areas, college graduates find the starting salary is about 400 U. S.

dollars a month, while the average rent is above ＄500. So what do they do? They have to share space—squeezed in very limited space to save money—and they call themselves "tribe of ants." And for those who are ready to get married and buy their apartment, they figured out they have to work for 30 to 40 years to afford their first apartment. That ratio in America would only cost a couple five years to earn, but in China it's 30 to 40 years with the skyrocketing real estate price.

Among the 200 million migrant workers, 60 percent of them are young people. They find themselves sort of sandwiched between the urban areas and the rural areas. Most of them don't want to go back to the countryside, but they don't have the sense of belonging. They work for longer hours with less income, less social welfare. And they're more vulnerable to job losses, subject to inflation, tightening loans from banks, appreciation of the renminbi, or decline of demand from Europe or America for the products they produce. Last year, though, an appalling incident in a southern OEM manufacturing compound in China: 13 young workers in their late teens and early 20s committed suicide, just one by one like causing a contagious disease. But they died because of all different personal reasons. But this whole incident aroused a huge outcry from society about the isolation, both physical and mental, of these migrant workers.

For those who do return back to the countryside, they find themselves very welcome locally, because with the knowledge, skills and networks they have learned in the cities, with the assistance of the Internet, they're able to create more jobs, upgrade local agriculture and create new business in the less developed market. So for the past few years, the coastal areas, they found themselves in a shortage of labor.

These diagrams show a more general social background. The first one is the Engels coefficient, which explains that the cost of daily necessities has dropped its percentage all through the past decade, in terms of family income, to about 37-some percent. But then in the last two years, it goes up again to 39 percent, indicating a rising living cost. The Gini coefficient has already passed the dangerous line of 0.4. Now it's 0.5—even worse than that in America—showing us the income inequality. And so you see this whole society getting frustrated about losing some of its mobility. And also, the bitterness and even resentment towards the rich and the powerful is quite widespread. So any accusations of corruption or backdoor dealings between authorities or business would arouse a social outcry or even unrest.

So through some of the hottest topics on microblogging, we can see what young people care most about. Social justice and government accountability runs the first in what they demand. For the past decade or so, a massive urbanization and development have let us witness a lot of reports on the forced demolition of private property. And it has aroused huge anger and frustration among our young generation. Sometimes people get killed, and sometimes people set themselves on fire to protest. So when these incidents are reported more and more frequently on the Internet, people cry for the government to take actions to stop this.

So the good news is that earlier this year, the state council passed a new regulation on house requisition and demolition and passed the right to order forced demolition from local governments to the court. Similarly, many other issues concerning public safety is a hot topic on the Internet. We heard about polluted air, polluted water, and poisoned food. And guess what, we have faked beef. They have sorts of ingredients that you brush on a piece of chicken or fish, and it turns it to look like beef. And then lately, people are very concerned about cooking oil, because thousands of people have been found refining cooking oil from restaurant slop. So, all these things have aroused a huge outcry from the Internet. And fortunately, we have seen the government responding more timely and also more frequently to the public concerns.

While young people seem to be very sure about their participation in public policy-making, but sometimes they're a little bit lost in terms of what they want for their personal life. China is soon to pass the U. S. as the number one market for luxury brands—that's not including the Chinese expenditures in Europe and elsewhere. But you know what, half of those consumers are earning a salary below 2,000 U. S. dollars. They're not rich at all. They're taking those bags and clothes as a sense of identity and social status. And this is a girl explicitly saying on a TV dating show that she would rather cry in a BMW than smile on a bicycle. But of course, we do have young people who would still prefer to smile, whether in a BMW or on a bicycle.

So in the next picture, you see a very popular phenomenon called "naked" wedding, or "naked" marriage. It does not mean they will wear nothing in the wedding, but it shows that these young couples are ready to get married without a house, without a car, without a diamond ring and without a wedding banquet, to show their commitment to true love. And also, people are doing good through social media. And the first picture showed us that a truck caging 500 homeless and kidnapped dogs for food processing was spotted and stopped on the highway with the whole country watching through microblogging. People were donating money, dog food and offering volunteer work to stop that truck. And after hours of negotiation, 500 dogs were rescued. And here also people are helping to find missing children. A father posted his son's picture onto the Internet. After thousands of unclear, the child was found, and we witnessed the reunion of the family through microblogging.

So happiness is the most popular word we have heard through the past two years. Happiness is not only related to personal experiences and personal values, but also, it's about the environment. People are thinking about the following questions: Are we going to sacrifice our environment further to produce higher GDP? How are we going to perform our social and political reform to keep pace with economic growth, to keep sustainability and stability? And also, how capable is the system of self-correctness to keep more people content with all sorts of friction going on at the same time? I guess these are the questions people are going to answer. And our younger generations are going to transform this country while at the same time being transformed themselves.

Thank you very much.

4. 汉译英翻译练习

（1）2009 年 10 月 16 日在湖北文理学院（襄阳）举办的"环境美学国际论坛暨第七届亚洲艺术学会襄樊年会·城市公共艺术研究国际会议"的开幕式发言辞

女士们，先生们：

我很荣幸代表国际美学协会在环境美学国际论坛暨第七届亚洲艺术学会襄樊年会的开幕式上发言。

首先，感谢主办方的盛情邀请，能够与众多享有盛誉的亚洲美学家齐聚一堂我深感荣幸。作为国际美学协会的主席，我很高兴见证亚洲同仁在美学领域日益活跃的身影，并在国际舞台上频繁现身。

在进行大会发言之前，请允许我对国际美学协会做个简要介绍，尤其是为在座的不熟悉这个组织的各位来宾。作为一个集国家性和地区性为一体的美学学会，国际美学学会目前拥有 25 个成员社团。目前，中国和日本位于该组织最大的社团之列。上周在阿姆斯特丹举办了美学会议，与会者均为国际美学协会的执行会员。在这次会议中，来自北京大学的高建平教授告诉我中国社团已拥有一千多名会员，其中五百名在该领域表现活跃。

仅次于国家学会，国际美学协会也拥有个人会员，这主要针对所在国家并没有国家美学学会的个人。国际美学协会拥有来自四十多个国家的六百多名美学家。

尽管国际美学协会于 1988 年在英国诺丁汉举行的第十一届美学国际会议上才正式成立，但它的历史可以追溯到成立之前的很多年。

第一届国际美学会议于 1913 年在柏林由德国学者马克斯·德苏瓦尔（Max Dessoir）主办。第二届于 1937 年在巴黎召开。由于二战的影响，第三届会议于 1956 年在威尼斯重新召开。从那时起，会议越来越有规律地举办。直到 1984 年，会议才由国际美学委员会主办。协会的会员中许多都是美学领域中最为知名的学者，他们都来自有着悠久美学传统的国家，包括法国、德国、英国、意大利、波兰、日本和美国。协会在成立后的不同时期，拥有许多著名的学者，例如法国美学学者艾蒂安·索里奥（Etienne Souriau）、米盖尔·杜夫海纳（Mikel Dufrenne）、英国美学家哈罗德·奥斯本（Harold Osborne）、德国美学家路易斯·帕莱松（Luigi Pareyson）、日本美学家今道友信（Tomonobu Imamichi）、米兰·达姆贾诺维奇（Milan Damnjanovic）、美国美学家托马斯·门罗（Thomas Munro）等等。1984 年在蒙特利尔召开的国际大会上，国际美学委员会转型成为一个美学国际协会，由一个选举产生的执行委员会领导。此执行委员会由 5 名官员、25 个国家协会代表、5 个普通代表，包括主席海因茨·佩茨沃德（Heinz Paetzold）、终身名誉会员阿诺德·伯林特（Arnold Berleant）、今道友信（Tomonobu Imamichi）和约瑟夫·马戈利斯（Joseph Margolis）。

国际美学协会的主要活动包括协调美学国际会议和临时国际会议，出版年报、简讯以及维护网站。

纵观历年国际会议，我们可以看到直到上个世纪末，所有的会议都是在欧洲召开的。这里顺便提一下，1966 年，会议是由 Jan Aler 组织在阿姆斯特丹召开的。出于对美学越来越大的兴趣以及对国际交流与联系的更多关注,国际美学学会扩展了会议在世界的覆盖面。因此后来会议召开的地点包括东京(2001),里约热内卢(2004),安卡拉(2007)。而且我们都知道下一届会议将于2010年在北京召开。到2013年,会议从柏林第一次召开以来将走过整整100年。这一年,国际会议将重新回到欧洲,走进波兰的克拉科夫。

在过去的几十年中,国际美学协会扩大了活动范围,其中包括出版国际美学协会简讯以及从1996年开始出版的美学国际年报。在幻灯片中,您可以看见第十二卷的扉页,它是由杰尔·艾尔桢(土耳其)编辑。与此同时,由柯提斯·卡特(美国)编辑的第十三卷正在印刷中,将于几个月后出版。简讯和年报可以在线获得,也可以在国际美学协会的网站上找到,网站上也提供了过去已召开的和未来将要召开的会议的具体信息。

我刚刚呈现给大家的国际美学学会的短暂历史表明,美学正日益成为一项全球化的事业。

当然,美学并不是孤立存在的,在全球化的时代,很多事物都日趋国际化。例如,城市化进程,是由于大批农村移民进入现在的城市而形成的。在世界范围内,城市居住人口比例已经由1900年的13％上升到现在的50％。虽然最初的城市化进程出现在西方国家,但现在93％的城市扩张出现在发展中国家,其中亚洲和非洲的城市发展占80％。从某些方面来看,城市化进程是能够起到一些积极的作用的,例如它能够通过增加就业机会促进经济增长,以及使更多人能够享受卫生保健,教育,文化和娱乐。但是另一方面,城市化进程也带来一些负面影响,比如贫富差距日益加大,环境污染以及社会凝聚力的下降,部分都是由城市近郊化所导致的。在过去的几十年中,我们见证了新型的城市化进程以及可持续性的城市化进程。这些运动的拥护者声称他们相信能够将设计的重点从以汽车为中心的郊区以及商业园,转变为以行人集中、中转中心和混合使用的社区。可持续性的城市化进程是结合了现在需求与旧式设计方案。这也是对使社区分裂,也使人类彼此孤立并对环境有严重影响的郊区蔓延时代的强烈反对。新都市主义概念,包括人民以及密集的充满活力的社区目的地,并降低对作为主要模式的过境车辆运输的依赖。在这种意义下的可持续性城市化进程中,城市公共艺术起到了很重要的作用。传统上看,艺术是与美以及和谐紧密相关的。和谐不仅是与自然的和谐,还要与社会、经济、生物物理、历史和文化相和谐。在这个意义上,艺术一直是可持续发展的。也许在日益全球化和城市化的时代,艺术的和谐功能可能比以往更加重要。世界各地都对艺术有着强烈需求,它产生于对工作以及社会、经济、生物物理、历史和文化环境之间关系的考虑,并追求其广泛影响。我衷心希望此次城市公共艺术国际论坛能够对这一重要任务有所帮助,也希望在座的各位能够在接下来的几天收获丰硕,不虚此行!

（2）

张业遂大使关于中美关系的讲话

尊敬的科恩前国防部长,

女士们,先生们:

首先,我感谢科恩前国防部长的热情介绍。我很高兴出席今天的晚餐会,同这么多重要人士见面。

我的工作从联合国转到美国,刚好已有半年。按惯例,我该向国内提交述职报告了。我希望今晚同大家的互动交流,能为我准备述职报告带来一些启发。

在中美关系进入重要发展阶段之时出任中国驻美国大使,我倍感荣幸。当前,中美两国的利益联系日益紧密,相互依存不断加深。现在,两国互为第二大贸易伙伴,过去 10 年美国对华出口增长了 330%,今年前 8 个月美国对华出口又增长了 34.4%。美国对华直接投资总额达 640 亿美元,美国继续是中国最大的外资来源国。两国之间每年人员往来超过 250 万人次。约 10 万名中国留学生正在美国学习深造。中美之间已缔结 161 对友好城市和 36 对友好省州。两国还在一系列国际和地区问题上保持着密切沟通与合作。

我高兴地看到,经过双方共同努力,中美关系已经克服今年初的困难局面,回到正常发展的轨道。通过这半年来的工作,我深切地体会到,保持中美关系稳定发展,确实太重要了。怎么保持中美关系的稳定发展呢? 我愿借此机会同大家分享以下三点看法。

第一,要牢牢把握中美关系发展的正确方向。

中美关系是当今世界最重要的双边关系之一,不仅关乎两国和两国人民的根本利益,而且具有日益重要的战略意义和全球影响。胡锦涛主席同奥巴马总统去年 4 月在英国伦敦首次会晤时,就共同努力建设 21 世纪积极合作全面的中美关系达成重要共识,为两国关系发展指明了方向。奥巴马总统今年 3 月 29 日接受我递交国书时也表示,"美中关系具有塑造 21 世纪的能力"。中美两国休戚与共,合则两利,斗则俱伤。显然,对话比对抗好,合作比遏制好,伙伴比对手好。

第二,要积极拓展各领域务实合作。

合作是中美关系发展的不竭动力。当前,中美两国都在积极转变发展方式。双方应支持彼此的经济结构调整,拓展在清洁能源、节能减排、环境保护和基础设施建设等领域的合作。中美在二十国集团峰会和应对国际金融危机方面进行了有效的磋商与协调,为两国经济恢复增长和世界经济的复苏做出了重要贡献。两国应继续密切关注全球经济复苏,与国际社会一道,加强宏观经济政策协调,继续推动国际金融机构改革。

中美在维护亚太乃至世界的和平、稳定与发展方面拥有广泛的合作基础,也肩负着重要的共同责任。双方应加强在反恐、防扩散、朝核、伊朗核、气候变化等重大国际和地区问题上的磋商与合作。

第三,要不断增进战略互信。

不少有识之士指出,中美两国之间不时出现分歧和问题,根源在于双方缺乏充分的战略互信。实际上,两国政府早已认识到这一问题的重要性,并在继续努力加以解决。我认为,双方应重点在以下三个方面作出努力,不断增进战略互信:

一是尊重和照顾彼此核心利益和重大关切。相互尊重主权和领土完整是指导中美关系的中美三个联合公报的核心。我们希望美方恪守在中美三个联合公报包括有关美售台武器问题的《八·一七公报》以及《中美联合声明》中所做的承诺。

二是加强对话与沟通。面对面的沟通对于减少误解、增进相互理解和建立互信是不可或缺的。近期,崔天凯副外长来美国举行了中美副外长级政治磋商,美国总统国家安全事务副助理多尼隆和白宫国家经济委员会主任萨默斯联袂访华,双方就中美关系中的一系列重大问题进行了有效的讨论。事实证明,这种深入沟通具有重要积极建设性意义。下周,温家宝总理将在纽约出席联合国大会期间同奥巴马总统举行双边会见。胡锦涛主席已接受奥巴马总统的邀请，将对美国进行国事访问。两国元首还有机会在二十国集团首尔峰会和横滨亚太经合组织领导人非正式会议等场合举行会晤。中美双方正在积极努力，为上述重要高层交往做好准备。

三是妥善处理分歧与摩擦。中美两国之间存在这样那样的差异，双方难免出现意见分歧。经贸问题就是经贸问题，不能政治化。中国正在进一步推进人民币汇率形成机制改革，增强人民币汇率弹性。人民币汇率问题不应被美国某些人用作实现国内政治目的的工具。外部施压只能适得其反。最好的办法就是本着平等和相互尊重的精神，进行对话与磋商。

在结束演讲之前，我还想告诉大家，我对中美关系的未来充满信心。因为我们两国关系的基本面是好的，对话与合作继续是中美关系的主流。而且，下阶段中美关系面临重要发展机遇。只要双方能够以理解和信任的心态看待彼此的政策意图，采取措施加强对话与合作，就能够不断减少分歧，增进互信，推动中美关系健康稳定发展。我衷心希望在座各位继续为此做出积极努力。

谢谢大家！

第十一章

学校及下属学院简介翻译

本章内容主要包括学校简介、行政各部门、各学院、各专业、各类课程、各类奖励的翻译。其中学校简介属于公司简介类,在第六章已详述,此处不再赘述。行政各部门、各学院、各专业、各类课程属于公示语的范畴,其特点和翻译方法在第五章有详细介绍。鉴于国内外学术交流日益频繁,越来越多的中国学生走出国门去海外求学,也有很多国际生来华学习深造,在此专用一章篇幅介绍有关学校简介及下属院系、专业、课程、奖励、成绩单等的翻译。更多的是提供案例和练习为广大翻译爱好者学习参考。

案例及习题

一、英译汉

1. 案例:加州大学简介

The University of California opened its doors in 1869 with just 10 faculty members and 38 students. Today,the UC system includes more than 238,000 students and more than 190,000 faculty and staff,with more than 1.7 million alumni living and working around the world.

For almost 150 years,UC has expanded the horizons of what we know about ourselves and our world. Our campuses are routinely ranked among the best in the world, but our reach extends beyond campus borders.

Our students,faculty,staff and alumni exchange ideas,make advancements and unlock the secrets and mysteries of the universe every day. They engage with their local governments,serve California schools,protect the environment and push the boundaries of space.

Education and research as pioneering as California itself.

From all backgrounds,ethnicities and incomes,UC attracts the best and brightest. UC undergraduates come from all over California,and they work hard to make it to college. In fact,over 40 percent of UC students come from low-income families.

UC's faculty are the drivers behind innovations in biotechnology, computer science, art and architecture—and they bring that knowledge, that greatness, directly to the classroom.

Thousands of California jobs, billions of dollars in revenues, and countless everyday household items—from more plentiful fruits and vegetables to compact fluorescent light bulbs—can be traced back to UC discoveries. Similarly, many of the state's leading businesses are based on UC technology, founded by our faculty or led by UC graduates.

UC is a part of your life, every day.

Besides world-class classrooms and labs, UC has dozens of museums, concert halls, art galleries, botanical gardens, observatories and marine centers—academic resources, but also exciting gathering places for the community. Another half million people benefit from UC Extension's continuing education courses and from Cooperative Extension's agricultural advice and educational programs located throughout the state.

2. 翻译工作坊课程规划

第一，文本解读。

（1）分析汉语学校简介的语言特征，结合英文商务文体确定翻译风格；

（2）结合公司简介、学校简介的翻译原则，确定具体的翻译方法。

第二，分组翻译（六人一组）。具体要求如下：

（1）按照所提出的翻译策略，各组成员分别进行翻译；

（2）组内进行翻译、修改，拟初稿；

（3）将初稿合并，六人进行小组讨论，统一术语，纠查错误，拟定稿。

（4）各组提交定稿。

第三，翻译教学讨论。

（1）以上各组分别由代表进行报告演示，说明本组翻译策略选择的依据；

（2）所有同学对各组所提出的翻译策略进行讨论；

（3）教师给出参考译文，结合学生译文进行评析，讲解相关翻译技巧。

3. 参考译文

加州大学在1869年建校并开放招生，当时只有10名教职工和38名学生。如今，加州大学有238 000多名学生和190 000多名教职员工，在世界各地的生活和工作的校友超过170万名。

近150年以来，加州大学扩大了对自身和世界的视野。加州大学校园常被评为世界之最，但其实我们的各种超越已经远胜于校园的建设本身。

我们的学生、教师、员工和校友不断交流思想、开拓进取，每天都在解开宇宙间的各种秘密和神秘之事。他们投身地方政府，为加州的各所学校提供服务、保护环境，在各个领域勇于打破空间限制。

正如加州一样，我们的教育和研究遥遥领先。

加州大学不分背景、种族、收入，只吸引最优秀、最聪慧的学生。加州大学的本科生来自加州各地，是他们自身的努力使他们成为一名大学生。事实上，加州大学有超过40%的学生来自低收入家庭。

　　加州大学的教师在生物技术、计算机科学、艺术和建筑的革新方面具有源源不断的驱动力，他们把知识和荣耀直接带进教室。

　　加州成千上万的工作，数十亿美元的收入以及无数的日常家居用品——从丰富的水果和蔬菜到紧凑型荧光灯泡，都可以追溯到加州大学的各项研究发现。同样，许多美国领先企业都基于加州的领先技术，都是由我们的教师成立或由加州大学的毕业生领导建立。

　　加州大学是你生活的一部分，是你的每一天。

　　除了世界级的教室和实验室，加州大学有许多博物馆、音乐厅、艺术画廊、植物园、天文台和海洋中心——学术资源，还有为社区提供的令人激动的聚会场所。另外五十万加州人们受益于加州大学扩展继续教育课程和合作推广的农业咨询以及遍布全国的教育项目。

4. 英译汉翻译练习

　　(1)

Administration	Administration
Office of the Party Committee	Graduate School
Office of Discipline Inspection Commission	Office of Student Affairs
Organization Department	Admission Office
Office of Veteran Cadres	Office of Continuing Education
Publicity Department	Office of Disciplines and Development
United Front Work Department	Personnel Department
Department of Student Affairs	Office of Science and Technology
Department of Graduate Student Affairs	Office of Social Science
Department of Armed Forces	International Exchange Division
Party School	Office of Hong Kong, Macao and Taiwan Affairs
Party Commission of Administrative Offices	Office of Liaison
Office for Letters and Calls	Office of Stated-owned Assets
Offspring Care Committee	Office of Equipment
Labor Union	Office of Information and Networking
Commission for Women	Office of Housing Reform
Youth League	Office of Supervision
President Office	Audit Office
Office of Development Planning	Treasury
Office of Academic Affairs	Office of Minhang Campus Construction

Administration	Administration
Office of Infrastructure	Logistics Group
Office of Logistics	Assets Management Co. , Ltd
Security Department	Institutions Attached to the Ministry of Education
General Office at Huaihai Rd. Campus	National Training Center for Secondary School Principals, Ministry of Education, P. R China
Library	
Archives	East China Training Center for Education Administrators, Ministry of Education, P. R China
ECNU Press	East China Training Center for Normal University Teachers, Ministry of Education
ECNU Journal Editorial Department	
Joint Service Center for Student Development	Shanghai National Center for School Computer Education, Ministry of Education
Global Education Center	Institutes of Global Chinese Language Teacher Education
International Center of Teacher Education	

（2）

Schools and Departments	Schools and Departments
Academy of International Transport & Logistics	Dept. of Tourism
Collage of Continuing Education	School of Chinese as a Foreign Language
College of Distance Education	Dept. of Chinese as a Foreign Language
Institute for Advanced Studies in Multidisciplinary Science and Technology	Dept. of Chinese Language
	School of Communication
Institute of Art	Dept. of Broadcasting & Television
Institute of Estuarine and Costal Sciences	Dept. of Communication
Institute of International Relations and Regional Development	Dept. of Journalism
School of Art	School of Design
Dept. of Fine Arts	School of Educational Science
Dept. of Music	Dept. of Curriculum and Instruction
School OF Business	Dept. of Educational Information & Technology
Dept. of Accounting	School of Finance and Statistics
Dept. of Business Administration	Dept. of Finance
Dept. of Conference and Exhibition Management	Dept. of Financial Engineering
Dept. of Economics	Dept. of Education
Dept. of Informatics	Dept. Of Intentional Trade
Dept. of Real Estate	Dept. of Risk Management and Insurance

(续表)

Schools and Departments	Schools and Departments
Dept. of Statistics and Actuarial Science	School of Preschool & Special Education
School of Foreign Language	Dept. of Preschool Education
Dept. of College English	Dept. of Special Education
Dept. of English	Dept. of Speech & Hearing Rehabilitation Science
Dept. of French	School of Psychology & Cognitive Science
Dept. of German	Dept. of Applied Psychology
Dept. of French	Dept. of Psychology
Dept. of Russian	Institute of Developmental & Educational Psychology
Dept. of Translation	
School of Humanities and Social Sciences	School of Public Administration
Dept. of Chinese Language & Literature	Dept. of Administrative Sciences
Dept. of History	Dept. of Educational Administration
Dept. of Law	Dept. of Resources & Environmental Sciences
Dept. of Philosophy	Dept. of Environmental Science
Dept. of Politics	Dept. of Geography
Dept. of Social Sciences	Dept. of Urban & Regional Economy
Institute of Ancient Chinese Books Studies	School of Sciences & Engineering
School of Informatics & and Technology	Dept. of Chemistry
Computer Center	Dept. of Mathematics
Dept. of Communication Engineering	Dept. of Physics
Dept. of Computer Science & Technology	School of Social Development
Dept. of Electronic Engineering	Dept. of Social Work
School of Life Science	Dept. of Sociology
Dept. of Biology	Institute of Anthropology and Folklore
Dept. of Life Medicine	Population Research Institute
School of Physical Education & Health Care	School of Software
Dept. of College Physical Education	Dept. of Digital Entertainment
Dept. of Kinesiology	Dept. of Embedded Systems
Dept. of Physical Education	Dept. of Software Engineering
Dept. of Sociology of Sports	Si-Mian Institute for Advanced Studies in Humanities

二、汉译英

1. 各类专业翻译

专业名称	专业名称
工业工程	工商管理（司法）
信息工程	工商管理（信息工程学院）
传播学	信息管理与信息系统
法学（司法）	信息管理与信息系统（信息工程学院）
光电信息工程	市场营销
光电信息工程（理）	市场营销（信息工程学院）
光信息科学与技术	人力资源管理
财务管理（信息工程学院）	电子商务
生物医学工程	电子商务（信息工程学院）
审计学	物流管理
机械设计制造及其自动化	电子信息工程
机械设计制造及其自动化（专升本）	电子信息工程（信息工程学院）
机械设计制造及其自动化（信息工程学院）	电子信息科学与技术
工业设计	电子信息科学与技术（信息工程学院）
工业设计（信息工程学院）	电子科学与技术
环境工程	光信息科学与技术（电子）
环境科学	集成电路设计与集成系统
车辆工程	计算机科学与技术
会计学	计算机科学与技术（专升本）
会计学（专升本）	计算机科学与技术（软件工程方向）
会计学（信息工程学院）	计算机科学与技术（信息工程学院）
统计学	网络工程
国际经济与贸易	数字媒体技术
国际经济与贸易（信息工程学院）	教育技术学
财务管理	软件工程
金融学	软件工程（信息工程学院）
金融学（信息工程学院）	自动化
经济学	自动化（信息工程学院）
工商管理	电子信息技术及仪器

（续表）

专业名称	专业名称
电气工程与自动化	英语
电气工程与自动化(信息工程学院)	英语(信息工程学院)
测控技术与仪器	社会学
信息与计算科学	编辑出版学
应用物理学	法学
数学与应用数学	会计学(2+2)
通信工程	电子信息工程(2+2)
通信工程(信息工程学院)	软件工程(专升本)
通信工程(计算机通信)	计算机科学与技术(2+2)
信息对抗技术	印刷工程
信息安全	包装工程
	软件工程(2+2)

2. 各种奖励翻译

国家奖学金	国家励志奖学金	三好学生标兵
三好学生	学习优秀生	突出才能奖
先进个人	优秀工作者	优秀学生干部
优秀共青团员	优秀毕业生	优秀志愿者
先进班集体	优秀团干部	学生协会优秀干部
学生协会工作优秀个人	精神文明先进个人	社会工作先进个人
文体活动先进个人	道德风尚奖	精神文明奖
最佳组织奖	突出贡献奖	工作创新奖
团队建设奖	十大学生修身楷模	学生科研创新奖

3. 各种证书翻译

大学英语四级	大学英语六级	英语专业四级
英语专业八级	普通话等级考试	日语能力考试
商务日语能力考试	商务英语证书	雅思
托福	剑桥商务英语初级	剑桥商务英语中级
剑桥商务英语高级	全国计算机等级考试	会计从业资格证书
初级职务(助理会计)证书	会计中级职称	管理会计师证书
注册会计师证书	注册金融分析师	特许公认会计师
电工证	技工证书	报关员资格证书

报关员证书	人力资源从业资格证书	驾驶证
国家司法考试证书	律师资格证书	国际电子商务师
证券从业资格证书	国际贸易单证员证书	报关员资格证书
报检员资格证书	公务员考试	网络工程师
软件设计师	数据库分析师	网络管理员
信息系统项目管理师	造价工程师	注册房地产估价师
公路造价师	工程造价师	药品检验员

4. 成绩单翻译

×××× 大学本科成绩一览表

中华人民共和国　湖北武汉

学号：＊＊＊＊＊＊

姓　名：×××　　　　　　　　　　　　　　入学时间：2001/09/01

院（系）：动力工程系　　　　　　　　　　　　学　制：四　年

专　业：热能动力工程　　　　　　　　　　　制表日期：2006/10/30

序号	课程名称	学分	第一年 09/2001—07/2002 学期		第二年 09/2002—07/2003 学期		第三年 09/2003—07/2004 学期		第四年 09/2004—07/2005 学期	
			1st	2nd	1st	2nd	1st	2nd	1st	2nd
1	体育	230	68	75	72	70	78	83		
2	英语	272	77	70	77	72				
3	高等数学	107	81	68						
4	机械制图	241	74	80						
5	算法语言	52	82							
6	线性代数	36		75						
7	物理	140		82	79					
8	物理实验	71		73	80					
9	理论力学	100			80	76				
10	复变函数与积分变换	46			87					
11	法律基础	30			70					
12	数理方程	36				68				
13	流体力学	80				87				
14	电工技术	60				76				
15	材料力学	80				94	通过			

（续表）

序号	课程名称	学分	第一年 09/2001—07/2002 学期		第二年 09/2002—07/2003 学期		第三年 09/2003—07/2004 学期		第四年 09/2004—07/2005 学期	
			1st	2nd	1st	2nd	1st	2nd	1st	2nd
16	金工实习				良					
17	机械原理	42					83			
18	机械零件	48					80			
19	工程热力学	70					82			
20	传热学	70					86			
21	电子技术基础	60					86			
22	金属材料及热处理	44					85			
23	微机原理及应用	60						88		
24	互换性与技术测量	48						74		
25	汽轮机原理	80						79		
26	锅炉原理	80						75		
27	换热器	30						91		
28	热力发电厂	50						80		
29	自动控制理论	68						91		
30	零件设计	2.5周						良		
31	英语六级							63		
32	生产实习	2周						优		
33	测试技术	50							88	
34	能源工程	44							86	
35	热工自动化	40							91	
36	现代管理概论	36							80	
37	泵与风机	30							81	
38	专业英语	30							通过	
39	锅炉课程设计	120							良	
40	汽机课程设计	1周							优	通过
41	汽轮机运行特性	30								通过
42	现代大型电站锅炉	30								通过
43	两相流动与传热	30							.	通过
44	沸腾燃烧	30								通过

注：采用以下三种记分制：

1. 百分制：60 分为通过，100 分为满分；

2. 四分制：优（85—100　A）、良（70—84　B）、中（60—69　C）、不及格（60 以下　D）；

3. 选修课：通过或不通过。

档案馆馆长：×××

×××大学

第十二章

......................▶

时事政要翻译

第一节　时事政要的翻译

随着我国改革开放的程度不断深化,经济全球化发展迅速,全世界对中国的关注度日益加深。中国和其他国家间的政治策略和措施有必要传播出去,有助于国际友好交往和合作。因而时事政要的翻译也引起了越来越多的重视。

时事政要从文体上讲属于第九章报刊的范畴,但是由于时事政要更具备时效性和政治性,虽具有又有别于报刊的文体特征,尤其反映在词汇的层面。因为时事政要记录的是真实发生并存在的政治政策和措施,一些政治术语必不可少的涌现出来并给翻译带来了一定的困难。概括来讲,政治术语具有以下特征:

1. 概括性

政治术语的一大特点就是常用缩写词来表达某些特定的含义,这类词寓意丰富内涵深刻,如"八荣八耻"、"三个代表"等都有高度概括性且丰富内涵。因此在理解过程中,要将词汇还原为本来的意义,再进行翻译。

2. 时代性

随着时代的发展和社会的进步,各类新的政治词汇频繁出现,这类词汇都有很强的政治色彩和时代特征,充分反映了政治的变化,但是其存在的时间并不是很长,通常都随着时代的变迁而结束。

3. 文化性

有些政治术语可以反映当时独特的国情、文化和思维方式。比如"奔小康"(strive for a relatively comfortable life)指积极努力地改善生活条件,提高生活水平,使生活水平达到小康。

4. 涵盖性

政治术语通常并不仅仅指的是政治事件本身,通常都涵盖并涉及许多领域,如经济、历史、文化、风俗等,这就使得各国的语言都具有自己的特色。"精神文明"(spiritual civilization)涵盖了思想道德、文化科学、民主法治等,属于上层建筑的所有方面,而从狭义上讲,它其实指的是道德伦理。

在进行时事政要翻译的时候,要遵循报刊翻译的几个原则:互文性视角、主述位推进模式及语域理论,同时要特别注意政治术语的翻译,译者除了要具有较强的语言和文化功底外,还应有一定的政治敏感性,能够深刻理解相关政策的内涵,所以,翻译时只有把语言因素、文学因素、文化因素以及政治因素结合起来考虑,才能从内涵意义和外延意义真正做到既忠实于原意又符合英语的表达。

第二节 案例及习题

一、英译汉

1. 案例

Presidential Candidates Walking a Tightrope Over the Fight on Terrorism

WASHINGTON—Ten hours before terrorists struck Brussels, Donald J. Trump was on television describing his strategy for confronting the Islamic State: He would pound it with airstrikes, but any ground action must be taken by the United States' partners in the region. He did not mention, if he knew, that this was a pretty close approximation of President Obama's approach.

But then Mr. Trump went further, saying that the American contribution to NATO—whose headquarters is in Brussels, smack between the airport and the subway station bombed by the Islamic State on Tuesday—should be scaled back.

It was a surprising signal to Europe at a moment when it is under attack, and a vivid reminder of the risks of running for president in an age of terrorism: What sounds reasonably cautious in the evening can ring weak or strategically incoherent by morning.

Most presidential candidates, with rare exceptions, are tempted to adopt far more hawkish stances on the campaign trail than presidents do in the Oval Office, where they must confront the realities of building coalitions, sorting through conflicting intelligence and pursuing comprehensive counter terrorism programs. But in the current atmosphere, a strike like the one on Tuesday in Brussels rekindles every debate about whether the United States should use diplomacy, isolation or military might.

Indeed, within hours of seeing images of the carnage in Belgium, Mr. Trump renewed his calls for a ban on Muslims entering the United States and for legalized torture to extract information from an Islamic State operative captured last week in Brussels. Senator Ted Cruz of Texas went beyond his promise of "carpet-bombing" to demand that the United States "empower law enforcement to patrol and secure Muslim neighborhoods before they become radicalized."

Even Gov. John Kasich of Ohio, who objected to Mr. Cruz's idea, called on Mr. Obama to abandon his trip to Cuba and Argentina, though it was not clear what more he could do from the White House than from the secure bubble in which he travels.

Hillary Clinton, while positioned at the hawkish end of the Democratic race, sounded mild compared with the Republicans scrambling to say how they would interrogate Muslims or separate them from the rest of the population.

A former secretary of state portraying herself as the steadiest, most experienced candidate to lead the United States and the world, Mrs. Clinton is promising continuity with the Obama administration. So she argued for doing more of what it is already doing: standing "in solidarity with our European allies," tightening the visa and passenger-list systems, and making sure, along the way, to remember that "torture is not effective."

Mrs. Clinton was headed next to Silicon Valley, however, and she dropped some of the hard language she has used before in siding with the F. B. I. in the debate about cracking encryption on smartphones, falling back to finding a "reasonable path forward" for gaining access for investigators to encrypted conversations and text messages.

Mrs. Clinton's aides said she would give a speech Wednesday at Stanford University detailing her plans to defeat the Islamic State.

"We've got to defeat them online," she said on Tuesday in Everett, Wash. "That is where they radicalize, and that's where they propagandize."

The responses reflect the different primary electorates the Republican and Democratic candidates face. Republican voters overwhelmingly support Mr. Trump's idea for a ban on Muslim immigrants, exit polls have showed.

But opinion polls have shown that most Democrats do not, and they remain deeply admiring of Mr. Obama—whom Mrs. Clinton has been loath to show up by responding more swiftly to international events.

Like Mr. Trump, Senator Bernie Sanders of Vermont said his piece on Monday, giving the first detailed foreign policy speech of his campaign.

But it was also notable for its generalities: He said that "the United States has the opportunity, as the most powerful nation on earth, to play an extraordinary role" in attempting "to put together a coalition in the region to destroy ISIS."

To Obama administration officials, this is not a new idea. They have been trying to accomplish exactly that, often with less success than they would like, for three years.

The instant responses to the attacks in Brussels highlighted the tightrope that all of the candidates find themselves walking when the subject turns to combating terrorism. The bitter lessons of the Iraq war loom over the 2016 election, as they loomed over the previous three, and none of the remaining candidates are calling for a ground force to take on the Islamic State in Syria or Iraq.

Some of the harshest messages and vaguest plans have come from Mr. Cruz. His carpet-bombing suggestion was immediately denounced because he appeared to be advocating a war crime; carpet-bombing is, by its nature, indiscriminate. So he now focuses on sealing the United States off from terrorist groups. Thus his call on Tuesday for patrols of Muslim neighborhoods, perhaps the ultimate step in ethnic profiling.

Mr. Trump's willingness to share his opinions over decades in the public eye has left a paper trail of noticeable shifts in his positions: from speaking approvingly of intervention inIraq early on, to opposing it, to his seemingly dueling impulses of aggressiveness and isolationism as the Republican front-runner.

After the terrorist attacks last year in Paris and San Bernardino, he set off a storm of outrage by calling for a ban on Muslims entering the United States, and he repeated that call on Tuesday in television interviews after the Brussels bombings.

He often promises to "knock the hell out of ISIS," and in a debate on March 10, he answered a hypothetical question about whether he would heed the advice of generals, if they recommended deploying 20,000 to 30,000 ground troops to Syria, by saying, "I would listen to the generals, but I'm hearing numbers of 20,000 to 30,000."

But on Monday, Mr. Trump suggested that he would reject any call to use ground troops, and appeared to suggest that he thought that American engagement could be effective even if it were limited to airstrikes—a view not held at the Pentagon.

"I'd get people from that part of the world to put up the troops, and I'd certainly give them air power and air support and some military support," Mr. Trump said on CNN. "But I would never, ever put up 20,000 or 30,000."

2. 翻译工作坊课程规划

第一,文本解读。

(1) 找出政治术语,并指出其语言特点;

(2) 分析政治术语的内涵,进行语内翻译;

(3) 结合互文性、主述位推进模式和语域理论三个方面提出相应的翻译策略。

第二,分组翻译(六人一组)。具体要求如下:

(1) 按照所提出的翻译策略,各组成员分别进行翻译;

(2) 组内进行翻译、修改,拟初稿;

(3) 将初稿合并,六人进行小组讨论,统一术语,纠查错误,拟定稿;

(4) 各组提交定稿。

第三,翻译教学讨论。

(1) 以上各组分别由代表进行报告演示,说明本组翻译策略选择的依据;

(2) 所有同学对各组所提出的翻译策略进行讨论;

(3) 教师给出参考译文,结合学生译文进行评析,讲解相关翻译技巧。

3. 参考译文

布鲁塞尔恐袭牵动美国大选，反恐考验候选人

华盛顿——布鲁塞尔恐怖袭击事件发生 10 小时之前，唐纳德·J·特朗普（Donald J. Trump）正在电视上谈论自己在对抗伊斯兰国方面的战略：他会发动空袭，轰炸伊斯兰国，但任何地面行动都必须由美国在那一地区的盟友进行。就算心里明白，他当时至少是没提——这和奥巴马总统的策略非常接近。

但接着特朗普就更进一步表示，美国应该减少对北约组织（NATO）事务的参与。该机构的总部位于布鲁塞尔，就在周二被伊斯兰国袭击的机场和地铁站之间。

对于正在遭受袭击的欧洲而言，这是一个让人意外的信号，它清楚地提醒人们，在恐怖主义年代竞选总统会存在什么样的风险：前天晚上听起来还算谨慎的提议，第二天早上听起来可能就显得软弱，或在战略上显得不合理。

除了很少数的例外，大多数总统候选人的立场，往往比正在椭圆形办公室里那位总统更强硬，因为后者必须面对真正的现实，要建立联盟，理清相互矛盾的情报信息，要展开全面的反恐行动。但在目前的气氛之下，周二在布鲁塞尔发生的这种袭击，会重新激起所有有关美国是否该使用外交、孤立手段，或动用军事力量的争论。

实际上，刚看到有关比利时惨剧的图像不到几小时，特朗普就再度发出了他此前的呼吁，即禁止穆斯林进入美国境内，以及修改法律，允许刑讯逼供，以便从上周在布鲁塞尔抓获的一名伊斯兰国特工人员那里获取情报信息。德克萨斯州参议员特德·克鲁兹（Ted Cruz）也突破了自己之前所做的对伊斯兰国进行"地毯式轰炸"的承诺，开始要求美国"授权执法机构在穆斯林社区进行巡逻，在他们变成激进分子之前就做好防范工作。"

就连反对克鲁兹观点的俄亥俄州州长约翰·卡西奇（John Kasich），也呼吁奥巴马总统取消访问古巴和阿根廷的计划，尽管他留在白宫，也不见得能比在访问途中的安全交通工具和住所中多做些什么。

尽管希拉里·克林顿（Hillary Clinton）在民主党候选人中属于强硬派，但与争相表示要审问穆斯林或将他们与美国其他人隔离开来的共和党人相比，她的话听起来就温和多了。

这名美国前国务卿将自己塑造成在领导美国和世界事务方面最沉稳、最有经验的候选人，她也的确很有希望接替奥巴马，组建下一届美国政府。因此她支持加强现在已经采取的措施："与欧洲盟友团结一致"，加强签证审核和旅客名单系统审查，与此同时，一定记住"拷问是没有用的"。

不过在破解智能手机加密一事上，她放弃了一些支持联邦调查局（FBI）的强硬言论，接下来要前往硅谷的克林顿夫人现在采取了更缓和的立场，称要为调查人员获取加密的通话和文本信息找到一个"合理的途径"。

克林顿夫人的助手表示，她将于周三在斯坦福大学发表讲话，详细讲述她在打击伊斯兰国方面的计划。

"我们必须在互联网上击败他们，"她周二在华盛顿州埃弗雷特市说道。"他们是在网上煽动人们走向激进，那是他们进行宣传鼓动的阵地。"

这些反应也证明了，共和党和民主党候选人面对着不同的选民主体。投票后的民意调查显示,共和党的绝大多数选民都支持特朗普的提议,即禁止穆斯林移民美国。

但多项民意调查显示,大多数民主党人并不支持这种提议,而且他们依然极为赞赏奥巴马——因此克林顿夫人一直不愿意在国际事务上太快做出反应,从而让他难堪。

和特朗普一样,佛蒙特州参议员伯尼·桑德斯(Bernie Sanders)也在周一发表了他的观点,第一次在选战中详细谈论了他在外交政策方面的想法。

但这次发言依然颇具他那显著的概括特征:他表示,"作为世界上最强大的国家,美国有这样一个机会,在当地组建联盟摧毁伊斯兰国"的行动中,"扮演特别的角色"。

对于奥巴马政府的官员而言,这不是什么新观念。过去三年,他们一直在努力达成的,恰恰就是这个目标,只不过效果往往差强人意。

这些针对布鲁塞尔袭击事件做出的快速反应,突显出所有候选人在话题转向抗击伊斯兰国时,都不免陷入一个困境。伊拉克战争的沉痛教训所留下的阴影,还像过去三年一样,笼罩在 2016 年的大选之上。在余下的这些候选人中,没有一位提议派地面部队到叙利亚或伊拉克,去对付伊斯兰国。

这方面最为刺耳的信息和最含糊其辞的计划出自克鲁兹。他的"地毯式轰炸"提议刚一出炉,就马上遭到谴责,原因是他似乎在鼓吹战争;而且地毯式轰炸本质上也的确是一种不加区分的盲目行动。所以,现在他把重点转向了建立封锁线,以避免恐怖组织渗入美国。因此他在周二呼吁派执法人员在穆斯林社区巡逻,这可能是走向种族定性的关键一步。

因为喜欢在大庭广众之下发表自己的观点,特朗普在过去几十年的明显立场转变是有书面记录的:从早期赞成在伊拉克实施干预,到反对这种做法,再到作为势头领先的共和党候选人所表现出的看似要与之决斗的雄心,以及孤立主义立场。

去年,在巴黎和加州圣贝纳迪诺恐怖袭击事件发生后,他呼吁禁止穆斯林进入美国,引起轩然大波。周二布鲁塞尔爆炸袭击事件发生后,他在接受电视采访时再次发出这种倡议。

他经常信誓旦旦地说,"要把伊斯兰国打得满地找牙"。在 3 月 10 日的一场辩论中,他回答了这样一个假设性的提问,即如果军方将领建议往叙利亚部署 2 到 3 万地面部队,他是否会听从。他回答说,"我会听取将领们的建议,不过这里说的可是 2 到 3 万人。"

但本周一,特朗普又表示,他会拒绝任何动用地面部队的请求。他似乎还暗示,他觉得哪怕只限于空袭,美国也可以有效打击伊斯兰国——五角大楼可不这么想。

"我会找当地人组建部队,我肯定会向他们提供空中打击的实力,给他们空中支持和一些军事支持,"特朗普在接受 CNN 采访时说。"但我永远、永远不会派 2 到 3 万人过去。"

4. 英译汉翻译练习

(1)

Obama to Nominate Merrick Garland to Supreme Court

WASHINGTON—President Obama on Wednesday said he would nominate Merrick B. Garland as the nation's 113th Supreme Court justice, choosing a centrist appeals court judge for the lifetime appointment and daring Republican senators to refuse consideration of a jurist who is highly regarded throughout Washington.

Mr. Obama introduced Judge Garland to an audience of his family members, activists, and White House staff in the Rose Garden Wednesday morning, describing him as exceptionally qualified to serve on the Supreme Court in the seat vacated by the death of Justice Antonin Scalia, who died in February.

The president said Judge Garland is "widely recognized not only as one of America's sharpest legal minds, but someone who brings to his work a spirit of decency, modesty, integrity, even-handedness and excellence. These qualities and his long commitment to public service have earned him the respect and admiration from leaders from both sides of the aisle."

He added that Judge Garland "will ultimately bring that same character to bear on the Supreme Court, an institution on which he is uniquely prepared to serve immediately."

Mr. Obama said it is tempting to make the confirmation process "an extension of our divided politics." But he warned that "to go down that path would be wrong."

Mr. Obama demanded a fair hearing for Judge Garland and said that refusing to even consider his nomination would provoke "an endless cycle of more tit for tat" that would undermine the democratic process for years to come.

"I simply ask Republicans in the Senate to give him a fair hearing, and then an up or down vote," Mr. Obama said. "If you don't, then it will not only be an abdication of the Senate's constitutional duty, it will indicate a process for nominating and confirming judges that is beyond repair."

In choosing Judge Garland, a well-known moderate who has drawn bipartisan support over decades, Mr. Obama was essentially daring Republicans to press their election-year confirmation fight over a judge many of them have publicly praised and who would be difficult for them to reject, particularly if a Democrat were to win the November presidential election and they faced the prospect of a more liberal nominee in 2017.

Judge Garland persevered through a lengthy political battle in the mid-1990s that delayed his own confirmation to the United States Court of Appeals for the District of Columbia Circuit by more than a year. Senator Charles E. Grassley, Republican of Iowa, argued at the time that the vacancy should not be filled.

Twenty years later, Mr. Grassley and other Republicans are again standing in the way of Judge Garland's appointment, arguing that the next president should be the one to pick the successor to Justice Scalia. Republicans in the Senate and on the presidential campaign trail vowed to stand firm against whomever Mr. Obama chose.

In remarks Monday, Mr. Obama chastised Republicans for taking that stand, demanding that the Republican-controlled Senate fulfill its responsibility to consider Judge Garland and hold a timely vote on his nomination. "To do anything else would be irresponsible," he said.

Judge Garland is often described as brilliant and, at 63, is somewhat older for a Supreme Court nominee. He is two years older than Chief Justice John G. Roberts Jr., who has been with the court for more than 10 years. The two served together on the appeals court and are said to be friends.

Supreme Court nominees tend to be in their early 50s. In choosing Judge Garland, Mr. Obama very likely gave away the possibility of a justice who would serve on the Supreme Court perhaps three decades. Instead, he imposed a sort of actuarial term limit on the nomination and thus his legacy, offering Senate Republicans a compromise not only on ideology, but also on tenure.

The Oklahoma City bombing case in 1995 helped shape Judge Garland's professional life. He coordinated the Justice Department's response, starting the case against the bombers and eventually supervising their prosecution.

Judge Garland insisted on being sent to the scene even as bodies were being pulled out of the wreckage, said Jamie S. Gorelick, then the deputy attorney general.

"At the time, he said to me the equivalent of 'Send me in, coach,'" Ms. Gorelick said. "He worked around the clock, and he was flawless."

White House officials on Wednesday noted that Judge Garland was confirmed to his current post in 1997 with the support of seven sitting Republicans: Senators Dan Coats of Indiana, Thad Cochran of Mississippi, Susan Collins of Maine, Orrin G. Hatch of Utah, James M. Inhofe of Oklahoma, John McCain of Arizona, Pat Roberts of Kansas.

In an email on Wednesday just before Mr. Obama was to appear in the Rose Garden to formally nominate him, one official said that Mr. Hatch said this year that Mr. Obama "could easily name Merrick Garland, who is a fine man." They noted that Mr. Hatch was quoted in 2010 as saying that Judge Garland would be a "consensus nominee" if he had been picked that year.

The White House also cited positive comments about Judge Garland from Chief Justice Roberts, the Republican governors of Oklahoma and Iowa, and former Republican officials in the Justice Department.

Because of his position, disposition and bipartisan popularity, Judge Garland has been on Mr. Obama's shortlist of potential nominees for years. In 2010, when Mr. Obama interviewed him for the slot that he instead gave to Justice Elena Kagan, Senator Orrin G. Hatch, Republican of Utah, said publicly that he had urged Mr. Obama to nominate Judge Garland as "a consensus nominee" who would win Senate confirmation.

"I know Merrick Garland very well," Mr. Hatch said at the time. "He would be very well supported by all sides."

In an email to supporters early Wednesday morning, Mr. Obama said he considered three principles in making his choice: whether the person possessed "an independent mind, unimpeachable credentials and an unquestionable mastery of law"; whether the nominee recognized "the limits of the judiciary's role"; and whether his choice understood that "justice is not about abstract legal theory, nor some footnote in a dusty casebook."

Mr. Obama said that he was "confident you'll share my conviction that this American is not only eminently qualified to be a Supreme Court justice, but deserves a fair hearing and an up-or-down vote."

At a news conference on Thursday, Mr. Obama said that Republicans must "decide whether they want to follow the Constitution and abide by the rules of fair play that ultimately undergird our democracy and that ensure that the Supreme Court does not just become one more extension of our polarized politics."

Republican senators have urged the president to hold off on a nomination, saying the next president should make the pick after voters express their preference in the presidential election. Senator Mitch McConnell of Kentucky, the Republican leader, has repeatedly said he would oppose any nomination until next year.

"President Obama is getting dangerously close to narrowing down the field of potential candidates for nomination to the U. S. Supreme Court," Mr. McConnell warned his supporters in a fund-raising appeal last month.

The outcome of the Washington clash could determine whether Mr. Obama gets to set the direction of American jurisprudence for decades. After the death last month of Mr. Scalia, a leading conservative, the court is evenly divided, with four liberal justices and four conservatives. A new justice appointed by Mr. Obama could be the deciding vote in several close cases.

(2)

Clinton and Black Voters

Mrs. Clinton is poised to sweep the South, but her margin of victory depends on how well she does among black voters.

Mrs. Clinton won 87 percent of the black vote in South Carolina—a larger share than President Obama won in the 2008 primary—helping her win the state in a landslide, 73 percent to 26 percent for Senator Bernie Sanders.

If Mrs. Clinton were to repeat that performance on Tuesday, she could post similar victories in states like Georgia and Alabama. She could top 60 percent of the vote in other Southern states with large black populations, like Virginia, Texas, Tennessee and Arkansas.

The margin matters, and for more than just appearances: Democrats allocate all delegates proportionally, so Mrs. Clinton will be rewarded if she maximizes her support among black voters.

二、汉译英

1. 案例

聚焦提质增效，推动产业创新升级。制定实施创新驱动发展战略纲要和意见，出台推动大众创业、万众创新政策举措，落实"互联网＋"行动计划，增强经济发展新动力。一大批创客走上创业创新之路。完善农业支持政策，促进农业发展方式加快转变。针对工业增速下降、企业效益下滑,我们一手抓新兴产业培育,一手抓传统产业改造提升。启动实施《中国制造 2025》,设立国家新兴产业创业投资引导基金、中小企业发展基金,扩大国家自主创新示范区。积极化解过剩产能,推进企业兼并重组。近三年淘汰落后炼钢炼铁产能 9 000 多万吨、水泥 2.3 亿吨、平板玻璃 7600 多万重量箱、电解铝 100 多万吨。促进生产性、生活性服务业加快发展。狠抓节能减排和环境保护,各项约束性指标超额完成。公布自主减排行动目标,推动国际气候变化谈判取得积极成果。

2. 翻译工作坊课程规划

第一,文本解读。

(1) 找出中国特色政治术语,并指出其语言特点;

(2) 分析中国特色政治术语的内涵,进行语内翻译;

(3) 结合互文性、主述位推进模式和语域理论三个方面提出相应的翻译策略。

第二,分组翻译(六人一组)。具体要求如下:

(1) 按照所提出的翻译策略,各组成员分别进行翻译;

(2) 组内进行翻译、修改,拟初稿;

(3) 将初稿合并,六人进行小组讨论,统一术语,纠查错误,拟定稿。

(4) 各组提交定稿。

第三,翻译教学讨论。

(1) 以上各组分别由代表进行报告演示,说明本组翻译策略选择的依据;

(2) 所有同学对各组所提出的翻译策略进行讨论;

(3) 教师给出参考译文,结合学生译文进行评析,讲解相关翻译技巧。

3. 参考译文

We worked to promote industrial innovation and upgrading to improve economic performance. To strengthen the new growth engines, an innovation-driven development plan was adopted along with guidelines on its implementation, policies and measures were introduced to encourage public participation in starting businesses and making innovations, and the Internet Plus action plan was implemented. A great number of makers started businesses and made innovations. Improvements were made to policies in support of agriculture to promote transformation of the agricultural growth model. In addressing the decline in industrial growth and the downward slide incorporate performance, we worked to foster new industries and upgrade traditional ones. We launched the *Made in China 2025* initiative to upgrade manufacturing, set up government funds to encourage investment in emerging industries and to develop small and medium-sized enterprises, and established more national innovation demonstration zones. We cut overcapacity and encouraged business acquisitions and restructuring. Cuts made in outdated production capacity over the past three years have included over 90 million metric tons of steel and iron, 230 million metric tons of cement, over 76 million weight cases of plate glass, and more than one million metric tons of electrolytic aluminum. The development of production- and consumer-oriented service industries picked up momentum. We took serious measures to conserve energy, reduce emissions, and protect the environment, exceeding obligatory targets. We released self-imposed emissions reduction targets and contributed to the positive outcomes of international negotiations on climate change.

4. 汉译英翻译练习

（1）时事政要（一）

1949 年 9 月 21 日至 30 日，中国人民政治协商会议第一届全体会议召开。会议代表全国各族人民意志，代行全国人民代表大会职权，通过了具有临时宪法性质的《中国人民政治协商会议共同纲领》和《中国人民政治协商会议组织法》、《中华人民共和国中央人民政府组织法》，做出关于中华人民共和国国都、国旗、国歌、纪年 4 个重要决议，选举中国人民政治协商会议全国委员会和中华人民共和国中央人民政府委员会，宣告中华人民共和国的成立。

（2）时事政要（二）

着眼开拓发展空间，促进区域协调发展和新型城镇化。继续推动东、中、西、东北地区"四大板块"协调发展，重点推进"一带一路"建设、京津冀协同发展、长江经济带发展"三大战略"，在基础设施、产业布局、生态环保等方面实施一批重大工程。制定实施促进西藏和四省藏区、新疆发展的政策措施。推进户籍制度改革，出台居住证制度，加强城镇基础设施建设，新型城镇化取得新成效。

第十三章

....

学术论文翻译

第一节　学术论文的语言特点及翻译方法

　　学术论文通常通过报道一项研究或实验的结果，来阐述某个学术观点或结论，其最终目的是说服读者相信其观点的正确性并接受其观点。学术论文不同于其他文体，它崇尚严谨周密，行文简练，概念准确，逻辑性强，重点突出，句式严整，表达客观。

一、英语学术论文在语言方面存在以下几个特点：

1. 名词化结构的使用

　　名词化结构是指大量使用名词和名词词组来充当本应由动词、形容词等词类充当的语法成分。充分利用名词化结构是英语学术论文的一个重要的语言特点。因为学术论文以描述客观事物为主，信息量大，要求行文简洁，名词化结构正好可以满足这些要求。

2. 被动语句的使用

　　被动语态在学术论文中被高频率使用有两方面原因：第一，学术论文论述的对象一般是客观的事物、现象和过程，被研究对象很方便被当做主语来组织句子；第二，学术论文强调客观性，如果用第一、二人称容易造成过于主观的印象。

3. 缩略词的使用

　　学术论文要求论述精简，频繁使用缩略词是其一大特点。

　　例：ESL：English as the Second Language（非母语英语）

　　例：EAP：English for Academic Purposes（学术用途英语）

4. 长句的使用

　　学术论文属于正式的书面语体，长句的使用可使结构严谨，逻辑严密，信息集中。

二、翻译方法

1. 名词结构的翻译方法有多种，可以翻译成

（1）汉语的名词结构；

例：Beyond the linking arrangement of language and content，additional components，such as social events and academic and personal counseling，are also included in the programs in order to create learning and social communities and provide academic and emotional support.

除与语言和内容相关的安排之外，这些项目中还包括一些其他要素，例如社会活动，学术以及个人辅导，从而能够帮助学生创建学习和社会团体，并提供学术和情感上的支持。

（2）动词的主谓或动宾结构；

例：These programs also require coordination of instruction，activities，and assignments between language and content instructors.

这些项目同样也需要语言指导者和内容指导者们在教学、活动以及课后任务方面进行合作。

（3）翻译成小句；

例：Due to changes in CUNY policies for financial aid which imposed time limits for completing ESL and developmental work as well as academic coursework for degrees，ESL students came under increasing pressure to be mainstreamed quickly into credit-bearing English courses and to succeed in courses in their major discipline.

纽约市立大学对资金援助的政策进行了调整，由于此调整对学生完成非母语英语课程、拓展性任务及学位学术课程的时间进行了限制，因此英语非母语学生就面临着更大的压力而要快速地加入学分英语课程并在他们的主要课程中取得成功。

2. 被动语态的翻译

（1）翻译成以原句主语为主语的主动句；
（2）翻译成以原句主语为宾译的主动句；
（3）翻译成主动形式的无主句；
（4）依照原句结构翻译成带有"……被……，为……所……"等结构的被动句。

3. 长句的翻译

长句的翻译主要遵循符合目的语的语言习惯，可使用主述位推进法，静态翻译与动态翻译结合，根据目的语的逻辑关系灵活掌握。如：

例：The study sought to compare content-linked ESL students' academic achievement with that of non-content-linked ESL students by using common measures such as GPA，graduation and retention rates as well as pass rates on English proficiency tests.

本研究试图通过利用常用衡量标准，例如平均分数，毕业和学籍保留率，以及英语水平测试通过率来比较参加以内容为依托英语作为第二语言教学项目的学生与没有参加此项目的学生的学术成就。

第二节 案例及习题

一、英译汉

1. 案例

SUMMARY OF THE INVENTION

The invention provides an information storage, searching and retrieval system for a large domain of archived data of various types, in which the results of a search are organized into discrete types of documents and groups of document types so that users may easily identify relevant information more efficiently and more conveniently than systems currently in use. The system of the invention includes means for storing a large domain of data contained in multiple source records, at least some of the source records being composed of individual documents of multiple document types; means for searching substanitially all of the domain with a single each query to identify documents responsive to the query; and means of categorizing documents responsive to the query based on document type, including means for generating a summary of the number of documents responsive the query which fall within various predetermined categories of document types.

The query generation process may contain a knowledge base including a thesaurus that has predetermined and embedded complex search queries, or use natural language processing, or fuzzy logic, or tree structures, or hierarchical relationship or a set of commands that allow persons seeking information to formulate their queries.

The search process can utilize any index and search engine techniques including Boolean, vector, and probabilistic as long as a substaintial portion of the entire domain of archived textual data is searched for each query and all documents found are returned to the organizing process.

The sorting/categorization process prepares the search results for presentation by assembling the various document types retrieved by the search engine and then arranging these basic documents types into sometimes broader categories that are readily understood by and relevant to the user. The search results are then presented to the user and arranged by category along with an indication as to the number of relevant documents found in each category. The user may then examine search results in multiple formats, allowing the user to view as much of the document as the user deems necessary.

2. 翻译工作坊课程规划

第一，文本解读。

（1）指出该篇论文的学术领域和专业术语，标记出其中的名词化结构、长句和被动语态；

（2）确定文体风格，分析语言特点，并根据文章的领域确定翻译策略。

第二，分组翻译（六人一组）。具体要求如下：

（1）按照所提出的翻译策略，各组成员分别进行翻译；

（2）组内进行翻译、修改，拟初稿；

（3）将初稿合并，六人进行小组讨论，统一术语，纠查错误，拟定稿；

（4）各组提交定稿。

第三，翻译教学讨论。

（1）以上各组分别由代表进行报告演示，说明本组翻译策略选择的依据；

（2）所有同学对各组所提出的翻译策略进行讨论；

（3）教师给出参考译文，结合学生译文进行评析，讲解相关翻译技巧。

3. 参考译文

系统概要

该系统主要应用于对大量数据进行信息存储，查询和检索，查询的结果将被导出成文件类型，比目前的系统更方便容易地找到用户想要查询的有关数据。该系统不仅包括存储广泛数据领域的复合数据源记录，还包括多个文件类型的某些原始记录。该方式提供了搜索大数据领域所进行的一次唯一辨认文件的重要查询部分；还提供了文件重要部分的查询，以及包括对文件数量的统计和属于各种各样的预先确定类别的文件查询。

查询创建过程包含一个知识库，该知识库包括被预先确定和嵌入复杂查询的分类词典，或者是自然语言的处理，或者模糊逻辑，或者树型结构，或者等级关系，或者是一套寻求信息的公式化查询命令。

搜索的过程可能利用到所有的索引和搜索引擎技术，包括布尔、传播媒介、几率查询。只要每次查询到一个原文归档数据的固有部分，所有建立的文档就能返回到其组织过程。

排序或分类的过程是通过调用搜索引擎检索查询的结果，从而为引入各种各样的基本文件类型做准备，然后组织安排这些容易被理解且与用户密切相关的基本文件类型。然后提供给用户相关查询的结果与在该查询结果中的每个类别相关文档数量的统计。用户可以多种形式来检查查询的结果，并且用户可以根据自己的需要来查看相关的文件。

4. 英译汉翻译练习

Environmental Aesthetics as Creative Dialogue with Otherness

The aim of this essay is to stress the vital need to understand the role played by *dialogue* in the ways cultural formations take shape, that is to say in the ways the latter become apparent and ultimately identifiable. What is meant here by *cultural formation* is a particular manifestation of human achievement not only in the arts, languages, forms of expression (whether secular or religious), and customs of all kinds, but also in practices that involve the mastering of particular techniques, such as architecture, design, and urban developments.

In the context of this essay, *dialogue* is a particular relationship between cultural formations and the *place* to which they relate, which can be, amongst others, the natural environment, the geographical location, the historical past, tradition, external cultural influences, contemporary trends, the community or the person to whom art practices are addressed, etc. The environment is therefore only a particular instance of *place* to which cultural formations relate. Thus, there might be a case for calling for an environmental aesthetics as creative dialogue with otherness.

The particular kind of environment on which I shall focus on this occasion is the natural environment, and indeed, unless we understand that humanly begotten cultural formations must be in *dialogue* with nature, we will run the risk of annihilating nature and in the mean time humanity itself. Needless to say, in some parts of the world, the process has already started. But why is it so important to be in *dialogue* with nature? After all, why shouldn't nature simply be conceived as a standing-reserve, to use Martin Heidegger's expression, ready-to-hand for the vital needs and therefore the survival of the human species? Why shouldn't the transformation of nature into, for example, urban designs such as the cities of Shanghai, Mexico, or Kaohsiung, be accepted as pragmatic priorities that enable the human species to survive by making the economy run, creating jobs opportunities, providing food, accommodations, education and culture for many of us? And why should we bother with the aesthetic delights that nature can give, as Western self-criticism and bad conscience tell us that such delights were only the privilege of the few romantic individuals or the bourgeoisie who could afford it? These are not questions asked for the purpose of academic research, for heuristic reasons, or for mere theoretical concerns. These are concrete questions whose answers are to be found in the fields of ethical reason and practice. What is the most striking is that, if the ethical issues raised in this essay have always been, are, and will remain common sense in the eyes of many people, instances of denying them, ignoring them, or failing to put them into practice can be found on a regular basis across history, wherever in the world, and concern each of us without exception albeit admittedly to varying degrees. The truth of the matter is that these ethical issues are obvious in theory but rarely resolved in practice. The point of this essay is not to foster any sense of guilt. It is rather to contribute to making us aware of the reasons why we have by and large so far, and more noticeably since the advent of modern technology, failed to live a healthy existence with nature.

The short-sighted view that consists in justifying grand urban developments and projects regardless of the damage caused to the natural environment, on the basis according to which the priority is to ensure the basic living standard of our fellow human beings in expanding communities, is to justify the means used, any means, as long as the end is that supreme entity in the name of *the human species*. In such a case, there is clearly no *dialogue* between the community and the natural environment. The relationship is unidirectional to the point that what was originally intended for the sake of humanity's well being, is actually destroying the same humanity. In too many parts of the world, we have forgotten that the survival of humanity depends on the preservation of something other than the human, in other words, on something that we have to accept we cannot always control.

Equally, a fatal mistake would be to believe that the ills of the relationships between humanity and nature come from the fact that human beings have traditionally been thought in the West as opposed to the world of things or from biological species of some kinds. Such an anti-humanism calls for *the human exception*, as French philosopher Jean-Marie Schaeffer calls it, to be put to an end. By doing so the same anti-humanism fails to understand that human beings constitute indeed the only species capable of giving shape to a better world by relating to otherness with responsibility, be it the natural environment, other species, other cultures, or other persons—assuming that a 'better world' is a world whereby different entities live in harmony with each others. In other words, the human exception lies precisely in its ability to relinquish its exceptional *self* in the light of *otherness*, with trust in order to learn from otherness and with responsibility in order to accommodate it.

Admittedly, the history of humanity East-West and North-South is not a linear unfolding of instances of ethical stances, which would suggest that rather than rejecting the concept of *human exception* the legitimate targets should be the *wrong forms* of human exception, such as the kind of self-interested humanism previously mentioned. Human being is exceptional, or perhaps I should say *should be* exceptional, in that it has the ethical ability to make decisions and to take action to prevent dominating forces to destroy otherness in its own image, and by doing so, to destroy itself. If we look at how ants build their habitat, they are well organised and efficient in the sense that each ant has a specific role that contributes to the edification of a structure made of thousands galleries. They also operate according to very complex biological patterns. To this extent they are no different from human beings, only that such behaviours are exclusively designed for self-survival. Just as these habitats can cause a lot of damage, they will disappear as soon as a stronger entity overwhelms them. Nature is of course full of mutations through overpowering and creations out of destructions. In this sense, urban and industrial developments that disregard the natural environment are similar in principle to how biological species operate. We can even go as far as to say that the same principle governs the mineral world, with the formations of mountains and seas, which end up being what they are to the detriment of what used to be at their place. A cultural formation, such as an urban design, that disregards otherness, such as the natural environment, indeed does not show any sign of a human exception. As a matter of fact, the ethical void that goes in hand with such an anti humanism can be held as the direct cause of much destruction and irresponsible behaviours and policies. Thus, and interestingly, what looked like a self-interested humanism from one angle now looks like an anti humanism. But in both cases they bring in destruction.

The human exception lies in *dialogical awakening*, the only way to let creativity be without destroying otherness. Or rather, the only way to enact an understanding of creativity fundamentally based on a responsible relationship with otherness. But what does it means for cultural formations to be in *dialogue* with otherness? What does it mean for the shaping of human habitats to be in dialogue with their natural environment? We usually think of a dialogue between two persons, sometimes between two philosophers. Much of philosophy emerged indeed from dialogues. For example, Plato and Xenophon put into writing the dialogues that their mentor Socrates had with his pupils in Athens. For Socrates, dialogue was the form of a particular way of thinking, that is to say the *dialectical* method. According to the Classical Greek etymology, δια-λέγειν, is made of the prefix δια (through), which thereby invokes a 'relationship', and λέγειν, which means 'to speak'; and the λόγος of 'dialogue' refers in this instance to the idea of 'principle' more than 'reason' or even 'order'. For Socrates, the relationship was a conversation between the master and the pupil, during which the master challenged the pupil who discovered something new, which, in turn, challenged the master who also ended up bringing the problem discussed to another level. Thus, from the very beginning of the history of Western culture, dialogue was fundamental to understanding how we conceive *reality*, and how such a conception depends on our relationships with our fellow human beings. In other words, dialogue was both philosophical and ethical. Dialogue was both the means by which we could understand our thinking through mutual challenges, and the means by which mutual consideration was shown. Dialogue was from the outset and by definition both relational and ethical, but it took different shapes in the course of the history of Western ideas. Indeed, if the mystics equally sought to bring to light the relational nature of *thinking*, or rather of the *soul* rather, it was not in the form of a dialogue between persons as it was the case with Socrates. Instead, the dialogue was thought to take place between the soul and the divine. A typical example is Jewish poet, statesman and philosopher Abravanel's *Dialogues of love* (originally published in Italian in 1535 as *Dialoghi di amore*). The reflections of the mystics did not really go beyond religious considerations, and it is only in the 20th century that all-encompassing philosophies of dialogue were developed. These philosophies attempted to understand all aspects of human experiences, and there is no doubt that the most influential philosopher of dialogue of that time in the Western world was Martin Buber, whose most significant work is a small and typically poetical text called in German *Ich und Du* (1923)—a work whose profundity, refinement and wisdom bear no possible comparison with nowadays *fast thoughts* and *take away philosophies* characteristic of much of the techno-world.

Let us first of all summarise, or recall, what Buber means by 'dialogue' in its broad lines, so that the idea of *creative dialogue with otherness* as natural environment will become clearer. What emerges from the practice and experience of dialogue according to Buber is the concreteness and problematic nature of human existence as a fundamental value. And, in our case, what is of paramount importance for understanding the shaping of non-destructive cultural formations is the idea of, for example, urban design, emerging from the way it relates responsibly to its natural environment.

Very succinctly, in *Ich und Du* Buber distinguishes between two ways human beings approach *existence*. One is called 'I-It' (Ich-Es); and the other is called 'I-Thou' (Ich-Du). Importantly, the distinction does not depend on the type of entities to which human beings relate, but rather on the way they *meet* such entities. For example, in the 'I-It' relationships, the 'It' is not always a thing or an animal, it can be another human being. Equally, in the 'I-Thou' relationships, the 'Thou' is not always another human being, it can be nature, a work of art, or whatever entity. Very importantly, what Buber means by the 'I-Thou' relationship involves a non-hierarchical reciprocity, and mutual openness, and for him it is through all these relationships that the ultimate and eternal Thou is experienced, that is to say God. We therefore meet God in the concrete experience of dialogue with other entities, whatever they are. Well-knowingly, Buber was initially influenced by Hasidism, whereby the mystical meeting with God can happen on an everyday life basis. In other words it was very much about a 'neighbour-to-neighbour' type of spiritual experience. This is what led Buber to think that the most authentic spiritual experience was found in the concrete and ethical nature of existence, in other words in the experience of the I-Thou dialogue. The 'I-It' relationship, by contrast, is like a subject-object relationship, whereby the 'I' relates to entities in order to manipulate them, or to use them as instruments for cognitive purposes. For example, the quest for scientific knowledge induces an 'I-It' type of relationship. Of course Buber does not suggest that the 'I-It' relationship should be altogether rejected. On the contrary, it is a necessary and enriching type of relationship, insofar as it alternates with the 'I-Thou' relationship. The danger is when the 'I-It' relationship begins to dominate our forms of understanding and our modes of existence, and when it becomes a type of control over other entities, whether they are human, inanimate, natural, or material.

Conceived as such, the I-Thou dialogue is clearly mutual and non-hierarchical. It is neither a self-interested humanism nor an anti humanism. For urban development to enter in dialogue with the natural environment is neither to use nature as a standing reserve ready-to-hand for the sake of the self-preservation of humanity; nor is it to ignore ethical consciousness as a human exception. Any selfhood that asserts itself by means of otherness or that identifies itself with otherness cannot experience the 'I-Thou' relationship, which can only happen in dialogue, and which teaches us how to meet other entities, including the natural environment. However, a creative dialogue with otherness should not lead to preserving differences, as letting ourselves being renewed in the light of otherness also means that a part of us accepts to be given up. A creative dialogue acknowledges the other side of the relationship in its uniqueness, but only insofar that this difference throws a renewing light on our inexorably vital relationship with otherness.

Of course, in the literal sense of the term and needless to say, a dialogue cannot take place between the natural environment, or any biological or mineral entity, and ourselves. The natural environment is not expected to *speak* to us. However, if we restrain from relating to nature in order to figure out how many stones would be needed to build a house, or what type of urban conglomerate would be the most economically sound for the sake of the well being of the community, and if we openly let the uniqueness of nature *call* us so that we start paying *attention* to it, if we let its voice speak in the sense it gives us the chance to give some part of ourselves up in order to be awakened to how much consideration it deserves, then we are establishing an 'I-Thou' relationship. As such, the 'I-Thou' relationships that we may establish with the natural environment can be understood in terms of creative dialogue, although it goes without saying that the spiritual awakening that emerges from such a dialogue only concerns human beings, communities, nations, and cultures.

As for our dialogue with the natural environment, what better way to be made aware of such a vital ethical dimension other than through the aesthetic experience of what has relatively recently come under fire for the same anti-humanist reasons as previously explained, that is to say the *landscape*, whether in its mental or poetical formulations, whether in the visualisations of 16th and 17th century Dutch painters or the over a thousand years Chinese tradition of landscape painting since the T'ang dynasty. Indeed, instead of seeing in any conception of landscape the symptom of a will to objectify or possess the natural environment according to the perceiving subject's perspective and criteria of aesthetic delights, such a form of representation, whether it is purely mental or artistic, can hide a more profound ethical dimension, a disinterestedness that tells us how to relate to the gift of otherness—through *creative dialogue*.

Prof. Dr. Gerald Cipriani
Affiliated Scholar
University of Helsinki
Institute for Art Research
Department of Aesthetics
Helsinki, Finland

二、汉译英

1. 案例

光肩星天牛幼虫脂肪体原代培养方法的研究

摘要 以光肩星天牛幼虫脂肪体组织为实验材料进行原代细胞培养,研究原代培养过程中,取材的虫龄、脂肪体组织块大小、组织块是否贴壁及培养表面等因素对原代培养及其细胞在体外分离和增殖的影响。结果表明,较高龄的光肩星天牛幼虫(4 龄或 8 龄)的较完整的脂肪体组织,在同培养表面紧密贴附的情况下,原代培养的成功率较高,其细胞在体外从组织块中游离出来并增殖的几率较大。

关键词 昆虫细胞培养;光肩星天牛;原代培养;细胞增殖

2. 翻译工作坊课程规划

第一,文本解读。

(1) 分析学术论文摘要的语言特点,并找出摘要中的生物学术语;;

(2) 分析中文摘要的语言特点,确定文体风格,并根据文章的领域确定翻译策略。

第二,分组翻译(六人一组)。具体要求如下:

(1) 按照所提出的翻译策略,各组成员分别进行翻译;

(2) 组内进行翻译、修改,拟初稿;

(3) 将初稿合并,六人进行小组讨论,统一术语,纠查错误,拟定稿。

(4) 各组提交定稿。

第三,翻译教学讨论。

(1) 以上各组分别由代表进行报告演示,说明本组翻译策略选择的依据;

(2) 所有同学对各组所提出的翻译策略进行讨论;

(3) 教师给出参考译文,结合学生译文进行评析,讲解相关翻译技巧。

3. 参考译文

Evaluation of Some Factors Effecting in Vitro Primary Culture of Larval Fat Body Cells of Anoplophora glabripennis

Abstract：Some factors effecting in vitro primary culture of larval fat body cells of the Asian longhorned beetle（Anopolphora glabripennis）were evaluated in the paper. The results showed that the insect stages, size and integrality of the fat body tissue, character of culture surface and whether the cultured tissues attaching to the culture surface were important for the success of the primary culture. Under the optimized conditions，which were in combination with higher larval stages（4th or 8th instar），more intact cultured tissue and close attachment of the cultured tissue and the culture surface，the fat body cells were inclined to separate from the cultured tissues and proliferate.

Keywords：insect cell culture; Anoplophora glabripennis; primary culture; cell proliferation

4. 汉译英翻译练习

从语言"象似性"看诗歌意象翻译

摘要：象似性理论揭示了语言形式与内容之间的象似关系，即二者之间的关系根本在于遵循"模仿原则"，即形式模仿意义。文章通过研究诗歌、文字与绘画三者的关系，揭示三者间的"模仿"本质。可以利用象似性原则帮助译者从词汇象似性、句法象似性及篇章象似性三个层面分解并阐释原诗：通过词汇象似性帮助阐释并翻译诗歌的"意象"，通过句法象似性揭示诗歌翻译中形式与内容的重要关系，通过篇章象似性分析诗歌翻译的完整性——歌意象的完整、诗歌形式与内容的完整。象似性理论为诗歌翻译提供了一个新的视角，有助于探讨诗歌意象翻译的原则及方法。

关键词：象似性原则；意象；诗歌翻译

第十四章

广告翻译

第一节　广告的语言特点及翻译策略

随着我国加入世界贸易组织,越来越多的外国企业及其产品不断进入我国市场。在这种产品市场争夺战中,最有力的武器之一就是商业广告。在经济全球化的今天,广告宣传的国际化趋势越来越明显。各国企业都存在着广告国际化、全球化问题——即广告翻译问题。广告翻译须充分考虑产品销售对象的语言习惯、文化积淀,因此熟知广告的语言特点及翻译策略就显得尤为重要。为了能够吸引读者,引起读者的购买兴趣,激发购买欲望,广告的语言具有大众性、简单易懂、生动形象、说服力强四大特点。对于广告的翻译而言,根据香港理工大学李克兴教授的分类,主要可以采取以下几种翻译策略:

1. 直译(Literal Translation)或语义翻译(Semantic Translation)

例:Challenge the Limits 挑战极限(SAMSUNG)

Wining the hearts of the world 赢取天下心(Air France 法国航空公司)

We're Siemens. We can do that. 我们是西门子,我们能办到(Siemens 西门子)

2. 意译(Free Translation)或动态对等(Dynamic Equivalence)

例:Whatever makes you happy. 为您设想周全,让您称心如意(Credit Suisse)

UPS. On time, every time. UPS——准时的典范(UPS 快递)

Every time a good time 秒秒钟钟欢聚欢笑(麦当劳)

3. 再创型翻译或创译(Creative Translation)

例:Connecting People 科技以人为本(诺基亚)

Good to the last drop! 滴滴香浓,意犹未尽!(雀巢咖啡)

A great way to fly 新加坡航空,飞越万里,超越一切。(新加坡航空)

It happens at the Hilton 希尔顿酒店有求必应(希尔顿)

4. 增补型翻译或超额翻译（Supplementary Translation/Over Translation）

这类翻译主要是对原文进行引申扩充或是将原文的深层意思加以发挥。

例：Elegance is an attitude 优雅态度 真我性格（浪琴表）

Beyond your imagination 意想不到的天空（大韩航空）

5. 浓缩型翻译（Condensed Translation）或欠额翻译（Under Translation）

这类翻译策略不太常见，主要是针对原文不够精练，信息过剩的情况。

例：Overseas. Time set free Overseas. 自有真义（江诗丹顿）

Wherever you are. Whatever you do. The Allianz Group is always on your side.

安联集团，永远在你身边（安联集团）

6. 编译

例：

What's in a name?

It sounds ordinary on paper. A white shirt with a blue check. In fact，if you asked most men if they had a white shirt with a blue check，they'd say yes.

But the shirt illustrated on the opposite page is an adventurous white and blue shirt. Yet it would fit beautifully into your wardrobe. And no one would accuse you of looking less than a gentleman. Predictably，the different white and blue check shirt has a different name Viyella House. It's tailored in crisp cool cotton and perfectly cut out for city life. Remember our name next time you are hunting for a shirt to give you more than just a background for your tie.

On women and children's wear as well as on men's shirts，our label says—quietly but persuasively—all there is to say about our good quality and your good taste.

Our label is our promise.

原译：

名字算什么？

写在纸上它听起来平平常常。带蓝格的白衬衫。事实上，如果你问大多数男人他们是否有带蓝格的白衬衫，他们都会说有。

但是，下页展示的衬衫是色调大胆的蓝格白衬衫。它会为你的衣柜横添风采，穿上它没有人会责怪你缺少绅士派头。可以预想，这种不同的蓝格白衬衫会有一个不同凡响的名字：维耶拉。它为都市生活选用凉爽的棉布精裁细制。下一次你寻购衬衫时请记住我们的名字，它给你的不仅是作为领带的背景。

对妇女和儿童的服装正如我们对男人衬衫的承诺，我们的品牌悄悄地动人地说，这里展示的是我们的上乘质量和你们的一流品位。

我们的品牌是我们的承诺。

编译：

名牌推荐

英国人以其衬衫的风度闻名世界。其知名品牌就是维耶拉衬衫，它以精纺棉布为面料，由英国维耶拉品牌精心裁制，质量上乘，畅销世界。维耶拉特此郑重地承诺：蓝格白底，是白马王子的首选，风度翩翩，惹来窈窕淑女的青睐。穿上维耶拉，男人闯天下。穿上维耶拉，生活真潇洒。维耶拉还请您关注我们出品的妇女和儿童服装，百分之百的一流品位，百分之百的质量保证。

第二节　案例及习题

一、英译汉

1. 案例

CUTTY SARK

SCOTS WHISKY

Some people wear trendy clothes to attract attention. Others drive flashy cars. A glass of Cutty Sark won't turn any heads. But if you insist on creating a stir, you can always ask the bartender for one of them.

Scots Whisky

Uncommonly Smooth

2. 翻译工作坊课程规划

第一，文本解读。

（1）分析广告英语的语言特征，针对广告商品的特征考虑目标语读者的心理特征。

（2）选择适当的翻译策略并给出理由。

第二，分组翻译（六人一组）。具体要求如下：

（1）按照所提出的翻译策略，各组成员分别进行翻译；

（2）组内进行翻译、修改，拟初稿；

（3）将初稿合并，六人进行小组讨论，统一术语，纠查错误，拟定稿。

（4）各组提交定稿。

第三，翻译教学讨论。

（1）以上各组分别由代表进行报告演示，说明本组翻译策略选择的依据；

（2）所有同学对各组所提出的翻译策略进行讨论；

（3）教师给出参考译文，结合学生译文进行评析，讲解相关翻译技巧。

3. 参考译文

（1）时尚引人夺目，飞车引人羡慕。

一杯卡特思，无人瞩目。

但，如果，想要追求激情——尽管举手要杯卡特思……

苏格兰威士忌

非凡的享受

（2）

有些人穿着艳丽时装引人注目，有些人驾着漂亮新车惹人羡慕。卡特思酒绝不上头，不会让你飘飘然。但君想尽显风流，还是卡特思酒。

苏格兰威士忌

非凡的享受

4. 英译汉翻译练习

（1）　　　　　　　　　　**Berried Treasure**

It's the shortcake you have been longing for. Ruby red strawberry in a light syrup over fluffy yellow cake. The crowning touch? A pearly puff of whipped topping.

And while you're treasuring every morsel，imagine this：German Chocolate Cake，richly wrapped in a chunky coconut walnut icing and strawberry cheesecake—smooth，silky sensational.

Sweet dreamers. Weight Watchers make desserts that'll make your day. And berried or not，you'll treasure them all.

（2）宣传语英译汉

Fresh up with seven up—seven up
Double delicious. Double your pleasure.
Only your time is more precious than watch.
Tasting is believing.
Give me a chance, and you'll have a big surprise.
If people keep telling you to quit smoking cigarettes, don't listen ... they're probably trying to trick you into living.

二、汉译英

1. 案例

瓶中装的不仅是酒，还有加拿大的精神。加拿大威士忌在行业中鹤立鸡群，有着持久的醇香、轻盈，带给你最美妙的品味。倘若你想喝酒的话，那就选洛德卡尔弗加拿大威士忌吧。

洛德卡尔弗加拿大威士忌

2. 翻译工作坊课程规划

第一，文本解读。

（1）分析汉语广告的语言特征，针对广告商品的特征考虑目标语读者的心理特征。

（2）选择适当的翻译策略并给出理由。

第二，分组翻译（六人一组）。具体要求如下：

（1）按照所提出的翻译策略，各组成员分别进行翻译；

（2）组内进行翻译、修改，拟初稿；

（3）将初稿合并，六人进行小组讨论，统一术语，纠查错误，拟定稿；

（4）各组提交定稿。

第三，翻译教学讨论。

（1）以上各组分别由代表进行报告演示，说明本组翻译策略的选择的依据；

（2）所有同学对各组所提出的翻译策略进行讨论；

（3）教师给出参考译文，结合学生译文进行评析，讲解相关翻译技巧。

3. 参考译文

The Unique Spirit of Canada：We Bottled It. Right to the finish，its Canadian spirit stands out from the ordinary. What keeps the flavor coming? Super lightness. Super taste. If that's where you'd like to head，set your course for Lord Calvert Canadian.

Lord Calvert Canadian

4. 汉译英翻译练习

宣传语汉译英

国酒茅台，相伴辉煌。（茅台）
鹤舞白沙，我心飞翔。（白沙牌香烟）
运动休闲，我行我速。（CBA 运动休闲系列）
我有我品质（龙的牌真空吸尘器）
爱您一辈子（绿世界化妆品）
随身携带，有备无患，随身携带，有惊无险（速效救心丸）
一切皆有可能（李宁）
拥有完美肌肤的秘诀（丁家宜）
中原之行哪里去？郑州亚细亚。（亚细亚商城）
稀世之美专属于你（钻石广告）

参考文献

1. 陈刚.旅游翻译与涉外导游[M].北京：中国对外翻译出版公司,2004:59.

2. 陈宏薇.新实用汉译英教程[M].武汉:湖北教育出版社,2000.

3. 程尽能,吕和发.旅游翻译理论与实务[M].北京:清华大学出版社,2008:308-312.

4. 邓忠.语篇指向性在演讲辞语篇分析中的应用——兼析美国总统布什对伊拉克开战演讲辞[J].西南民族大学学报（人文社科版）,2007(12):121-124.

5. 高静.中国时事政治术语的特点及翻译[J].文学界（理论版）,2012(10):185-186.

6. 辜正坤.中西诗比较鉴赏与翻译理论[M].北京:清华大学出版社,2003:340.

7. 贺学耘.汉英公示语翻译的现状及其交际翻译策略[J].外语与外语教学,2006(03):57-59.

8. 姜蓉.纽马克文本分类模式评析[J].西南民族大学学报（人文社科版）,2007(09):211-212.

9. 兰天,屈晓鹏.国际商务合同翻译教程[M].大连:东北财经大学出版社,2014.

10. 李克兴.论法律文本的静态对等翻译[J].中国语专业教学研究,2010(01):59-65.

11. 李克兴.论广告翻译的策略[J].中国翻译,2004(06):64-69.

12. 李明,仲伟和.翻译工作坊教学探微[J].中国翻译,2010(4):32-36.

13. 廖瑛.实用外贸英语函电（第三版）[M].武汉:华中科技大学出版社,2012.

14. 龙江华.从互文性视角看新闻英语语篇风格的翻译[J].高等函授学报（哲学社会科学版）,2006(01):58-60.

15. 卢颖,雷雨露.从语言"象似性"看诗歌意象翻译[J].湖北文理学院学报,2013(9):68-72.

16. 罗选民,黎土旺.关于公示语翻译的几点思考[J].中国翻译,2006(04):66-69.

17. 骆伟,朱晓华.试论地方文献与地方文化的关系[J].图书馆论坛,2000(5):3-6.

18. 彭红兵,张新红.英汉法律翻译的语用原则[J].西北民族大学学报（哲学社会科学版）,2007(2):147-150,156.

19. 彭琳.法律法文的语言特征及翻译策略[J].中国语专业教学研究,2013(12):276-290.

20. 宋平锋.浅谈"翻译工作坊式"翻译实践教学模式[J].内蒙古农业大学学报（社会科学版）,2011(1):140-143.

21. 谭克新.演讲文体特征及其翻译策略——以俄罗斯总统普京的演讲为例[J].中国俄语教学,2014(04):49-55.

22. 王方路.外贸函电特点与翻译刍议[J].中国科技翻译,2005(1):45-47.

23. 王树槐. 地铁公示语翻译：问题与原则[J]. 上海翻译, 2012(3)：30 - 33.

24. 王志娟. 寓语域理论于新闻报道的汉译之中[J]. 上海科技翻译, 2002(03)：11 - 15.

25. 徐聃. 联合国工发组织 2011 年《非洲投资者报告》的笔译实践及分析[D]. 对外经济贸易大学英语学院, 2013(5).

26. 杨元刚. 新编汉英翻译教程[M]. 武汉：华中师范大学出版社, 2012.

27. 张寰, 李瑄, 张永安等. 肩星天牛幼虫脂肪体原代培养方法的研究[J]. 细胞生物杂志, 2009, 31(2)：281 - 285.

28. 赵雁丽. 法律英语教程[M]. 西安：西安交通大学出版社, 2003.

29. 赵志刚. 英语海事公文的语言特点及翻译[J]. 上海海事大学学报, 2014(2)：89 - 94.

30. 朱慧芬, 厉义. 银行公示语翻译现状调查与研究——以浙江省 10 家银行为例[J]. 浙江金融, 2011(3)：49 - 51.